*Many other signs
therefore Jesus also
performed in the
presence of the disciples,
which are not written in
this book; but these
have been written that
you may believe that
Jesus is the Christ, the
Son of God; and that
believing you may have
life in His name*
(John 20:30-31).

The Gospel of JOHN

Classic Library Edition

Presented by
Marilyn Hickey Ministries

Marilyn Hickey Ministries
P.O. Box 17340
Denver, Colorado 80217

The Gospel of JOHN

Classic Library Edition

Formerly: Living in Victory Series

JOHN

Volume 5

Revised edition 2000

ISBN 1-56441-044-7

Printed in the United States of America

Unless otherwise indicated all Scriptures quoted in this volume are from The Open Bible, New American Standard Version.

The Gospel of John
Table of Contents

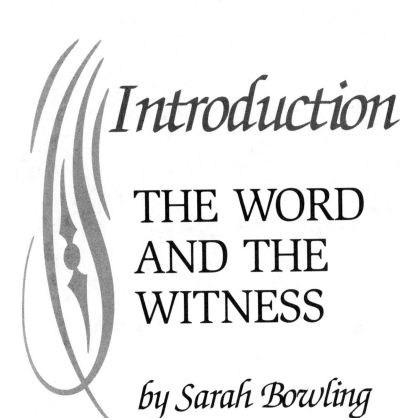

Introduction

THE WORD AND THE WITNESS

by Sarah Bowling

The Word and the Witness

In the beginning was the Word and the Word was with God, and the Word was God. He was in the beginning with God. All things came into being by Him, and apart from Him nothing came into being that has come into being. In Him was life, and the life was the light of men. And the light shines in the darkness, and the darkness did not comprehend it (John 1:1-5).

The Gospel of John is totally *unlike* the other Gospels. Matthew's Gospel begins the story of Jesus with a genealogy that starts with Abraham and shows that Jesus was a descendant of King David. Mark paints Jesus in vivid colors—you can almost see Him striding through the Judean countryside in this Gospel written to Gentiles. The Gospel of Luke is like a courtroom testimony of Jesus' life where eyewitnesses tell of the life and death of the Savior.

Before Time Began

John speaks of Jesus as the Eternal Son of God, and begins his story before time began with the words, "In the beginning." The first person we meet in the Book of John isn't called Jesus; it is someone John calls the *Logos*, or "the Word." John makes three powerful statements concerning the Word. He says the Word is timeless, the Word was with God from the very beginning, and the Word *is* God.

When John calls the Word "He," John begins to show that the Word is a Person, an individual with Whom there is the possibility of a relationship. Shining out of "Him" is light and life—not merely a cycle of existing and someday dying like an animal, but glorious *eternal* life.

John 1:5 says, *"And the light shines in the darkness, and the*

FAST FACTS

AUTHOR AND SETTING:
The Apostle John; Israel

PURPOSE:
John clearly sets forth Jesus Christ in His deity in order to spark believing faith in his readers.

BEHOLDING JESUS:
John presents seven signs to show the divinity of Jesus. John also gives us the seven "I Ams" of Jesus to prove that Jesus is the Christ, the Son of God.

THEME VERSES:
John 20:30,31

darkness did not comprehend it." Although John wrote this passage of Scripture many years after Jesus' death, he said the light "*shines* in darkness"—present tense. The light has shined, it is shining, and it will continue to shine. Salvation through Christ shines just as brightly today as it ever has.

The word, "comprehend" in the Greek means that the darkness couldn't extinguish or control the Light. It's a simple fact that darkness is subservient to light. When you put light and darkness in the same room, light always wins. When you turn on the light switch, darkness has to retreat—it has no choice. God, the Light, always wins over the darkness, the devil. He always has, He always does, and He always will. That means that you, too, as sons and daughters of the Light, should always win over Satan.

The Presenter

There came a man, sent from God, whose name was John. He came for a witness, that he might bear witness of the light, that all might believe through him. He was not the light, but came that he might bear witness of the light (John 1:6-8).

Suddenly, John, the writer, introduced an "outsider"—John the Baptist. Why? In ancient times and still today, when a world leader arrives for a visit, someone presents him or announces his arrival. When our own President enters a room someone says, "Ladies and gentlemen, the President of the United States." John the Baptist was the announcer of Jesus—the Word and the Light.

John the Baptist more than announced Christ—the Bible says that he "came for a witness." A *witness* is "someone who accurately describes a person or an incident." John had the distinction of being one of the few among the entire population of the earth who recognized the Son of God. When Mary (pregnant with Jesus) entered the room, Luke 1:44 says that John leaped for joy in his mother's womb. John the Baptist was born, sent, and anointed to tell everyone that Someone different from the rest of humanity had entered the world. That Someone is the Light.

A Stranger in a Strange Land

After this brief introduction to John the Baptist, the author John tells us that "his own," the Jews, didn't receive Jesus. The world did not perceive or recognize whom Jesus really was, not unlike much of the world today. Even the Jews, who were looking for their Messiah, failed to identify the Christ.

Nevertheless, there were individuals who received Jesus and believed in Him. John tells us that those individuals were given the right to become "children of God." By believing in Jesus and accepting Him for Whom He is—the Word of God, God in the flesh—we can become God's sons and daughters: *"But as many as received Him, to them He gave the right to become children of God,…"* (John 1:12).

This statement is the clearest expression of God's reason for everything He has ever done and why Jesus had to come to earth and suffer a sinner's death: God wants to make every man, woman, and child on the earth one of His children. This is *the* truth of the ages—whether we believe it or not, or receive it or not, it remains true. The entrance of Jesus into the world has caused humanity to question their "family identity." To whose family do we belong? Who is our father, creator, and god?

Speaking of Jesus, John said that he was *"…full of grace and truth"* (John 1:14). Without His grace, the truth would be like an anchor wrapped around our necks and would sink us. His "truth" exceeds the capacity of our lives to contain it. In Jesus, we find not only the fullness of God's truth, but also the fullness of His grace, and because of grace, we are able to walk according to the plumb line of truth. The Ten Commandments (truth) were given through Moses, but hard as they tried, man could not live up to God's expectations.

Through Jesus, mankind received truth and the abundant provision of grace that provided THE ONLY WAY for man to please God. Man could never measure up to the Law, so Jesus fulfilled it. As members of God's family, we can receive of His fullness. In John 1:16 it says, *"For of His fulness we have all received, and grace upon grace."* Can you think of anything Jesus lacks? The word for fullness in the Greek is *plethora*, which means "a massive variety of things, overwhelming abundance."

What do you need? Do you need healing? A miracle in your finances? Deliverance? Absolutely everything you need to live the overcoming life is found in the fullness of Jesus.

A Peculiar Herald

John, the writer, tell us a great deal about the *ministry* of John the Baptist, who played an extremely important role in introducing Jesus to the world, but we have to go to the other Gospels for more background information concerning John.

Luke tells us about John the Baptist's supernatural birth to Elizabeth and Zacharias, and Mary's visit to them. John's destiny was very precise and ordained *before* his birth. We, too, have a precise future and purpose designed by God before our birth. Regardless of how you were conceived, *you* were no accident. God wrote a plan for your life before He laid the foundations of the earth. If you don't know your God-given purpose, press into Him and discover your destiny.

In Matthew 3:4, John the Baptist's appearance is described in detail: *"Now John himself had a garment of camel's hair, and a leather belt about his waist; and his food was locusts and wild honey."* John wore strange clothes, ate strange food, and ministered in a strange way—yet, he spoke God's truth. Today, too, we have atypical ministers—but don't make the mistake of discounting what they say because of their appearance. Use God's Word as the standard by which you evaluate their words. God may use them to speak to you just as He used John the Baptist to speak to the people of his day.

Make Straight the Way

John had great favor among the Jews. Even the Jewish leadership came to be baptized by John. He challenged the hypocrites to make *real* repentance or face the judgment of the One Who was coming with a baptism of the Holy Spirit and fire. John's was a baptism of repentance—admitting sin and changing behavior. John was extremely intense because he had a compelling assignment—to introduce the Savior to the Jewish nation and the world.

Beholding Jesus in John

The name *John* means "Jehovah is gracious." John's home was Bethsaida. (See John 1:44; Luke 5:10.) He came from a family of four—the father and mother (Zebedee and Salome) and the two sons (James and John).

The father and sons were fishermen. (See Matthew 4:21.) Their mother, Salome, was ambitious for her sons. (See Matthew 20:20,21; Mark 10:35-37.) There is clear evidence that the family was prosperous because the family had hired servants.

John's family ministered to Jesus and His disciples out of their financial substance, and they were influential in official quarters. (See Mark 1:20; Matthew 27:56; Luke 8:3; John 18:15,16; 19:26,27.) John was first a follower of John the Baptist, and he left John the Baptist to follow Christ. (See John 1:35,40.)

It is interesting that water baptism, which played such a major role in John's ministry, is not found in the Old Testament. Yet, it was an accepted practice within Jewish tradition and was used in the ceremony of conversion for non-Jewish converts. Perhaps John used water baptism to signify a heart change rather than a mechanical, religious ritual without heart conviction.

God is looking for people who are devoted to Him in their hearts and with their behavior, not merely in a religious way. John the Baptist confronted this kind of surface living and we today are challenged to keep a pure heart toward God.

I Am a Voice

John replied in the words of Isaiah the prophet, "I am the voice of one calling in the desert, 'Make straight the way for the Lord'" (John 1:23 NIV).

When the Jews sent priests and Levites to ask John whom he was, he didn't waver and say he was a baptizer. Rather, John answered, "I am the voice of one crying in the wilderness." Often people think that *whom* they are is based upon *what* they do. Have you noticed that when people introduce themselves they often say their name and then their occupation? "I'm Chloe, an accountant." When John was asked, he knew whom he was based upon God's Word and he answered them with the Word.

We also know whom we are—God's dearly loved children— and we know what God's Word says about *us*—we are forgiven, healed, redeemed from destruction, favored with God's kindness and mercies, and blessed with every good thing. (See Psalms 103:2-5.) Yet how often do we declare to the world that we are sick, unlucky, poor, and victims? We need to do what John did—speak the Word concerning who we are and then confirm our identity with our actions.

When the day came that John saw Jesus coming to be baptized, he spoke words that have echoed around the world and down the corridors of time:

...Behold! The Lamb of God who takes away the sin

of the world! This is He of whom I said, "After me comes a Man who is preferred before me, for He was before me" (John 1:29-31 NKJ).

John knew that Jesus was the Son of God because his well-developed relationship with God enabled him to recognize the work of God. He knew Jesus when he saw the Holy Spirit descend and remain upon Him. The Holy Spirit to this day confirms Jesus; He is the Spirit of Truth, and He will lead us to the truth. The deeper your relationship with God, the better you can hear His Spirit—through the Bible, in the words of God's people, as a whisper in your heart, or through circumstances.

Baptizer—Baptized?

John baptized Jesus! John had foretold that Christ would baptize with the Holy Spirit, yet on that day, Jesus lined up with the sinners to be baptized for repentance from sin. Does it strike you as strange that a man without sin would come to be baptized for repentance? It seemed wrong to John also, but Jesus insisted. Even at the very beginning of His ministry, Jesus was identifying with sinful man.

Jesus had every right to skip this baptism of repentance, instead He humbled Himself and the result was extraordinary—for the only time mentioned in the New Testament, the Trinity was manifested at one time in one place on the earth—the Holy Spirit descended like a dove on Jesus and God spoke. God Himself announced Jesus, *"...This is my beloved Son, in whom I am well pleased"* (Matthew 3:17 KJV).

If you haven't received Jesus into your heart or if you have let your commitment slide and become cold in your relationship with Him, don't let another day, another hour, and no, not even another minute pass without making Jesus the Lord of your life. Take a moment now, and simply say, *Jesus, forgive me of my sins and cleanse me from all unrighteousness, I renounce sin and Satan. Come into my heart and be my Savior, and I will make you the Lord of my life.* If you prayed that prayer...get into your Bible...get in church…and get into fellowship with other believers, in a small group situation if possible.

You're going to love this book—my mother's study of the book of John. This Gospel is for everyone—it is the simplest yet most profound book of the Bible. New converts read it and are thrilled; theologians study it and discover great insights. When you turn the page, and begin to read it, *you'll find* the powerful, far-reaching truth about the Eternal Son of God and how He can change *your* life.

The Gospel According to John

Jesus: The Word Made Flesh

Prologue: Eternal Word
Jesus the Word
Chapter 1

Ministry to the World:
Jesus came to save the world
Chapter 1-12

Ministry to His own:
Fulfillment of the covenant
Chapter 13-17

Death & Resurrection:
Salvation is accomplished
Chapter 18-21

Location: Israel
Overview: Using miraculous signs, John proves that *"...Jesus is the Christ, the Son of God; and that believing ye might have life through his name"* (John 20:31).

Time:
Three-and-a-half years beginning around A.D. 30

Outline & Overview

I. Overview

There were at least three stages in John's fellowship with Christ:

A. Attachment: *"One of the two which heard John [the Baptist] speak, and followed him [Jesus], was Andrew, Simon Peter's brother [the other was John]"* (John 1:40 KJV).

B. Discipleship: *"And going on from thence, he saw other two brethren, James the son of Zebedee, and John his brother; in a ship with Zebedee their father; mending their nets; and he called them. And they immediately left the ship and their father; and followed him"* (Matthew 4:21,22 KJV).

C. Apostleship: *"And when it was day, he called unto him his disciples: and of them he chose twelve, whom also he named apostles; Simon, (whom he also named Peter,) and Andrew his brother; James and John, Philip and Bartholomew"* (Luke 6:13,14 KJV).

D. About John

1. John's relationship to Jesus was unique if, as conjectured, Salome, his mother, was the sister of Mary, the mother of Jesus. That would make John the cousin of Jesus.

2. John was one of the first two *disciples* to be called. (See John 1:35-40.) John was one of the first named an apostle. (See Matthew 4:18-22.)

3. He was one of the three *privileged apostles: "And he suffered no man to follow him, save Peter; and James, and John the brother of James"* (Mark 5:37). (See also Matthew 17:1; 26:37.)

4. John was one of the four who drew forth our Lord's great prophetic discourse: *"And as he sat upon the mount of Olives over against the temple, Peter and James and John and Andrew asked him privately, Tell us, when shall these things be? and what shall be the sign when all these things shall be fulfilled?"* (Mark 13:3,4 KJV).

5. John was one of the two sent to prepare the Passover: *"And he sent Peter and John, saying, Go and prepare us the passover; that we may eat"* (Luke 22:8 KJV).

6. He was the disciple whom Jesus loved: *"Now there was leaning on Jesus' bosom one of his disciples, whom Jesus loved"* (John 13:23 KJV).

7. It was to John that Jesus committed the care of His mother: *"Now there stood by the cross of Jesus his mother; and his mother's sister; Mary the wife of Cleophas, and Mary Magdalene. When Jesus therefore saw his mother; and the disciple standing by, whom he loved, he saith unto his mother; Woman, behold thy son! Then saith he to the disciple, Behold thy mother! And from that hour that disciple took her unto his own home"* (John 19:25-27 KJV).

8. John the Apostle wrote The Gospel of John, and eighteen years later he wrote the book of Revelation.

II. John appears three times in the book of Acts:

A. In the Temple: *"Now Peter and John went up together into the temple at the hour of prayer; being the ninth hour"* (Acts 3:1 KJV).

B. Before the council: *"Now when they saw the boldness of Peter and John, and perceived that they were unlearned and ignorant men, they marvelled; and they took knowledge of them, that they had been with Jesus"* (Acts 4:13 KJV).

C. In Samaria: *"Now when the apostles which were at Jerusalem heard that Samaria had received the word of God, they sent unto them Peter and John"* (Acts 8:14 KJV).

III. About the Gospel

A. Basically, John divided his Gospel into three themes: revelation, rejection, and reception. All three appear in every part of the Gospel.

B. There are six miracles in John's Gospel that only he recorded:

1. The turning of water into wine—John 2:7-9
2. The healing of the nobleman's son—John 4:49-53
3. The healing of the impotent man at Bethesda—John 5:6-9
4. The giving of sight to a man born blind—John 9:1,6,7
5. The raising of Lazarus from the dead—John 11:43

6. The multitude of fish—John 21:5,6

C. Beholding Jesus in John—In his Gospel, John shows that the Man of Galilee was God. The Gospel of John was written for the Christian Church as a whole, for the world at large, and presents the more profound aspects of the gospel.

IV. Division of the Gospel

A. Prologue—The Eternal Word • JOHN 1
B. Christ's Ministry to the World • JOHN 1-12
C. Christ's Ministry to His Own • JOHN 13-17
D. Christ's Death and Resurrection • JOHN 18-20

V. The Old Testament Quoted in John

John 1:23 quotes from Isaiah 40:3
John 2:17 quotes from Psalms 69:9
John 6:31 quotes from Exodus 16:4,15, Nehemiah 9:15 and Psalms 78:24
John 6:45 quotes from Isaiah 54:13 and Jeremiah 31:33,34
John 10:34 quotes from Psalms 82:6
John 12:13 Psalms 82:6
John 12:13 quotes from Psalms 118:26
John 12:15 quotes from Zechariah 9:9
John 12:38 quotes from Isaiah 53:1
John 12:40 quotes from Psalms 82:6
John 12:13 quotes from Psalms 118:26
John 12:15 quotes from Zechariah 9:9
John 12:38 quotes from Isaiah 53:1
John 12:40 quotes from Isaiah 6:9,10
John 13:18 quotes from Psalms 41:9
John 15:25 quotes from Psalms 35:19 and Psalms 69:4
John 19:24 quotes from Psalms 22:18
John 19:36 quotes from Exodus 12:46, Numbers 9:12 and Psalms 34:20
John 19:37 quotes from Zechariah 12:10

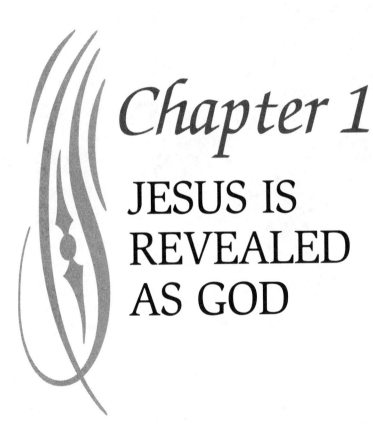

Chapter 1

JESUS IS REVEALED AS GOD

Jesus Is Revealed As God

The first four books of the New Testament are called *the Gospels* because they tell of the life of Christ. Yet these are not four separate books, but a *fourfold* revelation of THE Gospel. The correlation between the Gospels becomes clear when viewed in light of God's plan for the camp of the Israelites en route to the Promised Land. The book of **Matthew** is comparable to the whole of Israel camped surrounding the Tabernacle (which represents Christ). The Gospel of **Mark** brings us into the outer court of the Tabernacle where we see *the place of service and sacrifice.* **Luke** passes into the Holy Place where the seven-branched candlestick of witness and the table of shewbread are located. In **John** we enter within the veil into the Holy of Holies, where we learn without a doubt that *Jesus is really God!*

The miracles in John do not show Jesus laying His hands on people to heal them as frequently as He did in the other Gospels. He took Jairus' daughter by the hand and raised her up. He touched the hand of Peter's mother-in-law, and she received her healing. He put His fingers into the ears and upon the tongue of the deaf and dumb man who could immediately speak and hear! When the man who was "full of leprosy" fell on his face before Him, Jesus put forth His hand and touched him.

Instead, the Gospel of John shows Jesus speaking God's Word in power: He is the Word made flesh! At the marriage supper, Jesus didn't pour the water; instead, He **bid** the servants to fill the water pots. He did not personally go to a certain nobleman's home, but he **sent the Word** to heal the man's servant. Instead of laying his hand on Lazarus, or rolling the stone away from his grave, He **spoke the Word:** and the Word worked! The Word brings miracles! The Word brings life!

In the Gospel of John, Jesus has twenty-seven "personal interviews." His ministry to the individual is emphasized in more detail than His interaction with the masses. As you study this Gospel, allow Jesus to become more personal to *you* than ever before. God will reveal

Himself to you. Just as Jesus spoke and obeyed the Father's will, you, too, can learn to know Jesus, speak, and obey the Father's will.

John—the Book of Love

The book of John clearly reveals God's love for man. God loved us enough to send His Son to reveal Himself, and to give His life for our redemption. Jesus' love reaches out to the sinner and meets man's physical and spiritual needs. His love instructs in the Temple, on the hillside, in the garden. His love lights up our lives, dispels the darkness of sin and ignorance, and brings life in abundance to any who will receive it.

Christ demonstrated His love by serving, and He set the tone for His disciples to be servants also. Jesus taught them the principle of giving life in order to gain it. He showed them the way to the Father, and promised them the Comforter and Teacher in the Holy Spirit. He taught love by His life and then gave His life out of love for sinners. This kind of love conquers sin, death, and the world!

This Gospel starts with the words "In the beginning...."

In the beginning was the Word, and the Word was with God, and the Word was God (John 1:1).

The Bible tells us of many "beginnings": first, the beginning of the world (Genesis 1:1); second, the beginning of the Gospel of Jesus Christ (Mark 1:1); third, the beginning of sorrows (Mark 13:8); and fourth, the beginning of miracles (John 2:11). This beginning, from John 1:1, comes before all of these. Jesus Christ was not only from the beginning, but in the beginning. He was the Creator.

Jesus Is the Word of God

The Word existed before time began. Why is Jesus designated "the Word"? Because He is God's "alphabet." In Revelation 1:8, Jesus says, *"I am the Alpha and Omega...."* Christ is the One who spells out "deity." He is the One Who utters every Word that God has to say.

Jesus was God's means of manifestation. Just as words clothe thoughts to make them understandable, God's Word was made flesh—Jesus manifested an invisible God. When you know Jesus, you know God:

> *If you had known Me, you would have known My*
> *Father also; from now on you know Him, and have*
> *seen Him* (John 14:7).

Jesus was God's means of communication to mankind. Words transmit information from one person to another. Jesus, the "Divine Transmitter," communicates God's love and life to you.

Jesus revealed Who God is. Just as your words reveal who you are, Jesus' words unveiled the heart of God. He revealed God's perfect and holy character, His love and wisdom, and His will for men. Jesus explained the Father:

> *No man has seen God at any time; the only begotten*
> *God, who is in the bosom of the Father, He has*
> *explained Him* (John 1:18).

Jesus is God's spokesman. He came to explain the Father's "ways" to us and to give us His message of love. Nature can show us the orderliness of God and tell us about His power and His infinity, but we needed a special messenger to tell us of His character, and especially of His love. Listen to Jesus, He will explain the Father to you!

The Light of Men

The life of God was in Jesus, and that life was the light of men:

> *In Him was life, and the life was the light of*
> *men....There was the true light which, coming into*
> *the world, enlightens every man* (John 1:4,9).

Christ is our true Light, but Satan is a deceiving light:

And no wonder, for even Satan disguises himself as an angel of light (II Corinthians 11:14).

Christ is *the* Light because His light is not derived; He is light's source. This Light came into the world for every man. Yet not every man received that Light. Those who received the light of Jesus Christ became sons of the Living God.

But as many as received Him, to them He gave the right to become children of God, even to those who believe in His name (John 1:12).

And the Light shines on in the darkness, for the darkness has never overpowered it—put it out, or has not absorbed it, has not appropriated it and is unreceptive to it (John 1:5 TAB).

The Life of Men

Man became alienated from God because of "the fall" (Ephesians 4:18), but men became partakers of **life** through faith in the Lord Jesus Christ. (See John 3:15.) Jesus became the author of life to all who trust in Him (see Acts 3:15) and is the [zoe] **life** of the believer. (See Colossians 3:4.) The **life** that Jesus gives He maintains. (See John 6:35,63).

*Being darkened in their understanding, excluded—from the **life** of God, because of the ignorance that is in them, because of the hardness of their heart* (Ephesians 4:18).

*Jesus said to them, "I am the bread of **life**; he who comes to Me shall not hunger, and he who believes in Me shall never thirst....It is the Spirit who gives **life**; the flesh profits nothing; the words that I have spoken to you are spirit and are **life**"* (John 6:35,63).

ZOE

The word life here is the Greek word *zoe.* Vine's Expository Dictionary says: "Is used in the N.T. of life as a principle, life in the absolute sense, life as God has it, that which the Father has in Himself, and which He gave to the Incarnate Son to have in Himself, (John 5:26), and which the Son manifested in the world (I John 1:2)."

"For just as the Father has life in Himself, even so He gave to the Son also to have life in Himself;" (John 5:26).

"And the life was manifested, and we have seen and bear witness and proclaim to you the eternal life, which was with the Father and was manifested to us" (I John 1:2).

Eternal life is an actual possession of the believer because of his relationship with Christ.

> *Truly, truly, I say to you, he who hears My word, and believes Him who sent Me, has eternal life, and does not come into judgment, but has passed out of death into life* (John 5:24).

That **life** will one day extend itself to our human bodies because of the Resurrection of Christ.

> *For indeed while we are in this tent, we groan, being burdened, because we do not want to be unclothed, but to be clothed, in order that what is mortal may be swallowed up by life* (II Corinthians 5:4).

Life is not merely a principle of power and mobility, it has moral associations, such as holiness and righteousness. Death and sin, life, and holiness are frequently contrasted in the Scriptures. This is the life that you have been given! Let it be the "light of men" around you!

He Dwelt Among Us

> *And the Word became flesh, and dwelt among us, and we beheld His glory, glory as of the only begotten— from the Father, full of grace and truth* (John 1:14).

The word *dwelt* is the same word as tabernacled. You could say that Christ "pitched his tent [tabernacle]" in our world for thirty-three years! Let's look at some of the similarities between the purpose of the tabernacle and Christ's ministry:

Headquarters—The Tabernacle moved from place to place. Jesus also moved about in His ministry, never having a permanent headquarters. In Matthew 8:20, He said, *"...The foxes have holes, and the birds of the air have nests; but the Son of man hath not where to lay his head"* (KJV).

God's Dwelling Place—The presence of God remained in the middle of the Israelite camp. His presence was located above the mercy seat, between the cherubim. The shekinah glory manifested itself there, and that same glory manifested itself in Jesus on the Mount of Transfiguration:

> *And six days later Jesus took with Him Peter and James and John his brother, and brought them up to a high mountain by themselves. And He was transfigured before them; and His face shone like the sun, and His garments became as white as light* (Matthew 17:1,2).

Where God Met With Men

And you shall put the mercy seat on top of the ark...And there I will meet with you; and from above the mercy seat, from between the two cherubim which are upon the ark of the testimony, I will speak to you about all that I will give you in commandment for the sons of Israel (Exodus 25:21,22).

Jesus is the way to the Father, and He is the mediator between God and man:

> *Jesus said, to him, "I am the way, and the truth, and the life; no one comes to the Father, but through Me"* (John 14:6).

The Center of the Camp—The Levites were to camp around the Tabernacle. (See Numbers 1:50.) The tent of meeting was to be placed in the midst of the camps. (See Numbers 2:17.) When Moses gathered the seventy elders together, he would station them around the tent (see Numbers 11:24,25), which was the gathering center of the people. Jesus is our "gathering place," too, for He said that *"...where two or three are gathered together in my name, there am I in the midst of them"* (Matthew 18:20 KJV).

Where the Sacrifice Was Made—Animals were sacrificed

The Law

Look at the contrast between grace and the law.

1. **Law addresses men as members of creation; grace makes us new creations.**

2. **Law shows what is in man—sin; grace manifests what is in God—love.**

3. **Law demands righteousness from men; grace brings righteousness to men.**

4. **Law sentences a living man to death; grace brings a dead man to life.**

5. **Law speaks of what men must do for God; grace tells what Christ has done for men.**

6. **Law gives a knowledge of sin; grace puts away sin.**

7. **Law brought God out to men; grace brings men in to God.**

From the *Exposition of the Gospel of John* by A.W. Pink

on the brazen altar in the outer court. Jesus was the spotless Lamb of God Who was sacrificed on the Cross just outside the city.

> *For the bodies of those animals whose blood is brought into the holy place by the high priest as an offering for sin, are burned outside the camp. Therefore Jesus also, that He might sanctify the people through His own blood, suffered outside the gate* (Hebrews 13:11,12).

The Place of Worship—Only because of Christ can we come to the Father to worship. He has given us access to the Holy of Holies, through His blood.

> *Since therefore, brethren, we have confidence to enter the holy place by the blood of Jesus, by a new and living way which He inaugurated for us through the veil, that is, His flesh* (Hebrews 10:19,20).

The Witness of John the Baptist

John the Baptist was a witness sent from God: *"There came a man, sent from God, whose name was John"* (John 1:6). In clear contrast to Jesus, the Word Who was God, the Bible states that John the Baptist was a man who was to direct others toward God. His name means "the gift of God" and that He was! He was the subject of prophecy some 700 years before he was born:

> *A voice is calling, "Clear the way for the Lord in the wilderness; Make smooth in the desert a highway for our God"* (Isaiah 40:3).

John the Baptist's birth was due to the direct intervention of God. He was a gift to his parents in their old age:

> *And they had no child, because Elizabeth was barren, and they were both advanced in years....But the angel said to him, "Do not be afraid, Zacharias, for your*

petition has been heard, and your wife Elizabeth will bear you a son, and you will give him the name John" (Luke 1:7,13).

John the Baptist was filled with the Holy Spirit while in his mother's womb:

For he will be great in the sight of the Lord, and he will drink no wine or liquor; and he will be filled with the Holy Spirit, while yet in his mother's womb (Luke 1:15).

John the Baptist was sent with one mission—to prepare the way of the Lord.

For this is the one referred to by Isaiah the prophet, saying, "THE VOICE OF ONE CRYING IN THE WILDERNESS, 'MAKE READY THE WAY OF THE LORD, MAKE HIS PATHS STRAIGHT'" (Matthew 3:3).

Of John the Baptist, Jesus said:

Truly, I say to you, among those born of women there has not arisen anyone greater than John the Baptist; yet he who is least in the kingdom of heaven Is greater than he (Matthew 11:11).

John went before Christ, "in the spirit and power of Elijah."

And it is he who will go as a forerunner before Him in the spirit and power of Elijah, TO TURN THE HEARTS OF THE FATHERS BACK TO THE CHILDREN, and the disobedient to the attitude of the righteous; so as to make ready a people prepared for the Lord (Luke 1:17).

John the Baptist came into the world with only one purpose: to prepare a people for the Lord, and to that goal he dedicated his whole life!

A Witness for Jesus

A witness is one who "knows what he says and tells what he knows." John knew his message; he was not giving mere opinions or speculations. John the Baptist came to bear witness of the Light. Men in the world were blind and blind men cannot see the light. For that reason, they needed a herald—someone who would tell them plainly that the light had come to give them sight! Angels announced Christ's physical arrival in this world. John the Baptist announced the arrival of Jesus' ministry.

When John's disciples expressed their concern that Jesus was attracting more people, John said, *"He must increase, but I must decrease"* (John 3:30). John was *"...the lamp that was burning and was shining..."* (John 5:35), but Christ is the Light. A lamp has no inherent light of its own—it has to be supplied. A lamp has to be cared for by another. A lamp soon burns out—but the Light burns forever. Also, John the Baptist announced Jesus as the Lamb:

> *The next day he saw Jesus coming to him, and said, "Behold, the Lamb of God who takes away the sin of the world"* (John 1:29).

John the Baptist Bore a Sevenfold Witness

1. Jesus' Pre-existence
   > *John bore witness of Him, and cried out, saying, "This was He of whom I said, 'He who comes after me has a higher rank than I, for He existed before me'"* (John 1:15).
2. Jesus' Lordship
   > [John the Baptist said]...*I am A VOICE OF ONE CRYING IN THE WILDERNESS, MAKE STRAIGHT THE WAY OF THE LORD* (John 1:23).
3. Jesus' Immeasurable Superiority

> *It is He who comes after me, the thong of whose sandal*
> *I am not worthy to untie* (John 1:27).

4. Jesus' Sacrificial Work

> *The next day he saw Jesus coming to him, and said,*
> *"Behold, the Lamb of God who takes away the sin of*
> *the world"* (John 1:29).

5. Jesus' Baptism in the Holy Spirit

> *And John bore witness saying, "I have beheld the Spirit*
> *descending as a dove out of heaven, and He remained*
> *upon Him"* (John 1:32).

6. Jesus' Divine Right to Baptize Others in the Holy Spirit

> *And I did not recognize Him, but He who sent me to*
> *baptize in water said to me, "He upon whom you*
> *see the Spirit descending and remaining upon Him,*
> *this is the one who baptizes in the Holy Spirit"*
> (John 1:33).

7. Jesus' Divine Sonship

> *And I have seen, and have borne witness that this is*
> *the Son of God* (John 1:34).

John's Work Was Investigated

> *And all the country of Judea was going out to him,*
> *and all the people of Jerusalem; and they were being*
> *baptized by him in the Jordan River, confessing their*
> *sins* (Mark 1:5).

John the Baptist was the center of much attention. This aroused the interest of the Jewish leaders, especially the Pharisees. Soon they sent a delegation to get information. After all, John the Baptist was not a priest of the Jewish religion, a Pharisee, or a Sadducee.

Who are you? Are you Elijah? Are you the Prophet? John the Baptist said, "No, I am not, and I am not the Christ either." Being in the public eye and having such a following, it might have been a temptation to bolster his position a bit—but he said, "No, I am not a great prophet. No, I am not the Christ":

And it is he who will go as a forerunner before Him in the spirit and power of Elijah, TO TURN THE HEARTS OF THE FATHERS BACK TO THE CHILDREN, and the disobedient to the attitude of the righteous; so as to make ready a people prepared for the Lord" (Luke 1:17).

John the Baptist was not "the Prophet" spoken of in Deuteronomy—this was a prophecy of the Messiah:

The Lord your God will raise up for you a prophet like me from among you, from your countrymen, you shall listen to him....I will raise up a prophet from among their countrymen like you, and I will put My words in his mouth, and he shall speak to them all that I command him (Deuteronomy 18:15,18).

"Well then, who are you?" asked the Pharisees. "We need an answer to take back to the people who sent us. What do you have to say about yourself?"

His answer could have been, "I'm John, the son of Zacharias, the priest. I was filled with the Holy Spirit before I was born." But he drew no attention to himself. He said simply, *"...I am the voice of one crying in the wilderness, 'Make straight the way of the Lord,' as Isaiah the prophet said"* (John 1:23).

The investigators challenged John's authority. "Why are you baptizing, if you are not a great prophet?" They disputed his right to preach and baptize. After all, he had not been commissioned by the Sanhedrin!

But John, in the wisdom of the Holy Spirit, turned their attention from his actions to the Savior. *"I baptize in water, but among you stands One whom you do not know. It is He who comes after me, the thong of whose sandal I am not worthy to untie"* (John 1:26,27). They were upset with his baptizing, but John was concerned with Who Jesus was!

Studying John

Color coding your Bible can be a good way to study and remember topics. If you would rather not use your regular study Bible, buy an inexpensive paperback New Testament or Gospel of John, which you can mark and color. Colored pencils are best for color coding. As you read John, code the four most prevalent themes. Mark each word (or related word) with the appropriate color:

Light (Shine, Enlighten, etc.) — Yellow

Life (Living, Resurrection, Born Again) —Green

Word (My Words, Commandments, Believe, Believing) — Blue

Love (Loves, Loved) — Red

Christ's First Converts

In studying this passage, keep in mind that it deals with the **conversion** of these disciples, while other passages, such as Mark 1:16-20; Matthew 4:18-22; Luke 5:1-11, deal with the disciples' call to service a year later. Jesus used several methods of evangelism:

• A Preacher's Message

> *The next day he saw Jesus coming to him, and said, "Behold, the Lamb of God who takes away the sin of the world!"...Again the next day John was standing with two of his disciples, and he looked upon Jesus as He walked, and said, "Behold, the Lamb of God!" And the two disciples heard him speak, and they followed Jesus* (John 1:29,35-37).

The first two converts heard about Jesus from a preacher (John the Baptist), and as soon as they personally met Jesus they followed Him, because they wanted to know more. They were looking for fellowship. John, the preacher, lost two of his disciples, but he didn't care. He had pointed them to Jesus.

• Personal Witness, Word of Mouth

> *One of the two who heard John speak, and followed Him, was Andrew, Simon Peter's brother. He found first his own brother Simon, and said to him,—"We have found the Messiah" (which translated means Christ)....Now Philip was from Bethsaida, of the city of Andrew and Peter. Philip found Nathanael and said to him, "We have found Him of whom Moses in the Law and also the Prophets wrote, Jesus of Nazareth, the son of Joseph"* (John 1:40,41,44-46).

Andrew had fellowship with Jesus that was so sweet he had

to tell his brother. "We found the Messiah," he said, and he brought Simon Peter to Jesus. Philip found Nathanael and brought him to Jesus. Both Andrew and Philip knew they had found someone worth sharing. Are you sharing Jesus?

• No Human Instrument

> *The next day He purposed to go forth into Galilee, and He found Philip. And Jesus said to him, "Follow Me"* (John 1:43).

No human instrument brought Philip to Christ. But that did not deter our Lord! Jesus Himself went out and found Philip! He uses men, but when men are unavailable, God still has ways to get to men! *"...The Son of Man came to seek and to save that which was lost"* (Luke 19:10).

Jesus Dealt With Each Person Differently

> *And Jesus turned, and beheld them following, and said to them, "What do you seek?" And they said to Him, "Rabbi (which translated means Teacher), where are You staying?"* (John 1:38)

Jesus used a searching question to test their motives. "What do you seek?" He wanted them to understand their own purpose. No one sincerely seeks the Lord without finding Him. When they answered with another question "Where are you staying?" they revealed their motive: they wanted fellowship. Jesus always meets the needs of hearts, so He said, "Come." Jesus had won enough of their confidence for them to go and stay with Him.

Their desire for fellowship was satisfied. Yours can be, too— abide with Him now and someday it will be forever:

> *And if I go and prepare a place for you, I will come again, and receive you to Myself; that where I am, there you may be also* (John 14:3).

To Simon Peter, Jesus gave a declaration and a promise. (See John 1:42.) He said, "You are *Simon*," which means vacillating and unstable. You shall be called *Cephas* [Peter], which means Rock." To Philip Jesus gave a simple command:

> *The next day He purposed to go forth into Galilee, and He found Philip. And Jesus said to him, "Follow Me"* (John 1:43).

This same command is issued countless times as Jesus finds sinners. He says: "Follow Me for a love-filled life. Follow Me for a faith-filled life. Follow Me, and I will give you an abundant, eternal, joy-filled life!"

To Nathanael, Jesus gave a revelation. (See John 1:45-50.) It dispelled any prejudice that he might have had against the residents of Nazareth! Then Jesus revealed Himself as the Son of God. Nathanael responded immediately, *"...You are the Son of God; You are the King of Israel"* (John 1:49). Jesus answered, *"...Because I said to you that I saw you under the fig tree, do you believe? You shall see greater things than these"* (John 1:50).

The first revelation we need to have of Jesus is that He is the Son of God. Then, God wants to teach us many other things through "revelation knowledge." Nathanael knew that Jesus was operating on knowledge outside of His five senses and acknowledged Him as the Son of God. As a born-again child of God, you, too, can operate in revelation knowledge, "walking according to the Spirit not according to the flesh" (See Romans 8:4). Let Jesus show *you* "greater" things.

A Variety of Personalities Were "Called"

John the Beloved was one of the first two disciples called. (He is the unnamed one in Scripture.) *"Again the next day John was standing with two of his disciples"* (John 1:35). He describes himself as the "one whom Jesus loved." He started out as a "son of thunder," but became an affectionate, devoted person. He was the only disciple at the Cross when Jesus died; he was the one who leaned on Jesus at the Last Supper.

Andrew was the practical disciple. As soon as Andrew found the Lord, he went out immediately and found his brother. He thought, "If this is good for me, it is good for my brother too. I'd better get him to Jesus!" He had been satisfied with his encounter with Jesus, and he wanted to pass on the good news! Also Andrew was the one who noticed the little boy with the five loaves and two fishes when Jesus was teaching the multitude:

> *One of His disciples, Andrew, Simon Peter's brother, said to Him, "There is a lad here who has five barley loaves and two fish..."* (John 6:8).

Simon Peter was loud and impulsive. When he saw a problem, he had to speak, and many times it was the wrong thing! He often spoke before he thought, or acted impulsively without wisdom—like when he cut off the ear of a man in the garden of Gethsemane. He even impulsively denied the Lord three times, then wept bitterly at his sin. Yet, Christ knew his heart, chose him, and changed him!

Philip was skeptical and materialistic:

> *Jesus therefore lifting up His eyes, and seeing that a great multitude was coming to Him, said to Philip, "Where are we to buy bread, that these may eat?" And this He was saying to test him; for He Himself knew what He was intending to do. Philip answered Him, "Two hundred denarii worth of bread is not sufficient for them, for everyone to receive a little"* (John 6:5-7).

His natural mind could not comprehend how they were to feed so many people! Another time, Philip said to Jesus, "...*Show us the Father, and it is enough for us*" (John 14:8). He had been with Jesus for over three years at this point, but he still did not understand that Jesus had been revealing the Father all the time.

Nathanael was the meditative one. We don't know very much about him, since few of his actions are recorded. He was an

Israelite in whom there was no guile. Nathanael was open and honest. He asked Philip, "How can anything good come out of Nazareth?" He had some genuine difficulties, yet when he met Jesus, he recognized His divinity immediately. The eyes of his understanding were open.

Jesus "calls" many personalities to come to Him, to do His work, to be part of His body. He called you, too, and your unique personality fits perfectly into His Body.

The First Miracle of Jesus

In the account of Jesus' first miracle we see several significant symbols:

• Wine

Marriage is a feast of joy and wine was given as an emblem of joy. The same symbol is used in other passages in the Old Testament: Psalms 104:15 says, *"And wine which makes man's heart glad...."* In Judges 9:13 we read, *"But the vine said to them, 'Shall I leave my new wine which cheers God and men, and go to wave over the trees?'"* Just as the wine of the wedding had run out, so the joy of Judaism had run out.

• Six Water Pots

It is interesting to note that man's provision had run out. There was no more wine, and the water pots were empty. Judaism had no more joy. It had become a religious system that had nothing to offer the heart. Six water pots were used, six is the number of man, the number of the flesh. All that was left of Judaism were the efforts of the flesh. The feast of the Lord had now become the feast of the Jews:

> Speak to the sons of Israel, and say to them, "The Lord's appointed times which you shall proclaim as holy convocations—My appointed times are these:" (Leviticus 23:2).

Christ—the Son of God

And Jesus said to her, "Woman, what do I have to do
with you? My hour has not yet come" (John 2:4).

Jesus called His mother "woman." This was not out of
disrespect, it was a term of reverence and affection. However, it also
called attention to the fact that He was not speaking as a son to his
mother. He was speaking as the divine Son of God to a woman. At
the Cross, he also called her "woman."

Another reason for calling her "woman" was to dispel,
from the beginning, the notion that Mary had anything to do with
His divinity. She was blessed *among* women, but not blessed *above*
women.

In John 2:4 Jesus spoke of "His hour": this was the **hour** of
His Crucifixion, the hour when He would submit to the will of God
in order to complete His work of redemption.

Prepare for the Miracle

Follow instructions for a miracle. Mary, Jesus' mother, had some sound
advice for everyone: *"...Whatever He says to you, do it"* (John 2:5).
Apply this every day of your life. When Jesus says to do something,
there is no question whether you should do it or not, He is the Master.
His orders are always correct. His instruction will bring *joy* back into
a situation and satisfy any empty situation in your life!

He said to fill the water pots with water. This was the
means of bringing *joy* or wine back into the feast. The water is a
symbol of the Word, and we can bring joy into others'lives by
ministering the Word.

The servants filled the water pots, they drew some of the
water out, and they took it to the head of the feast. They did the
work, obeying every instruction of the Lord. The instructions probably
seemed foolish, especially when they took the water to the head of
the feast. They obeyed, and out of their obedience came a miracle
that blessed everyone!

God's instructions to you during a *joyless* time in your life

"His Hour"

And Jesus said to her, "Woman, what do I have to do with you? My hour is not yet come" (John 2:4).

These words He spoke in the treasury, as He taught in the temple; and no one seized Him because His hour had not yet come (John 8:20).

And Jesus answered them saying, "The hour has come for the Son of man to be glorified" (John 12:23).

Now My soul has become troubled; and what shall I say, "Father, save Me from this hour"? But for this purpose I came to this hour (John 12:27).

Behold, an hour is coming, and has already come, for you to be scattered, each to his own home, and to leave Me alone; and yet I am not alone, because the Father is with Me (John 16:32).

These things Jesus spoke; and lifting up His eyes to heaven, He said, "Father, the hour has come; glorify Thy Son that the Son may glorify Thee" (John 17:1).

From *Exposition on the Gospel of John* by A.W. Pink

can seem foolish. They might even appear contrary to sound reasoning! He is asking you to do a simple thing. Do it and watch Him fill your life!

The water turned into the best wine. The head of the feast was surprised that the host had kept his best wine until the last, but, he hadn't! He had given his best, and it ran out. Then it was time for Christ. God's supply is always the best! Your best can never equal what Jesus wants to give you!

The miracle that Christ most wants to do is change the hearts of sinners who are cold and lifeless like water pots—empty and useless. When filled with the Word the Word brings life! From water came wine. When a life receives the water of the Word, there is life and joy!

The obedient servants who worked with Jesus knew what had taken place. The bridegroom wasn't aware of it. The head of the feast knew only that the best wine had been served last. Not even the disciples had a part in this miracle, it was the humble servants. If you want to have a part in the miracles of Jesus, work closely with Him as an obedient servant! God reveals things to His servants:

> Surely the Lord GOD does nothing unless He reveals His secret counsel to His servants the prophets (Amos 3:7).

The Cleansing of the Temple

Judaism was faltering by the time John the Baptist came to minister and the Messiah was born. The priests, who were supposed to lead the people into spiritual truth were actually spiritually blind. They did not even recognize John the Baptist. They had to ask, "Who are you?" If they had been tuned in to what God was doing, they would have known that John the Baptist was sent from God and that Jesus was the Messiah:

> And this is the witness of John, when the Jews sent to him priests and Levites from Jerusalem to ask him, "Who are you?" And he confessed, and did not deny,

*and he confessed, "I am not the Christ." And they
asked him, "What then? Are you Elijah?" And he said,
"I am not." "Are you the Prophet?" And he answered,
"No." They said then to him, "Who are you, so that
we may give an answer to those who sent us?"*
(John 1:19-22).

Simeon, a righteous and devout man, did recognize the Messiah.
He identified Jesus and prophesied over Him. (See Luke 2:25-33.) How
sad that *"He came to His Own, and those who were His Own did not
receive Him"* (John 1:11). The nation of Israel had run out of joy.
Religion had become a ritual. The joy of a personal relationship
with God was not evident for the great majority of people. Jesus
promised, *"These things have I spoken to you, that My joy may be in
you, and that your joy may be made full"* (John 15:11). Jesus came
to give them joy.

The Temple Desecrated

Israel had desecrated the Temple and made it a den of thieves. Cattle
dealers and moneychangers had taken over the outer court.
Supposedly, they were there for the convenience of the worshipers
at Passover, who came great distances to celebrate the feast; but
Jesus knew their real motives and called them "thieves." In the Old
Testament, the people celebrated *the Lord's Passover*. Now they
celebrated the "Passover of the Jews." The Temple, a *house of prayer*,
had become a "den of thieves."

> *And He said to them, "It is written, 'MY HOUSE SHALL
> BE CALLED A HOUSE OF PRAYER'; but you are
> making it a ROBBERS' DEN"* (Matthew 21:13).

Because of the distance the people came to worship, they
did not bring their own animals for sacrifice. This gave shrewd
businessmen the opportunity to sell animals for this purpose. They
came closer and closer to the Temple until they were selling within
the outer court. Not only were they selling within the boundaries,

but they were charging double, making a great profit for themselves!

Foreign coins were not allowed to pollute the Temple; therefore, there also arose a need for moneychangers. Those with foreign currency could exchange it for the sacred currency and pay their Temple tax. The interest for this service was fifty percent! The Temple had become a place for personal profit, at the expense of the poor and the stranger, a place of covetousness! Recall how the Temple was built: first, there was the court of the Gentiles. Next, the court of the women, followed by the court of the Israelites and then the court of the priests. The commerce was taking place in the Gentile court, where Gentiles were to meditate and pray. This shut out the Gentiles from God. Watch how you treat those who are seeking God!

A Need for Cleansing

The desecrated Temple exemplified the need for cleansing in the lives of the Jews. They were sacrificing for their sins, but it was mere ritual, without praise and worship to the Father. It was the kind of sacrifice described in Isaiah, and God was weary of it.

> *"What are your multiplied sacrifices to Me?" says the Lord. "I have had enough of burnt offerings of rams, and the fat of fed cattle. And I take no pleasure in the blood of bulls, lambs, or goats. When you come to appear before Me, Who requires of you this trampling of My courts? Bring your worthless offerings no longer, Incense is an abomination to Me. New moon and Sabbath, the calling of assemblies—I cannot endure iniquity and the solemn assembly"* (Isaiah 1:11-13).

When Israel celebrated the Passover, the people were instructed to clean every bit of leaven out (which symbolized sin) of the house before the meal. Now, however, *leaven* had entered the Temple.

Jesus did not want the "old leaven," or sin, in their lives. The old leaven is discussed in I Corinthians 5:8-10 as—among other things—malice, wickedness, and covetousness:

Studying John

Start a scripture notebook. Get a three-ring notebook with alphabetical dividers and lots of lined paper. As you find scriptures that particularly speak to you, write them out and put them under a subject heading, then file them alphabetically in your notebook.

SAMPLE:
LIGHT
John 1:4
"In Him was life; and the life was the light of men."

John 1:7
"He came for a witness, that he might bear witness of the light, that all might believe through him."

John 1:9
"There was the true light which, coming into the world, enlightens every man."

File this page under "L." As you study John, the Lord will make certain verses meaningful to you, giving you new revelation of His truth. Write it down and file it—that way you are storing up knowledge and scriptures for meditation and for ministering to others.

*Let us therefore celebrate the feast, not with old leaven,
nor with the leaven of malice and wickedness, but
with the unleavened bread of sincerity and truth.*

Jesus in Action

Jesus acted, spoke, and moved with authority, and the whole
crowd fled before Him. Even sinners recognize authority:

*And He made a scourge of cords, and drove them all
out of the temple, with the sheep and the oxen; and
He poured out the coins of the moneychangers. and
overturned their tables;* (John 2:15).

Jesus was angry at what had become of His Father's house.
In righteous wrath, He cleansed the *leaven* from the house of God.
He showed them the holy, righteous character of God.

Jesus declared His deity. He called the Temple His "Father's
house." No prophet had ever spoken of the Temple like this. Christ
alone could claim divine Sonship:

*And to those who were selling the doves He said, "Take
these things away; stop making **My Father's house** a
house of merchandise"* (John 2:16).

Jesus still showed mercy. He drove out the large animals,
they could easily be located by their owners. He overturned the money
tables, the money could be picked up and recovered, and to the dove
owners He said, "Take these things away." If He had driven them
out, they might have flown away and never been caught again. Jesus
is righteous, but He is also merciful. He does not want *leaven* in
your life and He will point it out to you.

The disciples were watching Jesus and remembered the
scripture that said, "...*Zeal for Thy house will consume Me*"
(John 2:17). In thinking of this scripture in connection with Jesus,
they were acknowledging that He was indeed the Messiah.

Let Jesus go into action in *your* life. You are the temple of

God and the Holy Spirit lives within you. Do not allow the leaven of sin or bad habits to take over the courts of your temple. Let the blood of Jesus cleanse you and allow the water of the Word to wash out covetous ways. Your temple will then be a cleansed place of prayer and worship—filled with joy and new life!

Jesus Is Revealed

The Gospel of John concentrates on the deity of Jesus—the Word Who became flesh. God so loved you that He sent—and gave—His only Son. The Son spoke the Word and miracles happened! Watch what happens in your life when you speak that *same* Word! God's Word brings divine results!

Christ was revealed as God; He existed from the beginning; He created the universe. He came to earth to communicate to man exactly what God was like: His character, His love, His wisdom. He showed the world the mind of God. He brought God's light and life to a dark and dying world! He brought grace to men who were bound to the law.

John the Baptist was sent by God to prepare the way for the Lord Jesus. He took no glory for himself, but always pointed to the Greater One. John the Baptist was a lamp carrying the light. When questioned about who he was, John said only what the Word said about him. You, too, can be a herald for the King, carrying His light to people in darkness and keeping your confession about yourself in line with the Word!

Jesus used different methods of evangelism to win His disciples. He dealt with each one as an individual, knowing the strengths and weaknesses of each person, yet fitting them perfectly into His work. As Jesus filled the lives of the disciples, their weaknesses changed to strengths, and they began to act like their Lord!

When the wine ran out at the wedding feast, Jesus changed the circumstances of need and embarrassment to satisfaction and joy. That is what Jesus always does in your circumstances. Like the servants, do everything that He requests of you, and you will find empty places in your life satisfied and joyful!

Jesus saw the motive behind the merchandising in the Temple. The selling was not only a service to the worshipers, but a medium of covetousness, personal gain, and robbery of the poor. Speaking figuratively or literally, the Temple must be cleansed of "leaven" before the Passover. With authority and zeal for His Father's house, He evicted the sellers. Praise God that Jesus has made every provision for *you* (the present temple of God) to be cleansed—fit to be a temple of prayer and worship.

Personal Action Plan

1. Share the concept of Jesus as "the Light of the World" with a friend this week.

2. Study John 1:14. Write out three or four ways the glory and presence of the Lord affects your life.

3. In the "wilderness" of today's world, what lesson can you gather from John the Baptist and his ministry to the lost? How can you apply this to your personal life?

4. Study Christ's first miracle. What does this tell you about preparing for *your* personal miracle?

5. You are called "the temple of God." Pray about how you should cleanse your own temple.

Chapter 2

GOD SO LOVED THE WORLD

God So Loved the World

In the creation, the earth was dark, without form, and void. Then the Spirit of God moved, and God said, "Let there be light!"

> *In the beginning God created the heavens and the earth. And the earth was formless and void, and darkness was over the surface of the deep; and the Spirit of God was moving over the surface of the waters. Then God said, "Let there be light"; and there was light* (Genesis 1:1-3).

The **new** *creation* is similar. The sinner is in darkness; then the Holy Spirit works in the sinner's heart, convicting him of sin and convincing him that Jesus came to save him; then the Word of God brings light! The Holy Spirit is the One who produces the new life.

The kingdom of God has a different life source than this world, the natural realm. We are born of flesh and live in a material world. The kingdom of God is another dimension. You must be born again to enter the kingdom of God (John 3:5,6). You need a living spirit to enter that realm. It is a divine kingdom and you need divine life!

You do not need more religion, you need a totally new life— a new nature. The old nature is dead to the new kingdom. When you are born again, you become a partaker of the divine nature!

> *For by these He has granted to us His precious and magnificent promises, in order that by them you might become partakers of the divine nature, having escaped the corruption that is in the world by lust* (II Peter 1:4).

What is so exciting about this new nature is that it produces after its own kind. Just as the grass and trees yield after their kind, that which is born of the Spirit produces life after the Spirit:

> *But the fruit of the Spirit is love, joy, peace,*
> *patience, kindness, goodness, faithfulness,*
> *gentleness, self-control; against such things there*
> *is no law* (Galatians 5:22,23).

Romans 14:17 tells us that *"...the kingdom of God is not eating and drinking, but righteousness and peace and joy in the Holy Spirit."* Being born again gives you a new spiritual life source that produces good things, not only in your life, but in the lives of those around you!

Born of Water and the Spirit

> *Now there was a man of the Pharisees, named*
> *Nicodemus, a ruler of the Jews; this man came to*
> *Him by night, and said to Him, "Rabbi, we know*
> *that You have come from God as a teacher; for no*
> *one can do these signs that You do unless God is*
> *with him." Jesus answered and said to him, "Truly,*
> *truly, I say to you, unless one is born again, he*
> *cannot see the kingdom of God." Nicodemus said to*
> *Him, "How can a man be born when he is old? He*
> *cannot enter a second time into his mother's womb*
> *and be born, can he?"* (John 3:1-4)

It is obvious from the answer Nicodemus gave that he did not understand spiritual things at all—even if he was a teacher in Israel. The natural man does not perceive the things of the Spirit of God. Each time Jesus spoke of spiritual things, Nicodemus could not comprehend them or get past his natural way of thinking. Jesus was determined to teach Nicodemus that he needed to be made alive spiritually. A man cannot live before he is born, and you cannot control what is dead.

Jesus says, "Truly, truly...." This expression means that what follows has weighty significance and we are to pay attention. Without the born-again experience, you cannot enter, nor see, the kingdom of God. Spiritual life will not be yours, neither will you understand the things of God, unless you are born spiritually:

> But a natural man does not accept the things of the Spirit of God; for they are foolishness to him, and he cannot understand them, because they are spiritually appraised (I Corinthians 2:14).

> Jesus answered, "Truly, truly, I say to you, unless one is born of water and the Spirit, he cannot enter into the kingdom of God" (John 3:5).

Water is used symbolically in John 4:14 and Isaiah 12:3 for salvation; in John 7:37-39 for the baptism of the Holy Spirit; and in Ephesians 5:26 for God's Word.

> But whoever drinks of the water that I shall give him shall never thirst; but the water that I shall give him shall become in him a well of water springing up to eternal life (John 4:14).

> Now on the last day, the great day of the feast, Jesus stood and cried out, saying, "If any man is thirsty, let him come to Me and drink. He who believes in Me, as the Scripture said, 'From his innermost being shall flow rivers of living water.'" But this He spoke of the Spirit, whom those who believed in Him were to receive; for the Spirit was not yet given, because Jesus was not yet glorified (John 7:37-39).

Their Understanding Is Darkened

> Nicodemus answered and said to Him, "How can these things be?" Jesus answered and said to him, "Are you the teacher of Israel, and do not understand these things? Truly, truly, I say to you, we speak

THE WIND
OF THE SPIRIT

Wind is a symbol of the Holy Spirit. Man does not and cannot control the wind. It comes and goes at will. Neither can the Holy Spirit be controlled by man. You cannot see the wind, yet you can see the results. You cannot see the Holy Spirit, but it is evident when He produces new life. You cannot resist the power of the wind—it is a powerful force. The Holy Spirit is powerful when He comes into a life. He breaks down prejudices, changes wills, turns rebellion into repentance. The Holy Spirit may gently woo one soul on one side of town today, and tomorrow sweep across the entire city with a mighty revival. The Holy Spirit is indispensable—without Him we would not have a spiritual life.

that which we know, and bear witness of that which
we have seen; and you do not receive our witness"
(John 3:9-11).

Nicodemus had a *religious* mind; he could not understand the spiritual things Jesus was saying. "How can these things be?" was his reply. He was like the men in Ephesians 4:18, *"Being darkened in their understanding, excluded from the life of God, because of the ignorance that is in them, because of the hardness of their heart."* He did not mean to be hard, but that was his condition. He could not see what Jesus was trying to show him.

Jesus answered, "Are you the teacher of Israel, and yet you do not understand these things?" Nicodemus was designated as a light-holder in the nation, yet he was in the dark.

The reason for the ignorance of man concerning spiritual things is his refusal to receive God's witness concerning them. First, you receive what God says; then you have the knowledge. First, you believe what He says; then you understand it. *"By faith we understand...."* (Hebrews 11:3). Receive what God gives you in His Word, and He will give you enlightenment concerning it.

The Son of Man Lifted Up

And as Moses lifted up the serpent in the wilderness,
even so must the Son of Man be lifted up; that whoever
believes may in Him have eternal life (John 3:14,15).

Jesus showed Nicodemus what had to be done for the new birth to be available to mankind. Jesus must be lifted up, not as a conquering king, elevated to the throne of David (as the leaders pictured the Messiah), but as a sacrifice on the Cross. He must be lifted up as Moses lifted up the serpent in the wilderness.

Moses made a serpent in the likeness of one of the deadly serpents. So Jesus was made *"...in the likeness of sinful flesh..."* (Romans 8:3) and put on the Cross in our place.

He made Him who knew no sin to be sin on our behalf,

that we might become the righteousness of God in Him
(II Corinthians 5:21).

The serpent lifted up was a reminder of the curse that had come upon mankind. Jesus became the curse:

Christ redeemed us from the curse of the Law, having become a curse for us—for it is written, "Cursed is everyone who hangs on a tree" (Galatians 3:13).

This is the secret of being born again—believing Christ is the Son of God, and knowing that He was the perfect sacrifice for your sins.

God So Loved...

For God so loved the world, that He gave His only begotten Son, that whoever believes in Him should not perish, but have eternal life (John 3:16).

Christ, on the Cross, demonstrated to us the righteousness of God. (Sin had to be dealt with.) It also demonstrated to us the love of God. Love was the foundation of everything that God did for us. He wanted to make a way for sinful man to come back to Him, so that He could again have fellowship with him.

The one who does not love does not know God, for God is love...In this is love, not that we loved God, but that He loved us and sent His Son to be the propitiation for our sins (I John 4:8,10).

God did not send His Son to condemn the world, but to save the world. Love desires the good of those to whom it flows. Christ came to do good to the world:

For God did not send the Son into the world to judge the world, but that the world should be saved through Him (John 3:17).

If you believe in Him you are not judged. The believer is not judged guilty of sin because Christ took the guilty verdict upon himself.

> *He who believes on Him [who clings to, trusts in, relies on Him] is not judged [he who trusts in Him never comes up for judgment; for him there is no rejection, no condemnation—he incurs no damnation]; but he who does not believe (cleave to, rely on, trust in Him) is judged already [he has already been convicted and has already received his sentence] because he has not believed in and trusted in the name of the only begotten Son of God. [He is condemned for refusing to let his trust rest in Christ's name.]* (John 3:18 TAB).

Lovers of Darkness, Haters of Light

> *And this is the judgment, that the light is come into the world, and men loved the darkness rather than the light; for their deeds were evil* (John 3:19).

What a terrible condition: to see the Light and not want it, to prefer to stay in darkness rather than associate with the Light of the world. Men's deeds were so evil that they did not want the Light. They hated it, because it exposed their deeds. When men love their evil deeds, they do not want to read the Word. The Word lights up those deeds and exposes them.

> *But he who practices the truth comes to the light, that his deeds may be manifested as having been wrought in God* (John 3:21).

He who practices the truth comes again and again to the light of the Word to learn God's mind, to learn which deeds cannot stand up to the light, and to know which ones can. He who loves the truth wants his life constantly cleansed by the light of God's Word. When his deeds pass the "light inspection," he knows that he is on the right path! Nicodemus came by night as though he knew his deeds could not bear the light, so Jesus spoke to his conscience. We know Nicodemus responded because his later actions proved that he had received the testimony of Jesus.

Love Is Not Jealous

One day some of John the Baptist's disciples asked him whose baptism was most effective—his or Jesus'. They said to John, "That man whom you witnessed about, He is baptizing too. In fact, they are all following after Him!" (See John 3:26.) Did John the Baptist decide his ministry was over since a more popular preacher had come on the scene? Did he allow discouragement, jealousy, and hurt feelings to take over? No, instead he was filled with the **love** of God. Not only that, John knew *Who* Christ was. John the Baptist's crowds may have been decreasing, but his allegiance to Christ was not.

Moses had a similar situation during his ministry. Some men in the camp were prophesying, and immediately a young man ran to tell Moses. Joshua said, "Moses, make them stop." Then Moses lovingly answered, *"...Are you jealous for my sake? Would that all the Lord's people were prophets, that the Lord would put His Spirit upon them!"* (Numbers 11:29).

God has a place for each of us. There should be no competition in the Body of Christ. There is room for everyone! When you are filled with the love of God, you will never be jealous of someone else's ministry.

Increase vs. Decrease

John the Baptist rejoiced in the fact that the truth had come! John called himself a friend of the Bridegroom. He knew *Who* Jesus was!

> *The next day he* [John the Baptist] *saw Jesus coming to him, and said, "Behold, the Lamb of God who takes away the sin of the world!"* (John 1:29)

John the Baptist said he was the friend "who stands and

hears Him." *Stand* means "to stop activity and concentrate attention." He pointed men to Him and was filled with joy when Jesus spoke. His voice delighted John's soul! The Word—His voice—will also fill *your* life with joy. Stand still, listen to His voice, and rejoice!

The more Christ increases in your life, the less your own interests control you: *"He must increase, but I must decrease"* (John 3:30). As you stand and hear Him, Christ will become the primary object of your life, and you will be less and less preoccupied with yourself. You will be *"...transformed into the same image from glory to glory..."*(II Corinthians 3:18). John knew *his* place in God's scheme. He was sent "before" Christ. However, he saw with the eye of faith what was to happen. He saw the "bride of Christ" forming.

Receive the Witness of Christ

He who comes from above is above all, he who is of the earth is from the earth and speaks of the earth. He who comes from heaven is above all. What He has seen and heard, of that He bears witness; and no man receives His witness (John 3:31,32).

Christ testified of those things that He had both seen and heard. He had come down from above and was above all. He is God, and knows the mind of God.

The Jews thought that all men were following after Jesus, but John knew most were not accepting Jesus for Who He *really* was—God. John looked beneath the surface. He knew that most men were thinking earthly thoughts, speaking earthly ways, and did not receive Jesus as from heaven. Their hearts loved the darkness; they did not want to come to the Light.

He who has received His witness has set his seal to this, that God is true. For He whom God has sent speaks the words of God; for He gives the Spirit without measure. The Father loves the Son, and has given all things into His hand (John 3:33-35).

The person who dares to receive the testimony of Christ receives Him and knows that God is true. He seals the Truth to himself; he has it settled. He stakes his life on what the Son and His Word say is true. Christ had the Spirit without measure. The prophets had anointings that came and went, but the Spirit remained on this Man:

> *And John bore witness saying, "I have beheld the Spirit descending as a dove out of heaven, and He remained upon Him"* (John 1:32).

The prophets spoke portions of the truth—the Word of God, but Jesus speaks the whole Word. All things were given into His hand.

There are only two options: believing or refusing to believe in the Son. His testimony is true; accepting it brings life eternal. Rejecting it has only one possible result: the wrath of God:

> *He who believes in the Son has eternal life; but he who does not obey the Son shall not see life, but the wrath of God abides on him* (John 3:36).

Missions Journey

When Jesus learned that the Pharisees knew He was making more disciples than John, He left Judea. (John 4:1-3). Whenever a spirit of rivalry and jealousy enters, Jesus departs.

> *And He had to pass through Samaria. So He came to a city of Samaria, called Sychar, near the parcel of ground that Jacob gave to his son Joseph* (John 4:4,5).

Many Jews, because of prejudice towards the Samaritans, would travel across the Jordan, and through Perea (going far out of their way) in order not to have dealings with the Samaritans. (Samaria was the territory originally allotted to Ephraim and the half tribe of Manassah by Joshua.) When the ten tribes revolted, the inhabitants of this area no longer worshiped at the temple in Jerusalem, but worshiped idols introduced by King Jeroboam. (See I Kings 12:26-33.) After the exile of the ten tribes, the king of Assyria brought people of various nations to settle this territory. Each introduced various forms of idolatry, and the result was a mixture of Jewish principles and heathen practices.

> *They also feared the Lord and appointed from among themselves priests of the high places, who acted for them in the houses of the high places. They feared the Lord and served their own gods according to the custom of the nations from among whom they had been carried away into exile....So while these nations feared the Lord, they also served their idols; their children likewise and their grandchildren, as their fathers did, so they do to this day* (II Kings 17:32,33,41).

When the remnant of Judah returned from the Babylonian captivity, the Samaritans offered to enter into an alliance with the Jews, but were refused (Ezra 4:1-5). This caused a bitterness between the two lands.

During Jesus' time, the Samaritans accepted the Books of Moses as God's Word, but rejected the historic books written by the Jews—their worst enemies. The strength of this hatred is illustrated by the words of the enemies of Christ. When they wanted to especially insult Him—they called Him a Samaritan with a demon.

> *The Jews answered and said to Him, "Do we not say rightly that You are a Samaritan and have a demon?"* (John 8:48).

Sinner Seeker

By divine appointment, Jesus went to Samaria to meet a sinner. She was one of the sheep from the "other fold":

> *And I have other sheep, which are not of this fold; I must bring them also, and they shall hear My voice; and they shall become one flock with one shepherd* (John 10:16).

CHARACTER STUDY

Jesus loves and saves people from every walk of life! It is interesting to compare Nicodemus and the woman at the well.

1. Nicodemus was a Pharisee; she was an unnamed woman.

2. A master in Israel; a woman of low rank.

3. A favored Jew; a despised Samaritan.

4. Nicodemus had a good reputation; the woman had a bad reputation.

5. Nicodemus sought out Jesus; Jesus sought out the woman.

6. Nicodemus came by night; Christ spoke to the woman at midday.

7. To the one He said, "You must be born again"; to the other, "I will give you living water."

And Jacob's well was there. Jesus therefore, being wearied from His journey, was sitting thus by the well. It was about the sixth hour. There came a woman of Samaria to draw water. Jesus said to her, "Give Me a drink" (John 4:6,7).

Even though Jesus was tired, there was still a difference in the situation: His *divinity* was present. He lay asleep, at the bottom of the boat, yet He got up to still the storm! He groaned and wept when His friend, Lazarus, died; then called him back to life! At the well, Jesus was weary and resting, but also seeking to discern the heart of a troubled woman.

Jesus came looking for a woman who didn't know *Who* He was. He sought out one who was not seeking Him. Jesus went out to seek and to save the lost. He took the initiative. You, also, in your personal evangelism must take the initiative. Seek those who are not even looking for Jesus. Many are ripe and ready for harvest—they just don't know for what they are looking!

I permitted Myself to be sought by those who did not ask for Me; I permitted Myself to be found by those who did not seek Me. I said, "Here am I, here am I," To a nation which did not call on My name (Isaiah 65:1).

Paul testified of the same experience. He said, *"I was laid hold of by Christ Jesus!"*

Not that I have already obtained it, or have already become perfect, but I press on in order that I may lay hold of that for which also I was laid hold of by Christ Jesus (Philippians 3:12).

When Jesus spoke to Zacchaeus, He went right up to the tree where Zacchaeus was hidden and said "Hurry and come down. I'm going to your house today." That very day, salvation came to that house. (See Luke 19:5.)

We must remember that Jesus has already taken the initiative with sinners. He made complete provision. The next step is up to the sinner. He must believe:

> *And this is His commandment, that we believe in the*
> *name of His Son Jesus Christ, and love one another,*
> *just as He commanded us* (I John 3:23).

The sixth hour was when the sun was the highest and hottest, and the well was deserted. The woman came at this hour to avoid people, but she could not avoid God. Jesus Christ had an appointment with her; it was not an accident.

This woman had a low reputation, but Jesus spoke to her anyway, in broad daylight! Many rabbis would not talk to any woman in public, certainly not a Samaritan woman! Jesus was ministering to an adulterous Samaritan woman at midday, when He was weary and probably would have liked to take a nap. Concern about His reputation didn't stop Him, either.

Just a Cup of Water

Jesus asked for the simplest, cheapest gift that one man can give another, in order to give her the most precious gift that a person can receive! He said, "Give me to drink" so that she would say, "Give me that living water." He asked to have His physical thirst quenched so that He might show her how to quench her spiritual thirst.

> *The Samaritan woman therefore said to Him, "How*
> *is it that You, being a Jew, ask me for a drink since I*
> *am a Samaritan woman?" (For Jews have no dealings*
> *with Samaritans.)* (John 4:9).

We are full of "hows." She could only think of the prejudice of the Jews. She should have been thinking, "*Who* is this man?" Not, "Why is He, a Jew, talking to me?" Nicodemus also said, "How can it be?" He too, was preoccupied with human reasoning. Satan will try to keep you so busy with "hows and whys" that you forget "Who" is

The Well

The well was a figure of Christ; the water was a picture of salvation.

"Therefore with joy will you draw water from the wells of salvation" **(Isaiah 12:3 TAB).**

When in despair, look for the "well" in your situation. Ask God to open your eyes to the provision He has for you in Christ. The provision is *always* there!

talking to you. Be occupied with the Person of God and He will reveal to you the "hows and whys."

> *Jesus answered and said to her, "If you knew the gift of God, and who it is who says to you, 'Give Me a drink,' you would have asked Him, and He would have given you living water"* (John 4:10).

Her problem was that she was ignorant of God's greatest gift. She did not know about the love of God in sending His Son. That is the root problem of most sinners. They don't know the gift of God—Jesus. Let's spread the good news of THE GIFT!

The sinner must ask: "Ask and ye shall receive." The sinner must admit how needy and how thirsty he is, and go to the Giver of Living water. When he asks, he *will* receive.

> *And the Spirit and the bride say, "Come." And let the one who hears say, "Come." And let the one who is thirsty come; let the one who wishes take the water of life without cost* (Revelation 22:17).

Face the Truth

Jesus addressed her conscience. She had to face the truth of her life before she could accept *His* truth. He said, "go," but He also said, "come." Jesus wanted her to admit her sinful lifestyle. He wanted to change her life!

> *The woman answered and said, "I have no husband." Jesus said to her, "You have well said, 'I have no husband'; for you have had five husbands, and the one whom you now have is not your husband; this you have said truly"* (John 4:17,18).

Jesus showed this woman that He knew her heart. Jesus knows your heart, too. There is nothing you can hide from Him. He knows failures and heartaches, but He also knows your dreams and aspirations. And He says, "come" to you, too. He will take your heartaches and fulfill the visions and dreams He has given you!

> *Our fathers worshiped in this mountain, and you*
> *people say that in Jerusalem is the place where men*
> *ought to worship. Jesus said to her, "Woman, believe*
> *Me, an hour is coming when neither in this mountain,*
> *nor in Jerusalem, shall you worship the Father. You*
> *worship that which you do not know; we worship that*
> *which we know, for salvation is from the Jews. But an*
> *hour is coming, and now is when the true worshipers*
> *shall worship the Father in spirit and truth; for such*
> *people the Father seeks to be His worshipers. God is*
> *spirit, and those who worship Him must worship in*
> *spirit and truth"* (John 4:20-24).

When her conscience was pricked, the woman sought to change the subject. She saw Him as a prophet, so she asked a religious question *"Where should we worship?"* Then Jesus told her that the important issue was not WHERE, but HOW. One must worship in Spirit and *in truth*.

That is to say, outward rituals are not of great importance. It is your inner man, your spirit, that is worshiping. God is a Spirit, and your spirit was created to worship Him. Do not be so taken up with the outward temple or with buildings, services, etc. that you fail to recognize that *true* worship takes place within the spirit.

Your worship must also be in line with the revealed truth of God. You can do it from the heart, but if it isn't according to God's Word, it still isn't *true* worship. Worship is the activity of a reborn people. They worship, with their spirits, the God with Whom they have fellowship and Whom they want to spend time getting to know.

The Messiah Has Come!

When the woman said, *"I know Messiah is coming and then He will declare all things to us,"* she was declaring a desire.

The woman said to Him, "I know that Messiah is

Receive Living Water

Water is a figure or type of salvation:

Water is a gift. Man cannot create water. We depend on God for it. Salvation is a gift. It comes from God.

Water is indispensable. It is not a luxury. It is a basic necessity. So is salvation: "You *must* be born again."

Water is a universal need. This need is not limited to location, race, age, or any other qualification: neither is salvation.

Water comes from above—so does salvation.

Water never tires us. You might grow weary of some things, but water is welcome every day. You never grow weary of God's salvation.

Water refreshes, it satisfies your thirst and so does time with Him—the well of our salvation!

*coming (He who is called Christ); when that One
comes, He will declare all things to us." Jesus said to
her, "I who speak to you am He"* (John 4:25,26).

She was saying, *"I want to know Him."* Jesus said, *"I am
He."* Her eyes were opened; she saw *Who* He was and had no
more questions. She was a changed person. She had recognized
Him as a prophet, now her eyes were opened to the "well" that
was before her.

The woman at the well received the Living Water. She came
with a waterpot and left with a well of living water within her and
instantly, she became an evangelist. Good news *has to be* shared!

She had been alone with God. Every sinner must get alone
with Him. Now she went to tell all the people of the city. Before, she
wanted to avoid people—now she wanted to talk to them.

*"Come, see a man who told me all the things that I
have done; this is not the Christ, is it?"* (John 4:29).

It was amazing—not only had He told her what she had done,
but He loved her at the same time! There was not a word of
condemnation from the lips of Jesus. When the Jewish teacher spoke
kindly to the adulterous Samaritan, her life changed. She felt loved
and accepted. She had to share that with everyone.

That simple invitation brought results. They came to Jesus
because of *her* word, and they believed on Him because of *His*
Word. You may not make men believe, but you can take them to
hear His Word.

Love Reached Out

God's love reached out to Nicodemus, a ruler and teacher of Israel
who did not grasp spiritual things. Jesus showed him the necessity
of a new life source—a spiritual one—in order to understand spiritual
things. He had to be born of the Spirit and the Word—not just flesh
and blood. Meditate on the miracle that has taken place in your life.
You are a product of God's Spirit—you have a divine "life source"!

God loves the whole world. He sent His Son to a dark world to bring light and life. He initiated love and gave the solution to mankind's sin problem. Your sins have been totally dealt with in Jesus because of the Cross. Come daily to the Word and let its light shine on your life. Your love for God keeps you in the light, and the light shows up any ugly deeds which you can get rid of by the blood of Jesus.

John the Baptist understood *Who* Christ was and he pointed to Him. John knew that his ministry was only fulfilled when people went to Jesus. He was filled with the love of God. He was not jealous when others pointed out that Jesus' popularity was growing. You can have that attitude. Keep pointing men to Jesus, and you will fulfill your ministry.

Christ loves everyone—the adulterous woman as well as the rich Jewish ruler. Jesus went through enemy territory to meet a Samaritan woman at a well. He was not concerned with His own reputation. He was concerned with the life of an unhappy Samaritan. Jesus offered this woman a free gift of Living Water. He had a well of salvation for her—a well that would continually satisfy her thirst. She would never grow weary of its water as it refreshed her daily. Yes, Jesus knew about her unhappy, sinful condition, but He gave her a solution. Now it is your turn. You have the same Well—The Answer to a thirsty world. Share Him—share the Living Water with the lost.

Personal Action Plan

1. In your own words, paraphrase John 3:16-21 and write it in your notebook or journal. How does this affect you in today's world?

2. Read John 3:29 several times. What did you personally learn from this? Share it with a friend.

3. Jesus went through Samaria to reach a lost woman. What enemy territory are you facing today? What in the Gospel of John prepares you to face the enemy?

4. Meditate on a spirit of worship as described in John 4:21. Now write out some of the truths of this verse.

5. The well was a place of meeting with Christ, the water of salvation. What people in your life need the living water? Pray about how you can bring them to the Well.

Chapter 3

MEETING
MAN'S NEEDS

Meeting Man's Needs

Now when He heard that John had been taken into custody, He withdrew into Galilee; and leaving Nazareth, He came and settled in Capernaum, which is by the sea, in the region of Zebulun and Naphtali. This was to fulfill what was spoken through Isaiah the prophet, saying, "The land of Zebulun and the land of Naphtali, by the way of the sea, beyond the Jordan, Galilee of the Gentiles—the people who were sitting in darkness saw a great light, and to those who were sitting in the land and shadow of death, upon them a light dawned" (Matthew 4:12-16).

When Jesus heard that John the Baptist was cast into prison, He departed into Galilee, thus fulfilling prophecy. Jesus went into the land of darkness as the bright Light. In Samaria, Jesus had been honored as a prophet, but in Galilee, He was received because of a miracle.

So when He came to Galilee, the Galileans received Him, having seen all the things that He did in Jerusalem at the feast; for they themselves also went to the feast (John 4:45).

In Samaria, Jesus was honored for His Word. In Galilee, the people wanted miracles, and they received miracles, but it was still the Word that was at work!

A nobleman came to Jesus. He was a royal officer who belonged to Herod's court, a man of means—with servants. Money does not insure happiness or health. It is the Word that makes the difference, as this nobleman soon found out! His level of faith had not yet been developed. He did not know the Lord very well, but he did believe what he heard.

He thought, "If Jesus would just come to my house and be near my son, He could surely heal him. If He could do a miracle in Cana and turn water into wine, surely he could heal my son." He was like Jairus who said, *"If He would just lay hands on my daughter she would be healed."* (See Mark 5:23.) He was like the woman with the issue of blood who thought to herself, "If I could just touch the hem of His garment, I would be healed." (See Matthew 9:20.)

There is nothing wrong with this level of faith—it brought results—but Jesus was about to teach this nobleman a higher way. Jesus wanted the nobleman's faith to come because of His Word. He said, *"...Unless you people see signs and wonders, you simply will not believe"* (John 4:48). This did not deter the nobleman. He had a need, and he was convinced that Jesus was the answer. He asked again, *"Sir, come down before my child dies."* Jesus rebuked the nobleman. The man received the rebuke, but did not get discouraged. Jesus wanted the nobleman to fully trust Him, to trust His Word.

> *Jesus said to him, "Go your way; your son lives." The man believed the Word that Jesus spoke to him, and he started off"* (John 4:50).

A centurion came to Jesus. He was a Gentile and a man of means who was also from Capernaum. In Matthew 8, the centurion simply spread his need before the Lord. He did not dictate what needed to be done and Jesus said to him, *"I will come and heal him."* The centurion had great faith. He said, "I am not qualified for you to come under my roof, so just say the Word and my servant will be healed." Jesus said He had not seen such great faith in all Israel.

> *Now when Jesus heard this, He marveled, and said to those who were following, "Truly I say to you, I have not found such great faith with anyone in Israel"* (Matthew 8:10).

We cannot demand signs before we trust the Lord. Mark 16:17,18 says that the signs will follow those who believe:

And these signs will accompany those who have
believed: in My name they will cast out demons,
they will speak with new tongues; they will pick up
serpents, and if they drink any deadly poison, it
will not hurt them; they will lay hands on the sick,
and they will recover.

We are to expect signs to follow when we believe, but are not
to ask for signs in order to believe.

Jesus therefore said to him, "Unless you people see
signs and wonders, you simply will not believe"
(John 4:48).

Jesus knew where their hearts were. He wanted them to
believe His Word. The nobleman did believe His Word, because when
Jesus said, "Your son lives," he believed and went his way.

Ordinarily it would have taken the nobleman only four
hours to get home to Capernaum, but we notice that he did not
get home until the next day! Why? He had perfect faith that his
son was healed. Jesus had said so! He possibly stayed overnight
to complete his errands before returning home. His faith was
rewarded! His servants met him and told him the good news;
"Yesterday at the seventh hour he began to get better!" That was
the exact hour when Jesus had pronounced him well! His faith
may not have been perfect and mature when he came to Christ,
but when Christ gave him the Word, he believed, and his faith
took a giant leap!

The boy had been at death's door, but the Word came, and
the whole household received new life. Jesus said, *"I am the Way,*
the Truth, and the Life." The nobleman went his way believing that
the Word of Jesus was truth, and he found his son restored to health.
Jesus' words are truly "spirit and life."

It is the Spirit who gives life; the flesh profits nothing;
the words that I have spoken to you are spirit and are
life (John 6:63).

The Gate of the Sheep

This Sheep Gate is mentioned in Nehemiah 3:1:

Then Eliashib the high priest arose with his brothers the priests and built the Sheep Gate; they consecrated it and hung its doors. They consecrated the wall to the Tower of the Hundred and the Tower of Hananel .

It is the gate through which the sacrificial animals were brought to the Temple. The lamb was the predominant animal for sacrifice, so the gate was called the Sheep Gate. This gate points us to Christ—the Lamb of God who takes away the sin of the world.

Distance is no barrier to the Word. It brings healing regardless of the distance: *"He sent His word and healed them, and delivered them from their destructions"* (Psalm 107:20).

> *Now there is in Jerusalem by the sheep gate a pool, which is called in Hebrew Bethesda, having five porticoes* (John 5:2).

By this gate was the pool of Bethesda, which means "House of Mercy." The pool itself had five porches. The number five is significant. Five always stands for grace or favor.

> *And he took portions to them from his own table; but Benjamin's portion was five times as much as any of theirs. So they feasted and drank freely with him...To each of them he gave changes of garments, but to Benjamin he gave three hundred pieces of silver and five changes of garments* (Genesis 43:34; 45:22).

The five loaves fed five thousand men. The fifth of the Ten Commandments is the only one with a promise!

A Sick Nation

> *In these lay a multitude of those who were sick, blind, lame, and withered, waiting for the moving of the waters...* (John 5:3).

The multitude that lay at the pool of Bethesda was a picture of the condition of the nation of Israel. There were those who were impotent (no power), blind (in understanding and heart), lame (crippled, unable to walk), withered (unable to work), and waiting (for the promised Messiah, for some kind of deliverance).

The waters of the pool can be seen as a picture of the Sinai law, given to Israel "by the disposition of angels." An angel visited the pool periodically, stirred it up and made healing available for the first one who stepped into the waters. However, the pool was crowded with helpless people! They couldn't get into the water by themselves. The law was given for life, but no one could keep it, so it became death. Surely, God was preparing His people for a better way!

When one was healed at the pool, it was undoubtedly miserable for those who were still waiting—helpless and without power to get to the water. That is all religion can offer you. If you do some of the work and get into the water, then you can find healing. With Jesus it is so different! He knows your helpless state before salvation. When Jesus comes to you, He gives you the strength to get up and walk—to be healed! Jesus is all you need! He does not give you another requirement for healing, He gives you life! His life heals you.

Believing and Receiving

Jesus said to him, "Arise, take up your pallet, and walk." And immediately the man became well, and took up his pallet and began to walk (John 5:8,9).

Jesus asked this man if he wanted to get well. The sick man responded by reciting the circumstances of the past thirty-eight years! His eyes and hope had been fixed on men, and they had let him down. When Jesus spoke, His words entered the man's heart and he immediately transferred his hope and confidence to Jesus.

You may have a lot of negative circumstances, but the minute the Word enters there is hope. The man heard the Word. Then he acted on the Word, picked up his bed and walked and received a miracle. There was no provision for failure or relapse. He took that bed with him. He would never have to lie there again!

The Religious Persecute the Spiritual

And for this reason the Jews were persecuting Jesus, because He was doing these things on the Sabbath (John 5:16).

When the Jews saw the healed man, they asked him why he was carrying his bed. They were not interested in the fact that an impotent, powerless, sick man now had health and a new life. They were concerned that their laws had been broken. On the other hand, Jesus, the Master of the Sabbath, was not concerned with their laws. He was occupied with giving life and healing to a sick and dying man. Your vision should be the same. Concern yourself with giving life to dying people, not with petty disputings over religious rules. Christ's life leads to right and healthy living—religious rules will not!

My Father and I Do the Same Work

But He answered them, "My Father is working until now, and I Myself am working." For this cause therefore the Jews were seeking all the more to kill Him, because He not only was breaking the Sabbath, but also was calling God His own Father, making Himself equal with God (John 5:17,18).

Christ's response to the accusations of the Jews was that His Father was "working" and that He, too, was "working." They had just talked about the Sabbath, the "day of rest." Then Jesus talked about work. His work was spreading the Word. The Word works all the time—even on the Sabbath!

God *hallowed* the Sabbath, "set it apart for sacred use." That was the day in which God rested. Yet the Word worked while He rested (Hebrews 1:3). The Word is upholding all things; and that is *constant* work! Jesus saw the Word work at the beginning of the world. Now, He put the Word to work in the life of an impotent man. Christ's rest is not *from* work, but *in* work!

The Jews were "resting" on their Sabbath, but the Father and the Son were "working" to give sinners life and healing.

What I See My Father Doing

Jesus therefore answered and was saying to them, "Truly, truly, I say to you, the Son can do nothing of

> *Himself, unless it is something He sees the Father*
> *doing; for whatever the Father does, these things the*
> *Son also does in like manner* (John 5:19).

The word for *see* is the Greek word *plepo*, which signifies "to contemplate, to perceive, to know." When the Son used His divine power, it was always with the conscious knowledge that He was doing the Father's will. Christ stated that He did what the Father did, the way the Father did it using the same power and doing the same works. He was claiming absolute equality with God! Working together, they created the heavens and the earth. They both sustain the universe. They are both involved in our salvation. Someday, in the future, we will see the throne of God and Jesus the Lamb of God.

> *And he showed me a river of the water of life, clear as*
> *crystal, coming from the throne of God and of the Lamb*
> (Revelation 22:1).

The Father and the Son work in perfect unison!

The Father Shows the Son All Things

> *For the Father loves the Son, and shows Him all things*
> *that He Himself is doing; and greater works than these*
> *will He show Him, that you may marvel* (John 5:20).

The Father keeps no secrets from the Son. The Father can do this because the Son is of equal intelligence with the Father. The Son can understand what the Father is showing Him. Christ has the capacity to comprehend all things that the Father does. There is an exciting aspect to this truth—we also have the mind of Christ.

> *For who has known the mind of the Lord, that he*
> *should instruct Him? But we have the mind of Christ*
> (I Corinthians 2:16).

The Bible states in I Corinthians 2:12, *"Now we have received, not the spirit of the world, but the Spirit who is from God, that we might know the things freely given to us by God."* God wants us to know Him. He says that man cannot see, nor hear, nor even imagine the things God has prepared for us, but *"...to us God revealed them through the Spirit; for the Spirit searches all things, even the depths of God"* (I Corinthians 2:10).

Then, in John 15:15, Jesus affirms this truth when He says,

> *No longer do I call you slaves, for the slave does not know what his master is doing; but I have called you friends, for all things that I have heard from My Father I have made known to you.*

The Son Gives Life

> *For just as the Father raises the dead and gives them life, even so the Son also gives life to whom He wishes* (John 5:21).

Jesus declares His sovereignty. He says that He gives life to whom He wishes. Again, in John 15, He says, *"You did not choose Me, but I chose you, and appointed you that you should go and bear fruit, and that your fruit should remain..."* (John 15:16).

> *For not even the Father judges anyone, but He has given all judgment to the Son, in order that all may honor the Son, even as they honor the Father. He who does not honor the Son does not honor the Father who sent Him* (John 5:22,23).

The Father gave the Son all judgment. He is to have the same honor as the Father. The equality of the Son and the Father is so perfect that Jesus said, *"The one who listens to you listens to Me, and he who rejects you rejects Me; and he who rejects Me rejects the One who sent Me"* (Luke 10:16). Jesus and the Father are one.

> *Truly, truly, I say to you, he who hears My word, and*
> *believes Him who sent Me, has eternal life, and does*
> *not come into judgment, but has passed out of death*
> *into life. Truly, truly, I say to you, an hour is coming*
> *and now is, when the dead shall hear the voice of the*
> *Son of God; and those who hear shall live. For just as*
> *the Father has life in Himself, even so He gave to the*
> *Son also to have life in Himself* (John 5:24-26).

Jesus again linked Himself inseparably to the Father by saying that those who believed Him, believed the Father. You cannot believe Jesus and reject the Father. On the other hand, you cannot truly believe the Father and not the Son. Believing both, the Father and the Son, results in eternal life—not a life sometime in the future, but a "present-tense life." He that believes has eternal life. That's a guarantee of life for the present. Jesus has the power to give eternal life. This is divine power! He is equal with God. As God is love, so Jesus is life, it is His nature!

The Authority To Judge

> *...And He gave Him authority to execute judgment,*
> *because He is the Son of Man. "Do not marvel at this;*
> *for an hour is coming, in which all who are in the*
> *tombs shall hear His voice, and shall come forth; those*
> *who did the good deeds to a resurrection of life; those*
> *who committed the evil deeds to a resurrection of*
> *judgment. I can do nothing on My own initiative, As I*
> *hear, I judge; and my judgment is just, because I do*
> *not seek My own will, but the will of Him who sent*
> *Me"* (John 5:27-30).

Christ received the authority and power to execute judgment *because* He became a man. He was the Son of man. God originally gave authority on earth to man, but Adam forfeited that authority. Now a man, Jesus, got that authority back and earned the right to execute judgment. He walked on earth as a man—a perfect Man—and He will judge in perfection. Jesus is both Man and God—the perfect Judge!

Those who are dead will hear His voice. They would not listen to a mere human's voice. A human could not command the decayed remains of millions of men to rise and come to the judgment. However, they will listen to the Son's voice. It is the voice of God! At this judgment, Jesus will administer justice, and the "day of mercy" will be over. Even in speaking of judgment, Jesus said,

> *I can do nothing on My own initiative. As I hear I judge, and My judgment is just because I do not seek My own will but the will of Him Who sent Me"* (John 5:30).

Others Testify

"If I alone bear witness of Myself, My testimony is not true" (John 5:31). Jesus said He did nothing independently of the Father; He didn't even bear witness of Himself independently. If He did, it would not be true. However, He said, "there is Another that bears witness of me, and His witness is true," Jesus then presented His other witnesses.

It is possible to understand and accept the "witnesses" without accepting Jesus. It happened in Christ's day. Many Jews accepted John the Baptist's witness yet they did not accept the Christ. They saw the works of Jesus, even reaped the benefits of His miracles, yet still did not believe that He was the Son of God. Others searched the Scriptures, seeking eternal life, and yet missed the life towards which the Scriptures pointed. They heard the Father testify concerning Him, but they did not have His Word abiding in them, therefore they did not believe the Son the Father had sent.

> *There is another who bears witness of Me, and I know that the testimony which He bears of Me is true. You have sent to John, and he has borne witness to the truth. But the witness which I receive is not from man, but I say these things that you may be saved. He was the lamp that was burning and was shining and you were*

willing to rejoice for a while in his light (John 5:32-35).

Jesus reminded the people that they had sent inquiry to John and he had been a witness to the truth. John had witnessed concerning Jesus, but Jesus was not willing to receive mere human witness. *"But I do not receive [a mere] human witness—[the evidence which I accept on My behalf is not from man];..."* (John 5:34 TAB).

His Works Were the Greatest Witness

But the witness which I have is greater than that of John; for the works which the Father has given Me to accomplish, the very works that I do, bear witness of Me, that the Father has sent Me (John 5:36).

Jesus often appealed to His works as proof of His deity.

Jesus answered them, "I told you, and you do not believe; the works that I do in My Father's name, these bear witness of Me...but if I do them, though you do not believe Me, believe the works, that you may know and understand that the Father is in Me, and I in the Father" (John 10:25,38).

Believe Me that I am in the Father, and the Father in Me; otherwise believe on account of the works themselves (John 14:11).

If I had not done among them the works which no one else did, they would not have sin; but now they have both seen and hated Me and My Father as well (John 15:24).

Jesus' works bore witness to Who He is. As a child of God— your works will bear witness of who *you* are!

The Works of Jesus

There Were Many—Jesus did not stop with a few works and call them as witness to His deity. He did many works wherever He went.

They Were Great—Christ's miracles were extraordinary. They could not be mistaken for a magician's performance!

They Were Public—Jesus did His miracles publicly, for all to see. His works were not hidden in a corner and covered up.

They Were in Keeping With His Character— Jesus was full of love, mercy, and goodness. So were His works. He went about delivering those oppressed by the devil, freeing those who were bound, forgiving those who were sickened by guilt. There was always a purpose to His miracles. They were never to merely display power.

They Were Visible—Man could prove to his senses that the miracles were real. His works stood up to examination.

They Were Natural—Jesus went about doing good as He ministered. The miracles were a result of His ministry. He did not set up artificial situations to prove a point, but ministered to people in need. Miracles were the result of Who He is!

They Were Sufficient—When Christ did a miracle it was complete and sufficient. People knew they had received a miracle!

The Witness of the Father

And the Father who sent Me, He has borne witness of Me. You have neither heard His voice at any time, nor seen His form. And you do not have His word abiding in you, for you do not believe Him whom He sent (John 5:37,38).

Jesus said they had heard the Father's witness, yet had not believed it. His Father's witness had come through the prophets. Jesus had solemn charges for these people.
• You are unwilling to come to me: *"...And you are unwilling to come to Me, that you may have life"* (John 5:40).
• You do not have the love of God in you: *"...But I know you, that you do not have the love of God in yourselves"* (John 5:42).
• You do not receive me: *"I have come in My Father's name, and you do not receive Me; if another shall come in his own name, you will receive him"* (John 5:43).
    The Jews had been having difficulty receiving Him because they had not received the witness of the Father down through the centuries. Since the time of Moses, they had a history of unbelief and now it was directed at the very Son of God!
• You do not seek the glory that comes from God:

How can you believe, when you receive glory from one another, and you do not seek the glory that is from the one and only God? (John 5:44).

• You do not believe: *"But if you do not believe his writings, how will you believe My words?"* (John 5:47)

The Witness of the Word

You search the Scriptures, because you think that in them you have eternal life; and it is these that bear witness of Me; (John 5:39).

The Jews searched the Scriptures, but failed to come to the One of Whom they spoke, Jesus, to receive eternal life. If you allow it to, the written Word will lead you to the Living Word to receive life. You cannot separate the Scriptures from the Lord Himself. When you read the Word, or search the Scriptures, comparing one scripture with another, you are hearing the Lord speak. Expect the two always to work together! Open the book and, at the same time, open your heart to the Lord Jesus. As your eyes read the words, your mind will understand them, and your heart will be listening for the witness of the Holy Spirit.

If you reject the Scriptures you have nowhere else to go for testimony concerning Christ. There is no higher authority! First, Jesus appealed for proof of His divinity to His own works, then to the witness of His Father through the prophets, and then to the Scriptures which were written by the Holy Spirit. In these three Witnesses there is reference to the three Persons of the Trinity—all testifying of the deity of Jesus!

The Hungry Are Fed

And a great multitude was following Him, because they were seeing the signs which He was performing on those who were sick (John 6:2).

And when He went ashore, He saw a great multitude, and felt compassion for them, and healed their sick (Matthew 14:14).

Jesus looked at the great multitude and had compassion on them. He wanted to meet their needs—He loved them! Jesus knew they were not all following Him from pure motives, but He loved them nonetheless, and was moved to satisfy their physical hunger. A great multitude followed because they saw miracles. Christ is more than a Miracle Worker, He is our Bread from heaven. Do we follow Him for the loaves and the fishes? Remember, loaves and fishes follow those who believe!

And when it was evening the disciples came to Him, saying, "The place is desolate, and the time is already past; so send the multitudes away, that they may go into the villages and buy food for themselves." ...And He said, "Bring them here to Me" (Matthew 14:15,18).

When the disciples saw the multitudes and their need, they said, "Send them away to buy their own food." That was a logical solution to the hunger of such a great crowd. They were not particularly concerned with meeting their needs, they did not want a fainting crowd on their hands!

They looked around and saw that they were in a desolate place and could not see any provision. Sending the multitude to the surrounding villages for food was the only sensible thing to do. Philip observed that they did not have the money to buy enough for everyone to have even a little bit.

Philip answered Him, "Two hundred denarii worth of bread is not sufficient for them, for everyone to receive a little" (John 6:7).

Then Andrew noticed that a boy had brought a little lunch—five barley loaves and two fish! He probably felt foolish mentioning this small quantity in the face of such great need because no one yet realized the truth of Philippians 4:19, *"And My God shall supply all your needs...."* Their God was standing by their side and they were occupied with the negative circumstances. They looked at the circumstances and saw only lack. This was the language of unbelief! Philip spoke of everyone receiving a little in the presence of divine supply. Instead of counting on the Lord, he was occupied with natural resources. First, Philip made his unbelieving observation, and then Andrew followed. Unbelief is infectious!

The disciples said, "Send them away." Jesus said, "Bring them to me."

Jesus said, "Have the people sit down." Now there was much grass in the place. So the men sat down, in number about five thousand (John 6:10).

Christ did not act on the unbelief of His disciples. Instead of sending the people away, He had them sit down. There was much grass in that place. Jesus had even provided cushioned seats!

Why did Jesus have the men sit down in rows? Because He is a God of order. He is not the Author of confusion: *"...For God is not a God of confusion but of peace, as in all the churches of the saints"* (I Corinthians 14:33).

Also, when we are seated, we cease from our own striving; we rest to receive from Him. It is a cessation from self-effort and vain activity. They could do nothing to provide for their needs, so they sat down and allowed the Lord to provide!

> *Jesus therefore took the loaves; and having given thanks, He distributed to those who were seated; likewise also of the fish as much as they wanted* (John 6:11).

It did not matter to Jesus that the loaves were few, He took them and gave thanks. He used what was at hand. He acknowledged God as the giver of every good gift. Jesus blessed the loaves placed in His hands and God gave the increase. God increases what you give to Him—not what you keep!

God uses human instruments. He calls us laborers together with Him (I Corinthians 3:9). Jesus fed the multitude through His disciples. It was their work, too! Their hands distributed, but it was the hands of Jesus that caused the increase! They gave out what they received from Jesus. Give out freely what *you* receive from Jesus!

The Crowd Was Satisfied

> *And when they were filled, He said to His disciples, "Gather up the leftover fragments that nothing may be lost"* (John 6:12).

Jesus gave liberally to all—until they were filled. When Christ supplies, He leaves no deficiency. He wants you to be filled with peace, joy, filled and His love. He specializes in abundance!

*And so they gathered them up, and filled twelve baskets
with fragments from the five barley loaves, which were
left over by those who had eaten* (John 6:13).

God always supplies. He loves to give abundantly. There were
twelve baskets left over, one for each disciple. They had helped in
the work, and were rewarded. *"The generous man will be prosperous,
and he who waters will himself be watered"* (Proverbs 11:25).

When therefore the people saw the sign which Jesus had
performed, they said, "This is of a truth the Prophet Who is to come
into the world." This Man, they thought, would make a good king.
He could call into existence that which was not. When they tried to
force Him to be king, Jesus withdrew Himself. The crowd had no
concept of the real task of the Messiah. Jesus did not need to be
made a king—He was born one!

*Jesus therefore perceiving that they were intending to
come and take Him by force, to make Him king,
withdrew again to the mountain by Himself alone*
(John 6:15).

The Frightened Are Comforted

When Jesus is absent, there is darkness:

*And after getting into a boat, they started to cross the
sea to Capernaum. And it had already become dark,
and Jesus had not yet come to them* (John 6:17).

Thank God, it never needs to remain dark for the believer!
"Light arises in the darkness for the upright..." (Psalm 112:4).

*"And the sea began to be stirred up because a strong wind
was blowing"* (John 6:18). Sometimes your life may seem like a
storm-tossed sea. You may think Jesus has abandoned you, just
as the disciples did that night. Satan harasses you with hard
circumstances that threaten to swallow you. Jesus had not
forgotten them. It might have seemed so, but He was on the way

to perform a miracle for them.

You might be tempted to give up. Don't! Jesus has a plan for your situation! The disciples were frightened, but they did not give up. They kept on rowing. All the while Jesus saw them, and He sees you too, even when you feel like you are in a storm-tossed place!

Walking on Water

Jesus said we have the power to tread on all the power of the enemy.

> *Behold, I have given you authority to tread upon serpents and scorpions, and over all the power of the enemy, and nothing shall injure you* (Luke 10:19).

This enemy was a raging sea. How did Jesus approach His disciples? Walking on the water.

> *When therefore they had rowed about three or four miles, they beheld Jesus walking on the sea and drawing near to the boat; and they were frightened* (John 6:19).

He was on top of all the circumstances, treading on the power of the enemy.

What was the disciples' response to Jesus? Fear! They were not expecting deliverance. They were not looking for Jesus in this circumstance. They had forgotten the great miracle of the feeding of the five thousand, where Jesus had met their needs in a supernatural way—they probably still carried the twelve baskets. However, this was a different set of difficulties and they did not transfer their faith to the present situation. How many times have we done that? God does a miracle for us one day, and the next day we allow a circumstance to fill us with fear and paralyze our faith. Rebuke that fear! Do not let it be your master. No matter what is happening in your life, your Lord is right there, walking on top of the enemy, waiting for you to do the same.

Jesus dispelled their fears with the Word, "It is I, be not afraid." Then He calmed the sea. As soon as Jesus entered the boat, the wind ceased and the sea was calm. The act of turning their attention from the waves to the Savior calmed the disciples' fears. With Jesus in the boat, the wind ceased! Turn your eyes from the circumstances to Jesus; then invite Him into your situation. You *can* have a miracle!

Can you see the love of Jesus in this? He did not want them to be frightened and alone. He came with comfort, a miracle, and a change in the circumstances.

The Bread of Life

Christ reveals that He is acquainted with our innermost thoughts. He reads our motives!

Satisfaction Seekers—Many in the crowd were concerned with their physical needs. They were following Jesus for worldly blessings. *"Jesus answered them and said, 'Truly, truly, I say to you, you seek Me, not because you saw signs, but because you ate of the loaves, and were filled'"* (John 6:26).

Work Seekers—When they saw that Jesus knew their motives, they wanted to do something to earn God's favor. *"What shall we do, that we may work the works of God?"* The natural man always wants *to work* to receive from God.

The woman at the well could not understand the *gift* of God.

> *Jesus answered and said to her, "If you knew the gift of God, and who it is who says to you, 'Give Me a drink,' you would have asked Him, and He would have given you living water"* (John 4:10).

The rich young ruler said, "What shall I do?" *"And a certain ruler questioned Him, saying, "Good Teacher, what shall I do to inherit eternal life?"* (Luke 18:18). The Jews on the day of Pentecost said, *"...Brethren, what shall we do?"* (Acts 2:37).

The one thing that God requires is faith in Him. Though your faith will affect your works, your works will never develop faith.

Sign Seekers—*"They said therefore to Him, 'What then do You do for a sign, that we may see, and believe You? What work do You perform?'"* (John 6:30). They were asking for his credentials of divinity. Imagine their forgetfulness! They asked this question the morning after they had been fed miraculously along with the five thousand!

Then they turned the conversation to Moses (John 6:31,32). They were really saying, "How can you prove that you are greater than Moses? You fed five thousand once, but Moses fed a million or more for forty years!" Jesus immediately turned them from the human instrument to the Father Who gave it.

> *...I say to you, it is not Moses who has given you the bread out of heaven, but it is My Father who gives you the True Bread of heaven.*

Look beyond the instrument to the Source! Jesus was turning their attention from their fathers to God, from temporal bread to the Living Bread!

Manna for the World

Jesus carefully showed the people that the manna had no power to ward off death, but this Bread does: it gives life. The manna was only for Israel, but the True Bread is offered to the world:

> *Your fathers ate the manna in the wilderness, and they died. This is the bread which comes down out of heaven, so that one may eat of it and not die. I am the living bread that came down out of heaven; if anyone eats of this bread, he shall live forever; and the bread also which I shall give for the life of the world is My flesh* (John 6:49-51).

Jesus said, "I am the bread of life" (John 6:48). He is the true bread.

> *Jesus therefore said to them, "Truly, truly, I say to you,*

*it is not Moses who has given you the bread out of
heaven, but it is My Father who gives you the true
bread out of heaven"* (John 6:32).

He is the Bread from heaven: *"... the bread of God is that which
comes down out of heaven, and gives life to the world"* (John 6:33).

*I am the living bread that came down out of heaven;
if anyone eats of this bread, he shall live forever; and
the bread also which I shall give for the life of the
world is My flesh* (John 6:51).

Choose To Partake

*Jesus said to them, "I am the bread of life; he who
comes to Me shall not hunger, and he who believes in
Me shall never thirst"* (John 6:35).

You must choose to eat of the "Bread of Life" in order to
benefit from it. You may know all about Jesus, but if you have not
eaten of the Living Bread, it will do you no good.

Let's look at the action of eating. It is a necessary act. You
must eat, or you gain no benefit from food. Eating is the response to
a physical need. When you are hungry, you eat. It is the same
spiritually. When you begin to hunger for the things of God, you will
look for a place to "eat." The Father draws you and makes you aware
of the hunger within:

*No one can come to Me, unless the Father who sent
Me draws him; and I will raise him up on the last day*
(John 6:44).

Eating is an act of consuming. When you eat, you make the
food your own. You may believe everything someone else says about
the Living Bread, but until you taste Him for yourself and receive
Him on the inside, you reap no benefit.

Eating is intensely personal. You cannot eat by proxy. Each

person must partake personally. No one can get the benefits from
the Bread of Life for you, and you cannot partake for someone else.
However, you can lead someone to the Source!

Come and Dine

*He who eats My flesh and drinks My blood has eternal
life, and I will raise him up on the last day. For My
flesh is true food, and My blood is true drink. He who
eats My flesh and drinks My blood abides in Me, and
I in him* (John 6:54-56).

Jesus was predicting His death, and showing them that He was
now their Passover Lamb. They would no longer need to eat of the flesh
of the Passover Lamb and pour out the blood. They would live under a
new covenant! The Passover Lamb was killed in such a manner as to
separate all the blood from the flesh before it was eaten. The Lamb of
God also shed His blood and had to die before He was eaten.

To "eat His flesh" means to receive by faith all that Jesus did
by giving Himself as a sacrifice for our sins. To drink His blood is to
receive by faith all that was accomplished by His shed blood.

However, we know now that when we partake of Jesus' flesh
and blood, we are partaking of His death, identifying with His death
because it was ours, too! Yet, we do not worship a dead Christ, He is
alive! We are identifying with His death, but we are partaking of life.
Sin and death entered the human race through the act of eating the
forbidden fruit (Genesis 3); now in Christ we are made alive again
by "eating"!

How does one eat of Jesus' flesh and drink of His blood? It is
by feasting on the Word. His Words are spirit and they are life. Believe
His Words...accept His Word...make them your daily Bread. *"It is the
Spirit who gives life; the flesh profits nothing; the words that I have
spoken to you are spirit and are life"* (John 6:63).

*...Man shall not live on bread alone, but on every
word that proceeds out of the mouth of God*
(Deuteronomy 8:3 NKJ).

Why Is Bread Important?

Bread is a staple of life. It is called the "staff of life." There is no life or health without Christ.

Bread is food for everyone. Class makes no difference. Christ is for everyone. He meets the need of everyone regardless of class, culture, or education.

Bread is a daily food. Many foods are eaten only occasionally, but not bread. It is a daily part of our diet. We must also feed daily on Christ.

Bread is satisfying. One does not tire of bread though he eats it daily. So it is with Christ—He satisfies. Other things keep us searching for something better; Christ causes us to rest in Him.

Bread goes through a process. The grain was crushed to make bread. Christ was bruised for our iniquities!

Some Chose Darkness

Many of His disciples did not like to hear of Christ's death, or of eating His flesh and drinking His blood. *"As a result of this many of His disciples withdrew, and were not walking with Him anymore"* (John 6:66). They wanted to hear news of a conquering king establishing a new kingdom. Jesus gave the truth, and He gave it in the power of the Holy Spirit—yet some rejected it. Their withdrawal was because of the conflict in their hearts; not because of any weakness in the Messenger, or the message! This Word of God conflicted with their own traditions and views. They chose to stay with them! They did not take the Light. They chose to stay in their darkness!

They trusted in Moses, they enjoyed the light of John the Baptist, they quoted the Scriptures, yet they did not have saving faith.

Jesus turned to His twelve disciples and asked,

> ...*"You do not want to go away also, do you?"* Simon Peter answered Him, *"Lord, to whom shall we go? You have words of eternal life. And we have believed and have come to know that You are the Holy One of God"* (John 6:67-69).

Notice the order, they *believed* and then they came to *know*! Peter said, "We believe and know," but Jesus knew their hearts. He knew that one did not believe—Judas. Why then did Jesus choose him to be a disciple? Jesus came to do the Father's will: *"Then I said behold, I have come (in the roll of the book it is written of me) to do thy will, O God"* (Hebrews 10:7). His will is in His Word. Christ came to fulfill the Word. There is a prophecy that a friend would harm Jesus, *"Even my close friend, in whom I trusted, who ate my bread, has lifted up his heel against me"* (Psalm 41:9). Judas was chosen. He was that familiar friend.

Judas bore witness of Jesus' innocence: *"...Saying, 'I have sinned by betraying innocent blood.' But they said, 'What is that to us? See to that yourself!'"* (Matthew 27:4). Even the betrayer knew that Jesus was innocent.

Judas' actions show the wickedness of sin, and the sin is exposed just before Jesus went to the Cross to atone for all men's sin. Judas' actions are a warning. Here is an example of one who spent three years in the company of the Master Teacher, yet will spend eternity in hell. Nearness is not enough, the Word of life must be taken internally!

Judas was an example of a hypocrite among the true followers of Christ. Outwardly, Judas was no different than the other disciples—he preached, followed Christ, did miracles—but inwardly he was a wolf and not a sheep at all!

Some rejected the Bread of Life, but He still makes His life-giving offer today.

Your Miracle Worker

God wants you to learn to totally trust His Word, to rely on His Word more than you rely on your physical senses. When He says a thing is done, count it as done and act on it. Then He can meet your needs. Like the nobleman and the impotent man, you will reap miracles in your life.

Jesus and the Father are one—They do the same work. They have the same mind and the same intelligence. They both are due the same honor. Believing the Son means believing the Father. They both give life. Jesus earned the right and authority to execute judgment—He is perfect Man and God at the same time. Contemplate the unity between Jesus and His Father! Meditate on Jesus' prayer, *"That they may be one, just as We are One; I in them and Thou in Me, that they may be perfected in unity."* (John 17:22,23).

Jesus had compassion on the hungry crowd of 5,000. He wanted to meet their need. The disciples, too, saw the need, but could not see beyond the circumstances. They said, "Send them away." Jesus said, "Let them come." As they obeyed, Jesus took the only provisions they could find, and the disciples witnessed a miracle. You, too, can have a miracle for your need. Turn from your circumstances and look to Jesus. Give Him what you have and then obey all His instructions and you will see a miracle!

Life without Jesus is dark, especially during a storm. Your

enemy would like to fill you with fear and discouragement, but the Light is always with you. Jesus will never forsake you. He is watching and waiting to bring peace and security back to your life. Jesus is always on top of the stormy waters of stressful circumstances. Get to the top with Him, and tread the enemy under your feet! Invite Jesus into your situation and the storm will cease!

Jesus gives Himself as the Bread of Life. Bread that will satisfy and give you eternal life. This Bread is the only nourishment for a dying world. Each one must eat of this Bread for himself; no one can eat for another. Eat, draw strength from Him, and go and share Him with a starving world!

Personal Action Plan

1. What is the Bread of Life? Write out the meaning in your own words. How does it apply to you today?

2. Meditate on John 5:24. What does it mean to you to have eternal life? Share this revelation of eternity with someone this week.

3. Find two scriptures that describe the works of Jesus. How can you use them to improve your personal ministry to others?

4. Study the passages in John about the disciples in the storm. Are you in a storm today? How should you be reacting?

5. Look over John 3. In your journal write out the verses that personally speak to you about God's love.

Chapter 4

TEACHING AT THE TEMPLE

Teaching at the Temple

*And after these things Jesus was walking in Galilee;
for He was unwilling to walk in Judea, because the
Jews were seeking to kill Him. Now the feast of the
Jews, the Feast of Booths* [Tabernacles] *was at hand*
(John 7:1,2).

The sixth chapter of John took place during the Feast of the
Passover; this chapter takes place during the Feast of Tabernacles.
Because the Jews were seeking His life, Jesus had spent about six
months in Galilee. When it was time for all of the men to go to
Jerusalem for the feast, Jesus' half-brothers suggested that this would
be a good time for Jesus to go to Jerusalem, show Himself, do some
miracles, and get a little publicity! They were not yet believers and
were making this suggestion with no understanding of the truth.
They knew that many disciples had left Him and perhaps they were
suggesting He could find more in Jerusalem.

*His brothers therefore said to Him, "Depart from
here, and go into Judea, that Your disciples also
may behold Your works which You are doing. For
no one does anything in secret, when he himself
seeks to be known publicly. If You do these things,
show Yourself to the world." For not even His
brothers were believing in Him. Jesus therefore said
to them, "My time is not yet at hand, but your time
is always opportune. The world cannot hate you;
but it hates Me because I testify of it, that its deeds
are evil. Go up to the feast yourselves; I do not go
up to this feast because My time has not yet fully
come." And having said these things to them, He
stayed in Galilee* (John 7:3-9).

Jesus said, "My time is not yet come." He often spoke of His hour not having come, but this one time He used a different word, the Greek word *kairos* which means "opportunity" or "the best time to do something, the moment in which the circumstances are most suitable."

He said to His brothers, "*...any time is suitable for you and your opportunity is ready any time—is always here*" (John 7:6 TAB). Their presence did not stop confrontation, neither was anyone depending on them showing up. When Jesus arrived, however, people had to make decisions. His very presence revealed their sin, and His message told them He was the Messiah. Men had to either accept or reject Him—they could not remain neutral.

Remaining in Galilee was for protection—His hour had not yet come. (This was about six months before the Crucifixion.) Jesus did not needlessly expose Himself to danger, neither did He let danger keep Him from fulfilling the law! When the right time came, He went to Jerusalem secretly, not in a conspicuous caravan that would have warned His enemies.

> But when His brothers had gone up to the feast, then
> He Himself also went up, not publicly, but as it were,
> in secret (John 7:10).

Jesus had a definite purpose for going to Jerusalem. He had a special message for the middle and for the end of the feast. Jesus knew He would make an impact on the people at the festival.

How ironic—Jesus' half-brothers went on ahead to the feast to celebrate and worship God, yet they left Jesus, who truly was God, out of their celebration. How important it is not to get so caught up with all the festivity of worship that you leave out fellowship with Christ. He must be at the heart of everything we do in the name of worship!

Deliverance Dinner

The Jews celebrated the Feast of Tabernacles to remind themselves that God had delivered them from Egypt. They wandered in temporary homes for years, but found rest in the land of Canaan. Solomon celebrated this feast upon the completion of the Tabernacle. Someday, upon the completion of the spiritual tabernacle, we too will celebrate this feast in the New Jerusalem. Our journey in the temporary dwellings of our bodies will be over. We will find eternal rest.

> *And I saw the holy city, new Jerusalem, coming down out of heaven from God, made ready as a bride adorned for her husband. And I heard a loud voice from the throne, saying, "Behold, the tabernacle of God is among men, and He shall dwell among them, and they shall be His people, and God Himself shall be among them* (Revelation 21:2,3).

There, through the middle of the city, will flow the river whose waters give life. On either side of the river grow trees of life (this word is plural) with fruit, bearing a fresh crop of fruit each month. It will be continuous harvest time—an eternal feast of rejoicing and worship! Even Abraham, Isaac, and Jacob lived in temporary tents, but were looking forward to living in the city whose Builder and Architect is God.

> *By faith Abraham, when he was called, obeyed by going out to a place which he was to receive for an inheritance; and he went out, not knowing where he was going. By faith he lived as an alien in the land of promise, as in a foreign land, dwelling in tents with Isaac and Jacob, fellow heirs of the same promise; for he was looking for the city which has foundations, whose architect and builder is God* (Hebrews 11:8-10).

Jesus Was a Catalyst

Jesus' brothers did not believe in Him, but teased and taunted Him concerning the influence He could have if He went to Jerusalem.

The Pharisees and the chief priests hated Him because He saw right through their laws—their petty rules and regulations. The Pharisees and priests knew that if Jesus was right, they were wrong.

At the Feast of Tabernacles

• It was a grand harvest festival which began the fifteenth day of the seventh month (which corresponds to September in our calendar).

• It was celebrated for eight days.
(See Leviticus 23:34,39.)

• On each day of the festival they were to sacrifice a burnt offering to the Lord. On the eighth day, they were to gather together as a people and offer another offering by fire to the Lord.

• This was to be a joyous occasion.
  (See Leviticus 23:36,39 ; Deuteronomy 16:15.)

•The first and last day were to be days of solemn rest.
(See Leviticus 23:36,39.)

• During the seven days, native-born Israelites were to live in shelters made of tree boughs. On the first day, they were to take boughs of fruit trees, laden with fruit, and palm fronds and the boughs of leafy trees—such as willows that grow by the brooks—and build shelters with them rejoicing before the Lord for seven days.
(See Leviticus 23:33-36.)

• The purpose of this feast was to remind people that

God had rescued them from Egypt and had caused them to live in temporary shelter. They began celebrating this feast after they settled in Canaan.

• It was one of the three annual feasts that every adult male was required to attend. (See Deuteronomy 16:16.) The other two were the Feast of the Passover and the Feast of Pentecost. The Feast of the Passover was fulfilled in Jesus' death, the Feast of Pentecost was fulfilled in Acts 2 with the outpouring of the Holy Spirit. The Feast of Tabernacles will be fulfilled upon the completion of the spiritual temple. (See I Peter 2:5.)

• After the exile and before the foundation of the Temple was even begun, they rebuilt the altar of God and immediately began sacrificing. The first feast they celebrated was the Feast of Tabernacles. (See Ezra 3:3-6.)

• After the exile, the people added a ceremony of water-pouring to this feast. It was not prescribed in the Pentateuch but was carried on even in Jesus' time. This was the event that was reflected in the proclamation, *"If any man is thirsty, let him come to Me and drink"* (John 7:37). The practice of pouring water on the altar recognized that rain was a gift from God necessary for fruitful harvests. (See Deuteronomy 11:13-17.)

They had a system going and they did not want anyone upsetting their traditions. Were they really looking for a Messiah? NO! Their traditions and their systems which were politically and monetarily powerful, had become more dear to them than God Himself. Jesus was a threat! They had to either submit to Jesus or destroy Him. They chose the latter.

> *They were seeking therefore to seize Him; and no man laid his hand on Him, because His hour had not yet come. The Pharisees heard the multitude muttering these things about Him; and the chief priests and the Pharisees sent officers to seize Him* (John 7:30,32).

The "learned" Pharisees had an arrogant contempt for Jesus:

> *The Jews therefore were marveling, saying, "How has this man become learned, having never been educated?" The Pharisees therefore answered them, "You have not also been led astray, have you? No one of the rulers or Pharisees has believed in Him, has he? But this multitude which does not know the Law is accursed"* (John 7:15,47-49).

They said to themselves, "This Man has no special training in our rabbinical schools. He does not have a cultural background for this kind of teaching. What is He doing there? Teaching the crowd? How dare He! This crowd does not even know the law." They became so angry with the crowd for listening to this "unlearned" Man that they cursed them. Some of the crowd were grumbling:

> *And there was much grumbling among the multitude concerning Him; some were saying, "He is a good man"; others were saying, "No, on the contrary, He leads the multitude astray"* (John 7:12).

Others were afraid to say anything publicly: *"Yet no one was speaking openly of Him for fear of the Jews"* (John 7:13). The fear of man is a trap! People are even now afraid at times to speak openly of Jesus—afraid of what others will say or think. Jesus is still a very controversial figure! His danger was real at this festival, the Jews WERE trying to kill Jesus. On the one hand, they were religious and professed to worship God; on the other hand, they were planning to kill their Messiah, their only hope of eternal life. Religion, separated from the Living Word, is destructive.

Some believed. The evidence was overwhelming; they *knew* that Jesus was the Christ.

> *But many of the multitude believed in Him; and they were saying, "When the Christ shall come, He will not perform more signs than those which this man has, will He?"* (John 7:31).

There was division in the crowd: many believed, some were astonished, others wanted to seize Him.

> *So there arose a division in the multitude because of Him. And some of them wanted to seize Him, but no one laid hands on Him. The officers answered, "Never did a man speak the way this man speaks"* (John 7:43,44,46).

Nicodemus quietly defended Him: *"Our Law does not judge a man, unless it first hears from him and knows what he is doing, does it?"* (John 7:51). Nicodemus was not overwhelmingly bold in his defense, but he did make a stand. It had been eighteen months since his encounter with Jesus, and he hadn't forgotten it. His growth might have been slow, but it was steady and progressive.

The Verdict...Who Is This Man?

> *And there was much grumbling among the multitudes concerning Him; some were saying, "He is a good man"; others were saying, "No, on the contrary, He leads the multitude astray"* (John 7:12).

Jesus *was* a good man, but He was much more:

> *Some of the multitude therefore, when they heard these*
> *words, were saying, "This certainly is the Prophet"*
> (John 7:40).

He was a prophet. He gave His Father's message. He was
THE PROPHET. The Spirit of God was so foreign to them that they
did not recognize Him. They did not understand His words.

> *Therefore some of the people of Jerusalem were saying,*
> *"Is this not the man whom they are seeking to kill?*
> *And look, He is speaking publicly, and they are saying*
> *nothing to Him. The rulers do not really know that*
> *this is the Christ, do they?"* (John 7:25,26).

Jesus was speaking publicly when He knew the Jews were
seeking to kill Him. This impressed some of the people. It seemed to
them that the rulers had changed their minds because they were
doing nothing to Jesus. *"Never did a man speak the way this man*
speaks" (John 7:46). The men sent to arrest Jesus were in awe of
Him, and came back empty-handed. Power and authority emanated
from this Man, Jesus.

Jesus Surprised the Jews

Jesus stood up in the Temple and began to teach:

> *But when it was now the midst of the feast Jesus went up*
> *into the temple, and began to teach. The Jews therefore*
> *were marveling saying, "How has this man become*
> *learned, having never been educated?"* (John 7:14,15).

You can imagine what a surprise this was to the Jews. They
were seeking to kill Him, yet He was fearlessly speaking to them.

The second surprise was that He taught very well! They asked
themselves, "How did He learn to teach? He hasn't had a higher

education." Jesus knew their hearts, and even though those remarks were probably not directed to Him, Jesus answered their question. "My teacher is God. I say only those things that My Father speaks to Me." He told them He was not seeking His own glory, but the glory of the One who sent Him.

> ...*My teaching is not Mine, but His Who sent Me. If any man is willing to do His will, He shall know of the teaching, whether it is of God, or whether I speak from Myself* (John 7:16,17).

Then referring to the incident that began the rulers' hatred campaign—the healing of the impotent man at the pool of Bethsaida, He said:

> *Did not Moses give you the law, (the one you are so angry at me for breaking)—and yet none of you carries out the law. Why do you seek to kill Me?* (John 7:19).

Jesus had been debating with the rulers while the crowd listened, then the crowd broke in and shouted, "You have a demon! Who seeks to kill you?" The crowd was not aware of what the Pharisees and chief priests were planning.

Jesus paid no attention to the crowd. He did not even answer them.

> [Jesus was One] *WHO COMMITTED NO SIN, NOR WAS ANY DECEIT FOUND IN HIS MOUTH; and while being reviled, He did not revile in return; while suffering, He uttered no threats, but kept entrusting Himself to Him who judges righteously* (I Peter 2:22,23).

He continued to teach, "I did one work on the Sabbath, and you were upset, yet you do "works" on the Sabbath. *"And on the eighth day the flesh of his foreskin shall be circumcised"* (Leviticus 12:3). "You do that faithfully, whether it is the Sabbath or not. A lot of work is involved in circumcision. How can you be so angry with Me, when I make a man whole on the Sabbath? Be honest in your judgment." (See John 7:21-23.)

Some of the people of Jerusalem said:

...Isn't this the man they are trying to kill? Here He is speaking publicly, and they are not saying a word to Him. Have the authorities concluded that He is the Christ? But we know where this Man is from; when the Christ comes, no one will know where He is from. Then Jesus, still teaching from the temple courts, cried out, "Yes, you know Me, and you know where I am from. I am not here on my own, but He who sent me is true. You do not know Him, but I know Him because I am from Him and He sent Me" (John 7:25,27-29 NIV).

With that statement, Jesus caused a stir. They immediately tried to seize Him, but could not because "His hour" had not yet come.

Their anger was doubled. First, He healed on the Sabbath, and now He put Himself on intimate terms with God. That was blasphemy! He said they did not know God, and He did. The high priests, the Pharisees, those who knew and kept every law, didn't know God? Yet He, an unlearned man from Galilee, did? That made them furious!

They thought they knew all about Him—His upbringing, His family, His occupation. He could not be the Messiah! Jewish tradition said that the Messiah would appear mysteriously out of nowhere and traditions were respected! No, they concluded this man could not be the Messiah. No one should be allowed to make this kind of statement!

Actually, in some ways, they were right. To make the kind of statement that Jesus made required that He was either the Messiah or a mad impostor. One had to make a choice after hearing Jesus speak. It's the same today. You must make a choice every time you hear Christ speak. You cannot remain neutral.

They thought they knew Him, yet they really didn't. No one knew Him except the Father.

*All things have been handed over to Me by My Father;
and no one knows the Son, except the Father; nor does
anyone know the Father, except the Son, and anyone to
whom the Son wills to reveal Him* (Matthew 11:27).

Now, it is different, we know the Son! We have come to
know Him, love Him, and trust our very lives to Him. We know His
claim was true!

A Puzzlement

*Jesus said, "I am with you for only a short time, and
then I go to the one who sent me, You will look for me,
but you will not find me; and where I am, you cannot
come* (John 7:33,34 NIV).

You could misunderstand this as saying, "I'm going away
soon; then I won't bother you anymore."

His listeners did not really understand what He was talking
about. They wondered if Jesus was going to minister to the Jews outside
of Palestine, or if He was going to the Greeks. Was He just going to
disappear among the masses? They simply did not understand.

*The Jews therefore said to one another, "Where does
this man intend to go that we shall not find Him?
He is not intending to go to the Dispersion among
the Greeks, and teach the Greeks, is He? What is
this statement that He said, "You will seek Me, and
will not find Me; and where I am, you cannot come?"*
(John 7:35,36).

Jesus once said, *"Ask, and it shall be given to you; seek, and
you shall find; knock, and it shall be opened to you"* (Matthew 7:7).
Now He said, "You will seek me but you won't find Me." Why did
He say that? Because they had not sought Him as Savior—they had
not believed Him. Isaiah says, *"Seek the Lord while He may be found"*
(Isaiah 55:6).

Water Ceremony

Let's look into the background of this special water-pouring ceremony referred to by Jesus in John 7:37. William Barclay, in his book on the Gospel of John says, "This special ceremony is very closely connected with this passage and with the words of Jesus.

"Quite certainly He spoke with it in His mind, and possibly even as an immediate background. Each day of the festival the people came to the Temple with their palms and their willows and with them they formed a kind of screen or roof and marched around the great altar.

"At the same time, a priest took a golden pitcher which held three logs—that is about two pints—and went down to the Pool of Siloam and filled it with water. It was carried back through the Water Gate while the people recited Isaiah 12:3: *'With joy you will draw water from the wells of salvation.'*

"The water was carried up to the Temple altar and poured out as an offering to God. While this was being done, the

Hallel—that is, Psalms 113-118—was sung to the accompaniment of flutes by the Levite choir.

"When they came to the words, *'O give thanks to the Lord'* (Psalm 118: 1), and again to the words, *'O work now then salvation'* (Psalm 118:25), and finally to the closing words, *'O give thanks to the Lord'* (Psalm 118:29), the worshipers shouted and waved their palms towards the altar.

"The whole dramatic ceremony was a vivid thanksgiving for God's good gift of water; it was an acted out prayer for rain, and a memory of the water which sprang from the rock when they traveled through the wilderness. On the last day, the ceremony was doubly impressive for they marched seven times round the altar in memory of the sevenfold circuit round the walls of Jericho, whereby the walls fell down and the city was taken."

From *The Gospel of John* by William Barclay

There came a day when they could not find Him anymore. When the soldiers at the tomb found that Jesus had risen, they let the rulers know. Don't you think they scoured the city to find His body? They didn't find Him. They were not the ones to whom the risen Lord appeared. The time to seek Jesus is limited. God is patiently waiting and longing for the world to accept His Son, to be reconciled, but the time is coming to a close; it is not forever!

Jesus said, "Where I am going you cannot come." Scholarship and learning did not help these religious minds. They just didn't get it!

A Special Offer

On the last great day of the feast (the eighth day, which was a Sabbath or rest day), the crowd would have been large. Jesus waited for the maximum audience for His most important message. They had been feasting for seven days—much food, much meat. Physically speaking they were probably thirsty. Now, when the priests poured ceremonial water before the Lord, Jesus stood up and shouted, *"...If any man is thirsty, let him come to Me and drink"* (John 7:37). Can you imagine the reaction of the crowd? What kind of invitation was this? I'm sure He had the attention of everyone in that crowd!

Jesus said three key words, *Thirsty, come,* and *drink.* That is the gospel in a nutshell! The world is thirsty for God. They need only to come to Christ and drink. He is what they need. He will quench their thirst. They try to placate their thirst with money, goods, pleasure, ease, and fame. Nothing works! Our job is to present Jesus. Let them drink of Him—they will never seek another fountain. The Psalmist says, *"As the deer pants after the water brooks, So my soul pants for Thee, O God"* (Psalm 42:1).

When Jesus said that whoever believes in Him shall have streams of water flowing from within him, He was speaking of the Holy Spirit. Many men had been used by the Holy Spirit, but He had not been available to the masses—to the individual believer. Now Jesus was promising streams of living water to everyone who believed Him because of the Spirit Who would be within them!

Think of it! At salvation you receive a *well,* but when you are baptized with the Holy Spirit you receive a *fountain* that gushes out its streams of living waters. The *well* is salvation, the *fountain* is the baptism of the Holy Spirit. What cleans out pollution faster than good, clean water? What cleans out your life better than the water of salvation, the working of the Holy Spirit?

You must drink. Action is required to receive from God. He does not push it on you, you must freely come to Him and drink. You must make Christ your own. Remember, Jesus was not speaking to the heathen of the land, He was speaking to church-goers. Temple worship would not save them; they had to come to Him and drink. Jesus could *lead* them to water, but He couldn't *make* them drink.

> *He who believes in Me [cleaves to and trusts in and relies on Me] as the Scripture has said, out of his innermost being, springs and rivers of living water shall flow [continuously]* (John 7:38 TAB).

> *And the Lord shall guide you continually, and sanctify you in drought and in dry places, and make strong your bones. And you shall be like a watered garden and like a spring of water, whose waters fail not* (Isaiah 58:11 TAB).

The Jews believed that the Holy Spirit left with the last of the prophets, and yet a fresh outpouring would come during the Messianic age. The prophets had talked about it, and Peter quoted Joel in Acts 2:17:

> *And it shall be in the last days, God says, that I will pour forth of My Spirit upon all mankind, and your sons and your daughters shall prophesy, and your young men shall see visions, and your old men shall dream dreams.*

Another Joel prophecy was:

> *And it will come about in that day that the mountains will drip with sweet wine, and the hills*

> *will flow with milk, and all the brooks of Judah*
> *will flow with water; and a spring will go out from*
> *the house of the Lord, to water the valley of Shittim*
> (Joel 3:18).

At last, the *well and fountain* had come! Aren't you glad that the Holy Spirit has come to dwell in you? Are you allowing Him to flow through you? Become a well-watered garden, then allow the water to overflow into the lives of others!

Personal Action Plan

1. Write out three verses from John 7 that spoke to you in a special way and add them to your scripture notebook.

2. How does the enemy keep you from speaking of Jesus? Today, think of some ways that you can break out of that trap. Share them with a friend.

3. Write in your journal about ways the world views Jesus and how you viewed Him before you were saved (versus the way you see Him today). How can you use this knowledge to witness to others?

4. Meditate on Revelation 21:2,3 as discussed in this chapter. What does God want you to dwell in?

5. Pray about the bold statement made in John 7:37—does it still apply today?

Chapter 5

THE LIGHT WHO SHATTERED THE NIGHT

The Light Who Shattered the Night

Everyone went home after the festival, but *"...Jesus went to the Mount of Olives"* (John 8:1). He had no "home" to which to go. Here we have insight into the lifestyle of our Lord, Jesus. He became poor that we might become rich. He also went to the Mount to pray—to be with His heavenly Father. He often went alone and communed with God. Most likely He slept on the grass, under the trees that night.

> *And early in the morning He came again into the temple, and all the people were coming to Him; and He sat down and began to teach them* (John 8:2).

Early in the morning when the light first shone, Jesus, the Light of the world, went to the Temple. He took His light to the place that was built to house the light and glory of God. He put God first. He literally fulfilled the command He gave His disciples: *"But seek first His kingdom and His righteousness; and all these things shall be added to you"* (Matthew 6:33). Christ is our example. Seek the Lord early. Spend time with Him at the beginning of the day. Get His light first!

A New Scheme

As the Lord sat down to teach those who came to Him, the scribes and the Pharisees rudely interrupted, dragging a woman they had caught in the act of adultery. They had failed to have Jesus arrested the day before, so now they tried a new approach. They thought they could trap Him.

> *And the scribes and the Pharisees brought a woman caught in adultery, and having set her in the midst,*

*they said to Him, "Teacher, this woman has been
caught in adultery, in the very act. Now in the Law
Moses commanded us to stone such women; what then
do You say?" And they were saying this, testing Him,
in order that they might have grounds for accusing
Him...* (John 8:3-6).

Their plan was this: if He said, "Yes, stone her," He would
damage His reputation of being merciful and the friend of sinners.
Also, He would run the risk of incurring trouble with the Roman
government, since the Jews were not allowed to enforce the death
penalty. On the other hand, if Jesus said to let her go, they could
accuse Him of breaking the Law of Moses. They thought they had
Him trapped.

Sticks and Stones

"...Jesus stooped down, and with His finger wrote on the ground"
(John 8:6). Why did He write on the ground? He might have just
been drawing on the ground while He spent time receiving guidance
from the Father. Some manuscripts read, *"as though He did not hear
them."* Jesus might have been forcing the rulers to repeat their charges
in order for them to hear how terrible their words and attitudes
were. His writing on the ground reminds us of another time when
the finger of God wrote.

> *And when He had finished speaking with him upon
> Mount Sinai, He gave Moses the two tablets of the
> testimony, tablets of stone, written by the finger of
> God* (Exodus 31:18).

Jesus wrote on the ground twice, the tablets had also been
written twice. Some manuscripts translate this verse a little differently.
The Armenian translates the passage this way,

> *He himself, bowing his head, was writing with his
> finger on the earth to declare their sins; and they were*

seeing their several sins on the stones."

The MSV in St. Mark's in Venice reads: *"He wrote on the ground the sins of each one of them."*

God of the Second Chance

But when they persisted in asking Him, He straightened up, and said to them, "He who is without sin among you, let him be the first to throw a stone at her." And again He stooped down, and wrote on the ground. And when they heard it, they began to go out one by one, beginning with the older ones, and He was left alone, and the woman, where she was, in the midst. And straightening up, Jesus said to her, "Woman, where are they? Did no one condemn you?" And she said, "No one, Lord." And Jesus said, "Neither do I condemn you; go your way. From now on sin no more" (John 8:7-11).

Jesus had said, "He that is without sin cast the first stone." With that indictment before them, they dared not take action! No man could condemn her. They were smitten in their own conscience, and left. Jesus let them go quietly. He knew their sins, but He did not want to punish them. He is in the forgiving business!

> *A single witness shall not rise up against a man on account of any iniquity or any sin which he has committed; on the evidence of two or three witnesses a matter shall be confirmed* (Deuteronomy 19:15).

The Law required two witnesses before an execution could take place, but all had left. The witnesses had to not only accuse her, but assist in the carrying out of the sentence.

The hand of the witnesses shall be first against him

*to put him to death, and afterward the hand of all
the people. So you shall purge the evil from your
midst* (Deuteronomy 17:7).

No one was left but Jesus and the woman. He was the only
one without sin, but He didn't condemn her either! Jesus said,
"Neither do I condemn you," because He knew that in a short time
He was going to be condemned in her place. Justice was going to be
accomplished, the law would be fulfilled, but the execution would
fall on another—the Man without sin!

I believe the woman left Jesus as a believer that day, for she
called Him "Lord." Not "Master" as the Pharisees did, but "Lord."
Jesus became her Lord that day and there was no more condemnation
for her: *"There is therefore now no condemnation for those who are
in Christ Jesus"* (Romans 8:1).

This guilty woman met a Man who was Love and Light. She
came on the scene in darkness, surrounded by hatred. She left forgiven
and knowing someone loved her.

Several things are brought out in Jesus' attitude toward her:
He gave her a second chance. Jesus is merciful and compassionate.
He was not disputing her guilt, but He was extending His mercy and
giving her another chance. *"Go, and sin no more."* He is not so
interested in what a person has been as what a person can be. The
past definitely matters, but each person also has a future! Don't look
back, look to your future with Jesus!

Jesus had compassion. The Pharisees delighted in
condemning and exposing sin. Jesus delighted in covering and
forgiving sin. The Pharisees saw the woman with disgust and
self-righteousness. Jesus saw her with love and compassion.

"Go, and sin no more." Jesus didn't say, "Go, I know you
can't help it. You are doing the best you can." NO! He confronted
the sin and said, "Go, and live differently." He challenged her with
changing her lifestyle! Can you imagine simply telling an adulterous
woman to go and change her life? Jesus believed He could help her
change and He wanted her to know she could! Jesus brought light
into this woman's dark situation—He forgave.

Only Begotten Son

We have seen how Jesus spoke, during the Feast of the Passover, of being *the Bread of Life*. He announced He was the *Water of Life* at the well of Jacob. He proclaimed the coming of *a river of living water* during the pouring of the water at the Feast of Tabernacles. Now He had another picture for His audience. He announced that He is *the Light of the world*.

There was a ceremony connected with the Feast of Tabernacles to which He might have been referring. William Barclay describes it: "On the evening of its first day there was a ceremony called the Illumination of the Temple. It took place in the Court of the Women. The court was surrounded with deep galleries, erected to hold the spectators. In the center, four great candelabra were prepared. When the dark came, the four great candelabra were lit and, it was said, they sent such a blaze of light throughout Jerusalem that every courtyard was lit up with their brilliance.

"Then all night long, until the cock crowed the next morning, the greatest, wisest, and holiest men in Israel danced before the Lord and sang psalms of joy and praise while the people watched. Jesus is saying: 'You have seen the blaze of the Temple illuminations piercing the darkness of the night. I am the Light of the world, and, for the man who follows me there will be light, not only for one exciting night, but for all of his life. The light in the Temple is a brilliant light, but in the end it flickers and dies. I am the Light which lasts forever.'"

Follow the Son

Again therefore Jesus spoke to them, saying, "I am the light of the world; he who follows Me shall not walk in darkness, but shall have the light of life" (John 8:12).

The Greek word for "follow" here is *akolouthein*. Its different meanings help us understand how we are to follow Christ:

• *Follow* is used of **a soldier following his captain.** No matter where, nor how rough the terrain, the soldier follows his captain. The Christian follows his Commander, Christ, everywhere. He does not question where; he obediently follows.

• *Follow* is used of **a slave accompanying his master**. A slave is always on hand to carry out the wishes of his master. No matter what the task, the slave is to do what the master commands. We are bond slaves of the Lord Jesus Christ. We are to be constantly at His beck and call, willing and ready to do what He commands.

• *Follow* is used of **accepting a wise counselor's opinion**. A man who needs legal advice goes to the lawyer; the one who needs medical advice goes to the doctor. Then, if he trusts his advisor, he will follow his counsel. You have expert counsel awaiting you in Jesus Christ for every problem you may encounter. Follow His advice!

• *Follow* is used to mean **obeying the laws of a city or state**. Being a good citizen of a city, country, or state involves obeying its laws. You are a citizen of heaven. Being a good citizen compels you to obey the laws that the King sets forth.

• *Follow* is used of **following a teacher's line of argument**, or understanding his main thoughts. The Christian understands Christ's teaching. He receives the teaching, understands it, and follows it.

Following Christ means you never walk alone. You cannot take the wrong road when you are following an expert. Jesus Christ knows the way. He has a road map for your life, and when you follow Him, you walk securely.

Unregenerate man has the "light" to a certain extent: he is capable of making moral decisions and has a conscience.

> *...In that they show the work of the Law written in their hearts, their conscience bearing witness, and their thoughts alternately accusing or else defending them* (Romans 2:15).

Unregenerate man can also recognize evidence that points to a Creator, so he is without excuse. (See Romans 1:19,20.) What he does not have is *spiritual light*. He walks in darkness. Education and science will not further enlighten him. He needs to understand how much he is worth, that he is an eternal being who will spend eternity *somewhere*. He needs to know God, His character, and His love. Christ was sent to earth to light our way to eternal life. Just as the cloud led the Israelites out of Egypt to the Promised Land, so the Light of the world leads the believer from this world to the next! You do not walk in the darkness of ignorance and sin, but in the light of truth, holiness, and joy!

Sonrise Over Planet Earth

When Jesus said, "I am the Light of the world," the Jews listening understood Him to say He was the Messiah. The Light was God. The rabbis understood that the name of the Messiah was Light. Now Jesus was openly declaring that He was the Light of the world!

Old Testament prophecies refer to the Messiah as a light for the Gentiles:

> *I am the Lord, I have called you in righteousness, I will also hold you by the hand and watch over you, and I will appoint you as a covenant to the people, as a light to the nations* (Isaiah 42:6).

> *...I will also make You a light of the nations so that My salvation may reach to the end of the earth* (Isaiah 49:6).

> *But for you who fear My name the sun of righteousness will rise with healing in its wings...* (Malachi 4:2).

Be His Disciple

> *"I said therefore to you, that you shall die in your sins; for unless you believe that I am He, you shall die in your sins." And so they were saying to Him, "Who are You?" Jesus said to them, " What have I been saying to you from the beginning? I have many things to speak*

The Lord Is YOUR Light

The Lord is my light and my salvation; whom shall I fear? The Lord is the defense of my life; whom shall I dread? (Psalm 27:1).

YOU will have the Lord for an everlasting Light.

No longer will you have the sun for light by day, nor for brightness will the moon give you light; but you will have the Lord for an everlasting light, and your God for your glory (Isaiah 60:19).

By His light YOU walk through darkness.

When His lamp shone over my head, and by His light I walked through darkness (Job 29:3).

Though YOU might dwell in darkness, the Lord is a light for YOU.

Do not rejoice over me, O my enemy. Though I fall I will rise; though I dwell in darkness, the Lord is a light for me (Micah 7:8).

and to judge concerning you, but He who sent Me is
true; and the things which I heard from Him, these I
speak to the world." They did not realize that He had
been speaking to them about the Father. Jesus therefore
said, "When you lift up the Son of Man, then you will
know that I am He, and I do nothing on My own
initiative, but I speak these things as the Father taught
Me. And He who sent Me is with Me; He has not left
Me alone, for I always do the things that are pleasing
to Him" (John 8:24-30).

Your discipleship with Christ begins when you accept all that
He says about Himself, His Father, you, and your need of Him: *"As*
He spoke these things, many came to believe in Him" (John 8:30).
He disciples you as you abide in His Word:

Jesus therefore was saying to those Jews who had
believed Him, "If you abide in My word, then you
are truly disciples of Mine: and you shall know the
truth, and the truth shall make you free"
(John 8:31,32).

Listen to His Word. Listen for your Lord's voice. Make no
decision before you hear from the Lord. You *must* read His Word.
Jesus speaks to us through His Word. Read it continually, allowing it
to speak to your spirit.

Study the Word. You cannot *continue* in something unless
you understand it. Take time to find out what God's Word means.
In the parable of the sower, the enemy was able to steal the Word
from those who did not *understand it.* Understand what your Lord
is saying to you, and then the enemy cannot take it from you!

When anyone hears the word of the kingdom, and
does not understand it, the evil one comes and
snatches away what has been sown in his heart.
This is the one on whom seed was sown beside the
road (Matthew 13:19).

Practice the Word. If you never put the truth of God's Word into practice, you are a "hearer only" and not a true disciple. Jesus said that bearing fruit proves you are His disciple, but you cannot bear fruit without obedience.

> *If you abide in Me, and My words abide in you, ask whatever you wish, and it shall be done for you. By this is My Father glorified, that you bear much fruit, and so prove to be My disciples. Just as the Father has loved Me, I have also loved you; abide in My love. If you keep My commandments, you will abide in My love; just as I have kept My Father's commandments, and abide in His love* (John 15:7-10).

Follow Jesus and you will know the truth—you will know the answers to the great questions of life. What are you living for? Why are you working? What about life after death? Which value system do you live by? The closer you follow Jesus, the more you are infused with truth!

Truth or Trash—Freedom or Bondage

Discipleship with Christ leads to freedom. John 8:32 says, *"And you shall know the truth, and the truth shall make you free."*

You can be free from fear. You are walking with Jesus; how can fear abide when He is by your side? Be free from self. When you know the truth of how weak you are without Jesus, or how vile the old nature is, you want to be free of it. You want to live your life by His life.

> *I have been crucified with Christ; and it is no longer I who live, but Christ lives in me; and the life which I now live in the flesh I live by faith in the Son of God, who loved me, and delivered Himself up for me* (Galatians 2:20).

You can live a new life! You are a new creation! As a disciple, practice truth and live free from the dominion of self! A disciple of Jesus does not live for the applause or approval of men. He lives to please his Master. That means you can have a "single eye"!

For the disciple, the bonds of sin have been broken. The truth of Christ's death and resurrection has set him free. He is no longer enslaved by old habits. He has the power of the Greater One within! How does Jesus set you free? He teaches you truth. You become His disciple—one who believes the Lord and abides in His Word. When you hear His Word, listen for His voice, understand His Word, and then obey it, you are not only living as a disciple of Jesus Christ, but as a true child of God!

No Second-Generation Christians

They answered Him, "We are Abraham's offspring, and have never yet been enslaved to anyone; how is it that You say, 'You shall become free'? (John 8:33).

When Jesus spoke of making them free, the Jews were indignant. Jesus didn't argue with them. He went on with the truth He was teaching. They were proud of their heritage—and they should have been—but they had forgotten that Abraham's sons spent years as slaves doing hard labor for Pharoah in Egypt. During the time of the judges, the people of Israel were under bondage to surrounding nations seven different times. The whole nation was carried off to Babylon for 70 years! Now they were under Roman rule.

The Jews claimed to be free on the basis of their heritage. As Abraham's offspring they honestly believed that they had the favor of God simply because of whom they were.

Family ties are important, but what your parents did will not save you. *You* must decide for yourself to be a disciple. Your church may have a marvelous history, but that does nothing for you unless you are actively following the Lord.

..."If you are Abraham's children, do the deeds of Abraham," Jesus said. "But as it is, you are seeking to

> *kill Me, a Man who has told you the truth, which I heard*
> *from God; this Abraham did not do"* (John 8:39,40).

What a reprimand! They claimed to be Abraham's children. Jesus looked at their deeds and said, "No, you are not his children. He would not act like that! Your actions betray your true heritage."

Can you imagine the shocked looks on their faces? Jesus had dared to tell them not only that they were not true descendants of Abraham, but also that they were children of the devil! He said,

> *You are of your father the devil, and you want to do*
> *the desires of your father. He was a murderer from the*
> *beginning, and does not stand in the truth, because*
> *there is no truth in him. Whenever he speaks a lie, he*
> *speaks from his own nature; for he is a liar, and the*
> *father of lies. But because I speak the truth, you do*
> *not believe Me* (John 8:44,45).

They were seeking even then to kill Jesus. Murder was in their hearts—they were being deceived by the father of lies. They paid no attention to the Truth—Who was speaking to them.

> *Then Jesus challenged them with this question, "Which*
> *one of you convicts Me of sin? If I speak truth, why do*
> *you not believe Me? He who is of God hears the words*
> *of God; for this reason you do not hear them, because*
> *you are not of God"* (John 8:46,47).

The Jews were conscience-smitten. They could not accuse Him, yet they refused to believe Him. When Jesus told them they would not hear Him because they were not of God, they proved it by their words, *"Do we not say rightly that You are a Samaritan and have a demon?"* (John 8:48). They called the Son of God an enemy to religion, one possessed with a lying spirit.

Christ came to set them free, but they chose to remain slaves of sin. He came to give them light, but they would rather remain in the darkness of their traditions.

The Sighted Are Blind, But the Blind See

In Chapter 8, the people were unable to see Jesus because He hid Himself from those who would stone Him. In this next chapter, a man was unable to see Jesus because of blindness. In Chapter 8 the Light was despised and rejected; here it was received and worshiped. In Chapter 8 Jesus hid Himself from the Jews; in Chapter 9, He revealed Himself to a beggar. In Chapter 8 the Word found no reception; in Chapter 9, it changed a life! *Inside* the Temple, in Chapter 8, Jesus was accused of having a demon; in Chapter 9, *outside* the Temple, He was called Lord.

> *And as He passed by, He saw a man blind from birth. And His disciples asked Him, saying, "Rabbi, who sinned, this man or his parents, that he should be born blind?" Jesus answered, "It was neither that this man sinned, nor his parents; but it was in order that the works of God might be displayed in him. We must work the works of Him who sent Me, as long as it is day; night is coming, when no man can work. While I am in the world, I am the light of the world." When He had said this, He spat on the ground, and made clay of the spittle, and applied the clay to his eyes, and said to him, "Go, wash in the pool of Siloam" (which is translated, Sent). And so he went away and washed, and came back seeing. The neighbors therefore, and those who previously saw him as a beggar, were saying, "Is not this the one who used to sit and beg?" Others were saying, "This is he," still others were saying, "No, but he is like him." He kept saying, " I am the one." Therefore they were saying to him, "How then were your eyes opened?" He answered, "The man who is called Jesus made clay, and anointed my eyes, and said to me, 'Go to Siloam, and wash'; so I went away and washed, and I received sight." And they said to him, "Where is He?" He said, "I do not know"(John 9:1-12).*

This man was a beggar, dependent upon charity. Men could not cure him, but only share some coins. A spiritually blind man is also helpless; no one can cure him. We must lead him to Jesus Who opens blind eyes.

The disciples were more concerned with the cause of his sickness than with ministering to him. They asked Jesus, "Why was he born blind? Who sinned, this man or his parents?" They could not explain human suffering in any way except that it was "caused by sin." Most of the rabbis believed that Exodus 20:5 supplied the key:

> *You shall not worship them or serve them; for I, the Lord your God, am a jealous God, visiting the iniquity of the fathers on the children, on the third and the fourth generations of those who hate Me.*

John 9:3 corrects a belief quite common in that day, that all diseases were the result of a person's sin.

A Creative Miracle

Jesus did a creative thing. He spit on the ground, made some mud with the saliva, and put it on the man's eyes. Why did He use clay? Since this man was blind from birth, he might have been born without eyes at all. Jesus not only healed him, but did a creative miracle. Since man was made from the dust of the earth, He may have used dust to create new eyes:

> ..."*The man who is called Jesus made clay, and anointed my eyes, and said to me, 'Go to Siloam, and wash'; so I went away and washed, and I received sight*" (John 9:11).

We see, through Jesus' way of dealing with the blind man, a *picture* of mankind. Jesus saw the man's condition and He had compassion. God looked on the world, had compassion, and sent His Son. The beggar was created for the glory of God to be manifested through healing. God wants to be glorified in you, too. Jesus had to work while it was day. We do, too. He had to do the works of His Father. They are our works, too.

Jesus shines light into the darkness. So do we. He was THE Light of the world, and we are the lights to the world—the light-holders. (See Matthew 5:14-16.)

Jesus took the initiative to heal a blind man. Jesus restores our sight. The beggar had to respond; he had to obey and wash. We, too, must respond to Jesus' healing offer. We must not only hear the message, but also obey, and only then can we receive! The beggar received a miracle! Every time you obey Christ's word, you can count on results!

The healed man had a fearless testimony: *"Whether He is a sinner, I do not know; one thing I do know, that, whereas I was blind, now I see"* (John 9:25). This man knew a transformation had taken place, and no one was going to take that from him!

> *They said therefore to him, "What did He do to you? How did He open your eyes?"* (John 9:26).

They were concerned with the *how* rather than the *Who*. "What did He do to you?" They were more concerned with the method than the result!

> *He answered them, "I told you already, and you did not listen; why do you want to hear it again? You do not want to become His disciples too, do you?"* (John 9:27).

He did not answer according to their folly. *"Do not answer a fool according to his folly, lest you also be like him"* (Proverbs 26:4). He answered with unusual wisdom:

> *The man answered and said to them, "Well, here is an amazing thing, that you do not know where He is from, and yet He opened my eyes. We know that God does not hear sinners; but if anyone is God-*

fearing, and does His will, He hears him. Since the beginning of time it has never been heard that anyone opened the eyes of a person born blind. If this man were not from God, He could do nothing" (John 9:30-33).

"They answered and said to him, 'You were born entirely in sins, and are you teaching us?' And they put him out" (John 9:34). Sometimes, when a notable miracle takes place, the response of the religious world is total unbelief. Because they had not received the Word, they could not receive the results of the Word, either. Then they excommunicated him—they did their worst! The healed man was "put out" of the temple for his faith.

Jesus gave a special blessing for those that suffered excommunication:

> *Blessed are you when men hate you, and ostracize you, and cast insults at you, and spurn your name as evil, for the sake of the Son of Man* (Luke 6:22).

He warned His disciples that it would happen to them:

> *They will make you outcasts from the synagogue, but an hour is coming for everyone who kills you to think that he is offering service to God* (John 16:2).

Meeting Your Miracle

This man started out by calling Jesus a man, but he had never met anyone like Him!

> *He answered, "The man who is called Jesus made clay, and anointed my eyes, and said to me, 'Go to Siloam, and wash'; so I went away and washed, and I received sight"* (John 9:11).

Then he called Jesus a prophet:

"Put Out"

There were three kinds of Jewish "excommunication":

1. A "rebuke" that lasted from seven to 30 days.

2. A "thrusting out" that lasted 30 days and could be followed by a second period of 30 days. This could only be pronounced in an assembly of ten and it was accompanied by curses and the blast of a horn. The ostracized one could not come to public prayer and was kept at a distance of four cubits from others.

3. Finally, there was "excommunication" for an indefinite period of time. It was forbidden for others to eat, drink, or speak with the excommunicated one. This is what the blind man's parents feared, therefore they would not testify on his behalf.

The terror of excommunication for the Jews was that they believed it not only excluded them from people, but also from God.

*They said therefore to the blind man again, "What
do you say about Him since He opened your eyes?"
And he said, "He is a prophet"* (John 9:17).

Finally, he called Him "Son of God" and worshiped Him:

*Jesus heard that they had put him out; and finding
him, He said, "Do you believe in the Son of Man?" He
answered and said, "And who is He, Lord, that I may
believe in Him?" Jesus said to him, "You have both
seen Him, and He is the one who is talking with you."
And he said, "Lord, I believe." And he worshiped Him*
(John 9:35-38).

What happened to the blind beggar? He met the Light of the
world and became a new man. Jesus saw him, healed him, and
revealed Himself to him. Even the threat of excommunication could
not quiet his testimony. His response to the Light of the world was
worship!

Who received the invitation of light and guidance? Even the
Pharisees had the opportunity to be forgiven—to follow the Light
and have everlasting life. In this chapter they refused Jesus, yet many
"religious" people have accepted Him, because religion alone is dark
and lifeless. Only Jesus has the light and life to guide you. Once you
have met Jesus you must worship Him. He is your light in a dark
world; He is your sight in blind areas; He is your God. Worship Him!

Personal Action Plan

1. What impressed you most about the attitude of Jesus towards the adulterous woman? How does this attitude affect your life today?

2. Paraphrase these verses, making them into a personal declaration of your faith: John 8:12,31,32,36. Write them in your scripture notebook.

3. Describe "true discipleship" and how it fits into your ministry goals.

4. Look at the questions asked of the healed man in Chapter 9. How do they compare with questions asked of a new convert? List the similarities. Find someone to share them with this week.

5. Pray about how you can show the love of Jesus to someone who seems outcast or lonely. Record the answers in your journal.

Chapter 6

THE
LIFE
BRINGER

The Life Bringer

Christ is introduced as a"door"in John Chapter 10. A door can restrict access to protect those within. A door can be an entrance into something good or an exit from something bad. Jesus became each of these doors for us. There are three doors discussed in this chapter; the first is the Door to the Sheepfold:

> *Truly, truly, I say to you, he who does not enter by the door into the fold of the sheep, but climbs up some other way, he is a thief and a robber. But he who enters by the door is a shepherd of the sheep* (John 10:1,2).

In Palestinian villages, there was a large sheepfold, common property to the native farmers. The wall of the sheepfold was ten or twelve feet high. When night fell, a number of different shepherds would lead their flocks up to the door of the fold, leaving them in the care of the *porter* while they went home. The porter lay at the door all night. In the morning the different shepherds would return and they would call their sheep, the sheep would respond to the voice of their shepherd and follow him to pasture.

Jesus entered into this sheepfold to lead His people out:

> *When he puts forth all his own, he goes before them, and the sheep follow him because they know his voice* (John 10:4).

The porter opened the sheepfold door to Jesus. Who is the porter in John 10? It is the one who introduced Jesus to Israel—John the Baptist:

> And I [John] *did not recognize Him, but in order that He might be manifested to Israel, I came baptizing in water* (John 1:31).

In another sense the porter also represents the Holy Spirit, who revealed the truth of the Messiah as He was being presented to God's people. The Holy Spirit continually opens the door of the heart and presents Christ to the unsaved.

The true sheep of Israel recognized their Messiah. The shepherds came to worship Him at His birth. Simeon recognized Him in the Temple. The Holy Spirit had promised Simeon that he would not die without seeing the Messiah. When he saw the baby Jesus in the Temple, Simeon knew who He was and prophesied over Him, praising the Lord. (See Luke 2:25-32.) In the same chapter, Anna the prophetess came up to the Child, gave thanks to God, and then spoke about the Child to others who were looking forward to the redemption of Jerusalem.

> *And at that very moment she came up and began*
> *giving thanks to God, and continued to speak of Him*
> *to all those who were looking for the redemption of*
> *Jerusalem* (Luke 2:38).

During His ministry years, Jesus, like a sheperd, simply called men to "follow" Him. To Matthew He said, "Follow Me!" and Matthew rose up and followed Him.(See Matthew 9:9.) To Zaccheus He said, *"...Zaccheus, hurry and come down, for today I must stay at your house."* What was this man's response? *"...He hurried and came down, and received Him gladly"* (Luke 19:5,6). Even when Jesus spoke to a "dead sheep" (Lazarus), His voice was heard (John 11) and the sheep was restored. Others, like Jesus' half-brothers, had to be encouraged to follow. It took longer, but they, too, heard His voice and became a faithful part of the flock.

His own sheep responded. Those who did not listen were not His sheep: *"But you do not believe, because you are not of My sheep"* (John 10:26). He led His own sheep out of the dry places of Judaism into the rich pastures of new life in Christ.

The marks of a true shepherd are:
- He enters by the door, not as a thief or robber.
- The porter opens the door.
- The sheep recognize his voice.

The Second and Third Doors

Jesus therefore said to them again, "Truly, truly, I say to you, I am the Door of the sheep" (John 10:7).

When sheep are grazing on the hillsides in warmer weather, they do not return to the village each night. They sleep in sheepfolds made of simple wooden enclosures with an opening on one side. There is no door on this opening. The shepherd lies down in front of it and literally becomes the door. He keeps the sheep inside the fold and the enemies out.

The second door in John 10 is the Door of the Sheep—Christ Himself. People who truly sought God had to go beyond the system of Judaism to find a better way. They were passing from one covenant to another and Jesus was the Door.

I am the Door; if anyone enters through Me, he shall be saved, and shall go in and out, and find pasture (John 10:9).

Everyone who wants salvation must come to Him. He is the One who gives access to the Father. This is the third door, the Door of Salvation.

For through Him we both have our access in one Spirit to the Father (Ephesians 2:18).

Jesus is the new and living way. *"...And shall go in and out, and find pasture."* This was a way of describing perfect freedom. The ceremonial law hedged in the Jews; they were slaves of the law. Jesus came to give them freedom: *"By a new and living way which He inaugurated for us through the veil, that is, His flesh"* (Hebrews 10:20). They were separated from all the other nations by the law. Now the walls were going to be broken down.

"And find pasture." They would find nourishment in Christ; He was their food. He was their Shepherd and He would lead them to the choicest pasture.

A Shepherd's Life

The life of a shepherd was hard. He was always on duty, always caring for his sheep. Since there was not an abundance of grass in the Judean area, the sheep wandered about in search of food. The shepherd had to be close at hand, watching that they did not wander off or fall into danger. He was also on guard against thieves who robbed and wolves, bears, lions and other wild animals that might attack the flock.

The equipment of the shepherd was simple. He carried a bag for his food, and a sling and a staff for the protection of the sheep. Some Judeans were excellent marksmen with their slings. Judges 20:16 tells us there were some left-handed Benjamites that could "sling a stone at a hair and not miss." The staff was a short club with a thickened end that held nails. The staff hung by a leather strap from the shepherd's belt. He also carried a rod to aid in walking. It sometimes had a crook on it to help rescue sheep caught in underbrush. At night, the sheep were made to pass under the rod on their way into the fold while the shepherd checked for bruises and hurts.

"And for every tenth part of herd or flock, whatever

passes under the rod, the tenth one shall be holy to the Lord" (Leviticus 27:32).

The relationship between a Palestinian shepherd and his sheep was close. Since most of the sheep in Palestine were kept for wool rather than meat, they became almost like pets to the shepherd. He would have names for them like "brown leg" or "white spot." Some shepherds even had individual calls for their sheep—and the sheep knew their voice!

In the East, even to this day, the shepherd goes before his flock, not driving them ahead of him, as in the West. Sheep follow the shepherd who goes first to ensure a safe path for them. There are times when the sheep need extra encouragement to follow. One observer tells of a shepherd who was leading his flock towards a stream. The sheep were unwilling to cross. Finally, the shepherd picked up one of the lambs and carried it across the stream. The mother then crossed, and the whole flock followed.

Jesus likens us to sheep many times in the Word. Does He ever have to coax you to follow Him?

Jesus was the perfect leader Moses dreamed of for Israel. After Moses, Joshua led the people, but was only a *type* of the Savior who would lead His people out of the wilderness into the spiritual, eternal Promised Land.

> *Then Moses spoke to the Lord, saying, "May the Lord, the God of the spirits of all flesh, appoint a man over the congregation, who will go out and come in before them, and who will lead them out and bring them in, that the congregation of the Lord may not be like sheep which have no shepherd"* (Numbers 27:15-17).

True Shepherd or Hireling?

The "True Shepherd" was born to His task. He loved his sheep and risked His life to protect them. Like David, He would fight the wild beasts in order to protect his flock.

> *But David said to Saul, "Your servant was tending his father's sheep. When a lion or a bear came and took a lamb from the flock, I went out after him and attacked him, and rescued it from his mouth; and when he rose up against me, I seized him by his beard and struck him and killed him. Your servant has killed both the lion and the bear; and this uncircumcised Philistine will be like one of them, since he has taunted the armies of the living God"* (I Samuel 17:34-36).

The "hireling" is the shepherd who tends sheep only for money. Some true shepherds were also hired, but they had a true shepherd's heart. For example, Jacob kept sheep for his father-in-law, and Moses watched sheep for the priest of Midian in the wilderness. They were probably paid, yet both had the devotion of true shepherds. They protected their flocks. The usual hireling didn't care—he was a "false shepherd." When danger came, he

would run away and leave the sheep defenseless, and the flock
would be scattered.

> *For behold, I am going to raise up a shepherd in the*
> *land who will not care for the perishing, seek the*
> *scattered, heal the broken, or sustain the one standing,*
> *but will devour the flesh of the fat sheep and tear off*
> *their hoofs. Woe to the worthless shepherd who leaves*
> *the flock!...*(Zechariah 11:16,17).

There are enemies that come after Christ's sheep. Jesus
warned that the wolves would try to harm the flock of God, the
Church. Paul warned the Ephesian leaders:

> *I know that after my departure savage wolves will*
> *come in among you, not sparing the flock*
> (Acts 20:29).

The True Shepherd would stay and look after his sheep.
Character is revealed by the crises of life. How do you act when the
wolf is attacking? When stresses come, have you learned to lean
more heavily on your Lord Who is leading you to safety? Pastors or
under-shepherds should act like their Chief Shepherd in caring for
the flock that God has given them.

The Pharisees were the *hireling* shepherds of Israel. (See
Ezekiel 34:1-4.) They cast the healed beggar out of the synagogue
and their almsgiving was only for show. A true love for people
was lacking. Even fasting was done in order to *appear* holy.

Jesus is the Good Shepherd of Psalm 23. He loves His sheep
and leads them gently. He is the Good Shepherd Who risked His life
to save even one lost sheep:

> *What do you think? If any man has a hundred*
> *sheep, and one of them has gone astray, does he*
> *not leave the ninety-nine on the mountains and*
> *go and search for the one that is straying?*
> (Matthew 18:12).

Old Testament Shepherds

There are five individual shepherds in the Old Testament that point to Christ the Shepherd, and one that represents the Anti-Christ.

• Abel was a "keeper of sheep" and was slain by wicked hands. (See Genesis 4:2.)

• Jacob had a true shepherd's heart. (See Genesis 30:31; 31:38,39.)

• Joseph fed the flock: *"...Joseph, when seventeen years of age, was pasturing the flock with his brothers..."* (Genesis 37:2).

• Moses watered, protected, guided the sheep. (See Exodus 2:16,17; 3:1.)

• David risked his life for the sheep. (See I Samuel 17:34-36.)

• There is another shepherd, the foolish and worthless shepherd of Zechariah 11:16,17. How appropriate that he is the sixth shepherd (a type of the Anti-Christ)!

• The last Shepherd is Jesus—the *Perfect* Shepherd!

For the Sheep

"I am the Good Shepherd; the Good Shepherd lays down His life for the sheep" (John 10:11). The good Shepherd, Jesus, voluntarily laid His life down for the sheep. No one *took* His life. He was not a martyr! Jesus gave His life for "people"—not for fallen angels, a cause, His beliefs, or for a principle. He died for people! He died so that we wouldn't have to:

> *For while we were still helpless, at the right time Christ died for the ungodly. For one will hardly die for a righteous man; though perhaps for the good man someone would dare even to die. But God demonstrates His own love toward us, in that while we were yet sinners, Christ died for us* (Romans 5:6-8).

Are You Sheep-Like?

> *I am the Good Shepherd, and I know My Own, and My Own know Me, even as the Father knows Me and I know the Father;...* (John 10: 14,15).

Sheep have certain characteristics that set them apart from other animals: sheep are among the few animals considered by the Jews to be clean. Each of Christ's sheep has been cleansed from all sin:

> *If we confess our sins, He is faithful and righteous to forgive us our sins and to cleanse us from all unrighteousness* (I John 1:9).

Sheep are harmless:

> *Behold, I send you out as sheep in the midst of wolves; therefore be shrewd as serpents, and innocent as doves* (Matthew 10:16).

Sheep are helpless: without Christ you can do nothing:

> *I am the vine, you are the branches; he who abides in
> Me, and I in him, he bears much fruit; for apart from
> Me you can do nothing* (John 15:5).

Sheep are gentle, but prone to wander: sheep need to keep their eyes on the Shepherd. *"Keep watching and praying, that you may not come into temptation;..."* (Mark 14:38).

Sheep are useful: We have been created for good works:

> *For we are His workmanship, created in Christ Jesus
> for good works, which God prepared beforehand, that
> we should walk in them* (Ephesians 2:10).

Who *Really* Knows You?

Jesus knows each of us intimately. He knew the heart of Nathanael. He knew that Judas was a betrayer when no one else suspected. He knew that Peter would become an overcomer even though he would deny Jesus. Jesus knows you better than you know yourself.

> *I am the good shepherd; and I know My own, and My
> own know Me, even as the Father knows Me and I
> know the Father; and I lay down My life for the sheep*
> (John 10:14,15).

Never hesitate to confide in your Shepherd. He loves you, knows each of your weaknesses and strengths, and the secret desires of your heart. He knows your potential and is willing to help you to live life to the very fullest.

> *The thief comes only to steal, and kill, and destroy; I
> came that they might have life, and might have it
> abundantly* (John 10:10).

Jesus gives you "abundant" life—physically, socially, spiritually, and emotionally. *"The Lord is my Shepherd, I shall not want"* (Psalm 23:1). You need not want for forgiveness, spiritual blessing, health, strength, ability, money—or opportunities to use them all according to His plan.

Lost and Found

And I have other sheep, which are not of this fold; I must bring them also, and they shall hear My voice, and they shall become one flock with one Shepherd (John 10:16).

Jesus revealed to His disciples that the Gentiles are also part of His flock. Isaiah said that Israel was given "for a light to the **nations.**" (See Isaiah 42:6; 49:6.) Even at the beginning of the Abrahamic covenant, Jesus said that through Abraham's Seed ALL the nations of the earth would be blessed. Jesus sent His disciples only to Israel and proclaimed that was His mission. (See Matthew 10:5,6.)

But He answered and said, "I was sent only to the lost sheep of the house of Israel" (Matthew 15:24).

Even during this phase of ministry, Christ met the needs of Gentiles that came to Him: the Roman centurion who had such strong faith; the Samaritan leper who was the only one of the ten to return to give thanks; the Syrophenician woman whose daughter was healed.

God's plan was to ultimately save the world. God so loved the world—but He began with a man, Abraham; then a family, Jacob; then a nation, Israel. Finally, the blessing spread to the entire world. The Gentiles were strangers to God, but now, through Christ, were brought near. They are part of the flock.

Therefore remember, that formerly you, the Gentiles in the flesh, who are called "Uncircumcision" by the so-called "Circumcision," which is performed in the flesh by human hands—remember that you were at that time separate from Christ, excluded from the commonwealth of Israel, and strangers to the

166   The Life Bringer

Christ Is Your Shepherd

John 10:14 presents the Good Shepherd in death:

I am the good shepherd; and I know My own, and My own know Me, even as the Father knows Me and I know the Father, and I lay down My life for the sheep

Hebrews 13:20 presents the Great Shepherd in resurrection:

Now the God of peace, who brought up from the dead the great Shepherd of the sheep through the blood of the eternal covenant, even Jesus our Lord

First Peter 5:4 presents the Chief Shepherd in the glorious return:

And when the Chief Shepherd appears, you will receive the unfading crown of glory

covenants of promise, having no hope and without God in the world. But now in Christ Jesus you who formerly were far off have been brought near by the blood of Christ. For He Himself is our peace, who made both groups into one...(Ephesians 2:11-14).

Jesus planted the gospel in Israel for three years. The fourth year, He laid down His life as a sacrifice and the *first* fruits of that sacrifice were the apostles. In the fifth year, the fruit was no longer within the confines of Judaism, but was being seen in all nations. A few years later Christianity had spread everywhere—the fruit of Christ's life. You are part of the abundance of that harvest!

Behold the Lamb

The first ten chapters of John have to do with the *public* ministry of Jesus. The last part has to do with His *private* ministry where Jesus presented Himself as Messiah and offered Himself as a sacrifice.

"At that time the Feast of the Dedication took place in Jerusalem; it was winter..." (John 10:22,23).This feast pointed to Jesus' death: He was dedicating Himself for sacrifice as the "Lamb of God."

The Feast of Dedication (of the Temple) was observed at Jerusalem in remembrance of the purification of the Temple after it had been polluted by the idolatries of Antiochus Ephiphanes. The feast was instituted by Judas Maccabaeus about 165 B. C. This eight-day feast was celebrated every year in the month of December. It is also called the "Festival of Lights," or what we know as "Hanukkah." This is the only place this feast is mentioned in Scripture, and there are only two other places where the word is translated *dedication* in the New Testament—Hebrews 9:18 and 10:19,20. Both verses speak of the shedding of blood of the Son of God.

Before a lamb was sacrificed, it was set apart for a few days. Jesus talked of Himself as sanctified or set apart in John 10:36.

The feast was to commemorate the Dedication of the Temple. Jesus talked of Himself as the Temple in John 2:19. *"...Destroy this temple and in three days I will raise it up."* His Temple was dedicated to do the will of God, even to the shedding of blood!

One last time, the Jews asked Jesus if He was the Messiah. He said, "By now you should know, because of what I have done. But you do not believe because you are not of My flock." They could not hear Him and did not know His voice because they were not His sheep. Jesus' sheep know His voice and respond. They are the chosen ones. Jesus described His sheep by saying they hear His voice and follow Him. They cannot be taken away from Him. They are secure in His Father's hand and He gives them eternal life!

> *My sheep hear My voice, and I know them, and they*
> *follow Me; and I give eternal life to them, and they*
> *shall never perish; and no one shall snatch them out*
> *of My hand. My Father, who has given them to Me, is*
> *greater than all; and no one is able to snatch them*
> *out of the Father's hand* (John 10:27-29).

The Seventh Sign

Six miracles were performed by Christ in the first ten chapters of the book of John. In Chapter 11 we have the seventh.

He turned the water into wine, healed the nobleman's son, restored the impotent man, multiplied the loaves and fishes, walked on the sea, and gave sight to a blind man. In Chapter 11 is the seventh miracle—Jesus raised the dead. This man was not recently dead, or one who had not been buried. Jesus raised a man who had been dead four days.

The miracles in John portray the state of natural man: he has no more wine, no divine joy, he is sick; impotent, without strength. He is storm-tossed, heading for destruction. He is blind, cannot see his own danger. In the most helpless state, he is dead— dead in trespasses and sins.

Martha, Mary, and their brother Lazarus lived in Bethany. They were close friends of Jesus. Martha was probably the oldest of the three, for the Bible says that Martha received Jesus into *her* house. (See Luke 10:38.)

Martha was the one who served while Mary sat at Jesus' feet absorbing His teaching. When Martha became distracted and expressed her resentment for having to do all the work, Jesus rebuked her. One sister ministered *to* Christ while the other received *from* Him. Jesus commended the latter.

Then came the day their brother, Lazarus, became deathly ill. They notified their friend, Jesus, *"...Lord, behold, he whom You love is sick"* (John 11:3). They cast their care on the Lord. They appealed to His love. Mary and Martha knew just where to go in time of trouble—to the Lord.

How did the Lord answer the messenger? *"...This sickness is not unto death, but for the glory of God, that the Son of God may be glorified by it"* (John 11:4). Jesus knew what the end results would be! He let the sisters know that He knew about the situation and had it under control, but He did not tell them exactly what would happen. Sometimes when you are in trouble, you may give your burden to the Lord and yet not get a specific answer. You only know He will meet your need. Rest in that! He does not always give us specifics. He allows us to exercise our faith!

Timing—Yours or God's?

"Now Jesus loved Martha, and her sister, and Lazarus" (John 11:5). Why did He wait two more days before He went to see them? Jesus waited for God's timing. When the time was right, even a death threat wouldn't stop Him.

> The disciples said to Him, *"Rabbi, the Jews were just now seeking to stone You, and are You going there again?"* (John 11:8).

His enemies could not lay a hand on Him until the time appointed by the Father. In Chapter 10, His enemies had tried to seize Him *"...but He eluded their grasp."* Jesus said, *"...If anyone walks in the day, he does not stumble, because he sees the light of the world"* (John 11:9). To walk in the day means to walk with God who

Glorified as Divine

In the preceding chapters of John, Jesus was repeatedly rejected and scorned. In John 5:16, He was rejected because of His works. In John 8:58, He was rejected because of His Words. Then, in John 10:30, it was because of His diety.

In Chapter 11 and 12, God glorified Jesus in three ways: in Lazarus' resurrection, Jesus was glorified as divine. In the entrance to Jerusalem, He was glorified as the Messiah, King of Israel. To the Gentiles, He was glorified as the Son of Man:

"And Jesus answered them, saying, 'The hour has come for the Son of Man to be glorified'" (John 12:23).

is Light, to fellowship with Him and walk in obedience. You will not stumble if God's Word is a lamp to your feet and a light to your path.

In the next breath Jesus gave us a solemn warning: *"But if anyone walks in the night, he stumbles, because the Light is not in him"* (John 11:10). Don't be foolish enough to go anywhere without Jesus, or contrary to the light of the Word—that guarantees stumbling.

When Jesus determined to go to the grieving family in Bethany, the disciples could only think of the danger. Their minds were filled with death—Lazarus was dead. We see the devotion of Thomas, he refused to be parted from Jesus even if it meant death.

> *Thomas therefore, who is called Didymus, said to his fellow disciples, "Let us also go, that we may die with Him"* (John 11:16).

Thomas was as afraid of dying as the rest of the disciples, yet he had the courage to say, "Let us go with Him."

A Jewish Funeral

Burial followed death as soon as possible in Palestine because of the warm climate. The body was wrapped in linen. The feet and hands were swathed in bandage-like wrappings. The head was wrapped in a towel. The Jews believed that the spirit of the dead person hovered around the tomb for four days, seeking entrance to the body. They had a funeral march. The women mourners walked first, for it was said that they first brought death. Mourners were not to be bothered with idle chatter, but left alone.

In the house of mourning, as long as the body was there, they were not to eat meat, drink wine, wear phylacteries, or engage in any kind of study. When the body was taken out, the furniture was reversed and mourners sat on the ground or on low stools.

When mourners returned from the tomb, their friends prepared a meal of bread, hard-boiled eggs, and lentils. The round eggs and lentils symbolized life, which was always rolling toward death.

Deep mourning lasted seven days—the first three were

devoted to weeping. During these seven days, mourners didn't anoint themselves, wash, put on shoes, or do business. The week of deep mourning was followed by 30 days of lighter mourning. As the mourners passed the tomb, they all said, "Depart in peace." The louder they wailed, the more honor they paid to the dead.

Questioning God

Martha, the sister who loved action, came to meet Jesus. She had reproach in her voice when she said, "Lord, if You had been here my brother would not have died." Perhaps in her mind she was saying, "Why did You wait two days after You heard my brother was sick? You waited too long!" As soon as her words were spoken, she followed them with faith-filled words. *"Even now, I know that whatever You ask of God, God will give You"* (John 11:22). She had just said words that defied the circumstances. Jesus answered, *"...Your brother shall rise again"* (John 11:23). She thought it was too good to be true, and said, *"...I know he will rise again in the resurrection in the last day"* (John 11:24).

Jesus gave her more words to feed her faith. He said, *"I am the Resurrection and the Life."* When Mary saw Jesus, she fell at His feet. In Luke 10, she honored Him as a Prophet. In John 12:3, she acknowledged Him as King. In Matthew 26:7, she anointed His head. In John 11 she acknlowledged Him as Priest.

Notice that Mary's words were precisely the same as Martha's: "Lord, if You had been here, my brother would not have died." Yet Jesus' response was not the same. He saw her weeping and was Himself overcome with compassion. Jesus felt her loss:

> When Jesus therefore saw her weeping, and the Jews who came with her, also weeping, He was deeply moved in spirit, and was troubled, and said, "Where have you laid him?" They said to Him, "Lord, come and see." Jesus wept (John 11:33-35).

Jesus wept three times—over Jerusalem, over Lazarus, and in Gethsemene. Each time, He wept over the consequences of sin.

The Dead Return to Life

Jesus sought the glory of God in raising Lazarus. The miracle of Lazarus' resurrection led to his triumphal entry into Jerusalem. Bethany to this day is called *Azariyeh* which means "Lazarus."

Lazarus had been dead four days. When Jesus arrived on the earth, man had been spiritually dead four *thousand* years. He came to call mankind forth from death.

Man was helpless to do anything about Lazarus' death, but Jesus arrived—the Resurrection and the Life! What did He do? He called the dead man's name:

> *When he had said this, Jesus called in a loud voice, "Lazarus, come out!" The dead man came out, his hands and feet wrapped with strips of linen, and a cloth around his face. Jesus said to them, Take off the grave clothes and let him go"* (John 11:43,44 NIV).

He called because His voice was *life-giving*. He had called the worlds into existence. Now, He spoke life into a dead man. His Words went forth into that dead situation with power! When you have a dead circumstance in your life, use the life-giving Word of God. Speak it forth and watch a miracle take place. God's Word is power-packed. It is the Word of *life*!

To the amazement of those watching, Lazarus came forth. The people rolled away the stone, they saw him come forth out of the grave, and they loosed him from his grave clothes.

The raising of Lazarus from the dead was the last great sign that Jesus performed before witnesses. Located about two miles from the temple, many saw this miracle with their own eyes. There was no excuse left for rejecting Him.

Mary and Martha had a house full of mourners. By waiting four days, Jesus had many witnesses to the work of His Father. The leaders could not deny it—many of them had personally seen it. It was impossible for the Sanhedrin to deny the last sign of the Messiah of Israel.

When God seemingly delays in answering a desperate need that you lay at His feet, hold on and trust Him. God is on your side!

He cares about your grief and He has a miraculous plan to overcome the enemy in every situation. Don't give up!

Love Brings Life

Your Good Shepherd loves you, goes before you and protects you. He never leaves you. He knows you well; He knows all your inner thoughts, emotions, and desires. Trust His care and praise God for your Good Shepherd.

Your Shepherd gives you abundant life. That means He provides everything you need for living life to its fullest! To do this, Jesus gave His life. He *gave* that you might *have*—and not only you, but all His sheep. His flock consists of people from all nations and races. All born-again people are one flock with one Shepherd.

Jesus was a beloved friend to Martha, Mary, and Lazarus. When they faced a crisis, they took their burden to the Lord. The Lord didn't act as quickly as they had hoped. Sickness led to death. Had Jesus let them down? No, He was waiting for God's perfect timing to do a perfect work—raise Lazarus from the dead! Many Jews were there to witness the work of the Father. They could not honestly deny His deity.

You too, can take all your crises to your Good Friend. He sticks closer than a brother, and He knows exactly how to solve each problem. Depend on His wisdom. Depend on Him to give you a scripture or His wisdom. Jesus is your resurrection and life! Not only in the future, but in any situation where death is working in this life!

Personal Action Plan

1. Study the Good Shepherd in John Chapter 10. Share with a friend what this concept can mean to your lives.

2. Meditate on the three doors spoken of in chapter 10. What does each represent to you. Record it in your journal.

3. Read John 10:9,10. What personal lesson do you draw from these verses?

4. What were Martha's faith-filled words to Jesus? (See John 11:22.) Apply these words to a crisis about which you know.

5. Pray and ask God to bring resurrection life to a "dead" situation in your family, work, or neighborhood.

Chapter 7

GIVING
AND
SERVING

Giving and Serving

We know that Mary loved Jesus. One day she chose a unique way to show her love. She had a box of precious spikenard ointment, and she poured it on her Lord. The ointment was valued at a year's wages!

Mary therefore took a pound of very costly perfume of pure nard, and anointed the feet of Jesus, and wiped His feet with her hair; and the house was filled with the fragrance of the perfume (John 12:3)

The ointment had been diligently preserved. She broke the box, first anointing Jesus' head and feet, then wiping His feet with her hair. She recognized the worship that was due Him. Her hair was her glory—and she used it to bring glory to Jesus Christ. The aroma not only filled the room, but the whole house. Sooner or later all would know what she had done for the Lord. (See John 12:1-8.)

They were at dinner in the home of Simon the leper, who had probably been healed of leprosy. Martha was doing what she did best. Martha was a server; that was her ministry. She showed her love to the Savior with the work of her hands. We can serve Jesus in the kitchen or behind a pulpit.

Mary gave the most precious thing she possessed to Jesus. She counted the cost, and she did it anyway. It was a sign of honor to anoint the head, but Mary didn't stop there. She also anointed His feet.

Thou dost prepare a table before me in the presence of my enemies; Thou hast anointed my head with oil; My cup overflows (Psalm 23:5).

She sat at Jesus' feet to learn, she fell at His feet in grief, and she anointed His feet. Mary was so engrossed in her worship and adoration of Jesus that she was unaware of what people thought of her. She had let her hair down when "respectable" women always had their hair bound in public! At that moment she was not thinking of her reputation. She was worshiping her Lord!

The whole house was filled with the aroma of Mary's ointment and since then, the entire Church has been filled with the sweet memory of Mary's action. Not only did Jesus smell of the precious ointment, but so did Mary—she smelled like Jesus. The best way to smell like Jesus is to spend time in His presence worshiping Him!

Mary anticipated Jesus' death and had some understanding of the value of His death. Other woman brought sweet spices to anoint Him after He died, but Mary anointed Him before His burial.

> *And when the Sabbath was over, Mary Magdalene, and Mary the mother of James, and Salome, bought spices, that they might come and anoint Him* (Mark 16:1).

> *For when she poured this perfume upon My body, she did it to prepare Me for burial* (Matthew 26:12).

She expressed her love by anointing Jesus while He was yet alive. She anointed Him, the Resurrection and the Life, in the presence of Lazarus whom He had recently raised from the dead. It was like an affirmation of Jesus' own resurrection which was yet to come!

Mark 14 and Matthew 26 tell us more of the story. What a convincing group they were: Simon, a healed leper; Lazarus, a resurrected man; Martha, the server; and Mary, the devoted worshiper. Mark and Matthew mentioned that Jesus' head was anointed. John, who emphasized the deity of Christ, speaks of Mary at His feet. That was her accustomed place. She loved, worshiped, and absorbed His teaching at His feet—the place of a student!

Matthew and Mark also mention the result of this incident. After the anointing, Judas went to the chief priests and sold Jesus. This act of anointing might have triggered Judas' decision and finalized his suspicion that being a disciple of Jesus was not going to be immediately profitable or politically powerful.

Notice the contrast between Judas and Mary. Mary freely *gave* three hundred denarii worth of ointment and Judas *sold* Christ for thirty pieces of silver. She was in Simon's house; Judas was the son of another Simon.

She had an ointment box; he had a moneybox. She was a worshiper; he was a thief. Mary drew the attention of all to the Lord. Judas would try to turn away the thoughts of all from Christ to the poor. At the very time Satan was goading Judas to do his worst, the Holy Spirit moved on Mary to give her best for Jesus. Mary became famous for her act and Judas became infamous for his.

Love is never wasted! Generosity is never wasted! You cannot give enough to the Lord when He gave His all. Giving to God and to each other is a sweet smell to the Lord. Paul said,

> *But I have received everything in full, and have an abundance; I am amply supplied, having received from Epaphroditus what you have sent, a fragrant aroma, and acceptable sacrifice well pleasing to God* (Philippians 4:18).

It Was Accepted

Mary was criticized by Judas for her extravagant act, but Jesus approved. He defended her and said, "Let her alone." He knew her motive and commended her action. Jesus is still defending His own against the accusations of others.

> *My little children, I am writing these things to you that you may not sin. And if anyone sins, we have an Advocate with the Father, Jesus Christ the righteous* (I John 2:1).

God is our Judge and Father, Jesus is our Advocate (Attorney) and Elder Brother. How can we lose?

> *For when she poured this perfume upon My body, she did it to prepare Me for burial. Truly I say to*

you, wherever this gospel is preached in the whole world, what this woman has done shall also be spoken of in memory of her (Matthew 26:12,13).

Wolf in Sheep's Clothing

Judas was the ministry's treasurer. He was in charge of money that was given by those who supported Jesus and His disciples.

> *For some were supposing, because Judas had the money box, that Jesus was saying to him, "Buy the things we have need of for the feast"; or else, that he should give something to the poor* (John 13:29).

Judas also did the buying and giving of money to the poor, but he only *pretended* to care for them. *"Why was this ointment not sold for three hundred denarii and given to poor people?"* (John 12:5). These are the first recorded words of Judas in the Gospels. The other Gospels do not tell us who began the grumbling over the ointment. Judas tried to hide his true feelings. If the ointment had been sold, it would have come to him before going to the poor and he would have had a chance to "help himself." Judas' heart was evil, therefore he did not see the beauty of Mary's sacrifice. That which is in your heart determines what your eyes see!

> *Now he said this, not because he was concerned about the poor, but because he was a thief, and as he had the money box, he used to pilfer what was put into it* (John 12:6).

The Greek tense of *pilfer* in this verse is a continuous one and a better translation would be: He was in the habit of continually stealing the contents of the purse. We know he used some of these funds to buy a field.

> *Now this man acquired a field with the price of his wickedness; and falling headlong, he burst open in*

the middle and all his bowels gushed out. And it became known to all who were living in Jerusalem; so that in their own language that field was called Hakeldama, that is, Field of Blood (Acts 1:18,19).

Peter called it *"the price of his wickedness."* The money used to purchase the property was not the thirty pieces of silver, he threw that back at the chief priests and elders! They used that money to buy a potter's field for the burial of strangers.

Then when Judas, who had betrayed Him, saw that He had been condemned, he felt remorse and returned the thirty pieces of silver to the chief priests and elders....And he threw the pieces of silver into the sanctuary and departed; and he went away and hanged himself....And they counseled together and with the money bought the Potter's Field as a burial place for strangers (Matthew 27:3,5,7).

Judas the Taker—Took the Silver

As one of the twelve disciples, Judas had healed the sick and cast out demons. I'm sure he was elated over their success and felt that Jesus would announce His Messiahship and be crowned King. Then he could have one of the high offices in the kingdom!

When Jesus was performing many miracles, public opinion was in His favor. The crowd tried to make Him earthly king after He fed the 5,000. Judas must have been extremely disappointed when Jesus declined their offer.

When Christ preached that He was the Bread of Life, many disciples left Him. The hope of establishing a powerful earthly kingdom dwindled. It might have been at that time that resentment began to grow in Judas' heart, for shortly afterward Jesus said, *"Did I Myself not choose you, the twelve, and yet one of you is a devil?"* (John 6:70).

This may have added fuel to Judas' anger, resentment, disappointment, and guilt. Such an emotional combination is the breeding ground for murder and betrayal.

When Jesus said about Mary, "She did it for My burial, leave her alone," Judas was rebuked and angry. He went to the chief priests and asked, *"What are you willing to give me to deliver Him up to you?"* (Matthew 26:15).

Judas made an agreement with the chief priests to deliver Jesus to them secretly, when no one would be there to protest. Then he took the thirty pieces of silver. Judas had come to a place in his greed and lack of faith in Jesus that he was willing to sell Jesus for the price of a common slave!

Jesus treated Judas no differently than the other disciples, no one suspected that he was *the* traitor that Jesus spoke of:

> *"Truly, truly, I say to you, that one of you will betray Me." The disciples began looking at one another, at a loss to know of which one He was speaking. There was reclining on Jesus' breast one of His disciples, whom Jesus loved. Simon Peter therefore gestured to him, and said to him, "Tell us who it is of whom He is speaking." He, leaning back thus on Jesus' breast, said to Him, "Lord, who is it?" Jesus therefore answered, "That is the one for whom I shall dip the morsel and give it to him." So when He had dipped the morsel, He took and gave it to Judas, the son of Simon Iscariot. And after the morsel, Satan then entered into him. Jesus therefore said to him, "What you do, do quickly"* (John 13:21-27).

For the host to offer the guest a special morsel, *the sop*, from the dish, was a sign of special friendship. When Boaz wished to show how much he honored Ruth, he invited her to come and dip her morsel of food in the wine.

> *And at mealtime Boaz said to her, "Come here, that you may eat of the bread and dip your piece of bread in the vinegar." So she sat beside the reapers; and he served her roasted grain, and she ate and was satisfied and had some left* (Ruth 2:14).

One Last Appeal

On the night of the Last Supper Jesus made one last attempt to show His friendship to Judas. William Barclay explains,

"It is quite clear that Jesus could speak to him privately without the others overhearing, if that be so, there is only one place Judas could have been occupying. He must have been on Jesus' left, so that just as John's head was on Jesus' breast, Jesus' head was on Judas'. The revealing thing is that the place on the left of the host was the place of highest honour, kept for the most intimate friend. When that meal began, Jesus must have said to Judas, 'Judas, come and sit beside me tonight; I want specially to talk to you.' The very inviting of Judas to that seat was an appeal."

From *The Gospel of John* by William Barclay

Jesus was trying to get Judas to reconsider their friendship and commitment, but when Judas left the room that night, Satan was in him, guaranteeing that the betrayal would occur as planned.

Imagine Judas' guilt when he went to the garden and betrayed Jesus with a kiss and heard Him say, "Friend." Think of the terror that must have gone through him when, by the power of God, he, along with the others, fell to the ground.

Suddenly all the memories of Jesus' kind words and actions must have flooded his mind! The man he had betrayed was *innocent*! His guilt drove him back to the Sanhedrin to throw down the money!

> *Saying, "I have sinned by betraying innocent blood."*
> *But they said, "What is that to us? See to that yourself!"*
> (Matthew 27:4).

He repented of his deed, but to man, not God. He felt sorrow, but not the kind that changes lives. His sorrow turned to despair, and he hung himself. (See Matthew 27:3-10.) He had not accepted the love that Jesus offered.

Jesus the Giver—Gave His Life

And I, if I be lifted up from the earth, will draw all men to Myself (John 12:32). Crowning Jesus was not God's plan for making Jesus King. You may wonder, "Why didn't Jesus take advantage of the cheering and praising crowds? Why didn't He build His Church on that enthusiastic crowd?" Life can only come through death. There is no salvation in kingship; salvation for mankind had to come through death. When he was "lifted up" on the Cross, then He would draw all men to Himself.

Why did Jesus initiate the Triumphal Entry? Why did He arrange for a donkey to ride and encourage the crowd to praise Him, knowing that, in four days, many of these people would be shouting, "Crucify Him!"

> *Saying to them, "Go into the village opposite you, and*
> *immediately you will find a donkey tied there and a*

*colt with her, untie them, and bring them to Me. And
if anyone says something to you, you shall say, 'The
Lord has need of them,' and immediately he will send
them"* (Matthew 21:2,3).

Jesus did it to fulfill the Scriptures! The Father's Word
prompted Him to go through with every detail! Jesus told the Jews,
"The Scriptures bear witness of Me" (John 5:39). *"And after He had
said these things, He was going on ahead, ascending to Jerusalem"*
(John 19:28). Jesus moved totally by the divine clock. He did the
Father's work in the Father's time.

The manner in which Jesus rode into Jerusalem sitting on a
colt was prophesied in Zechariah 9:9, hundreds of years earlier! He
sat on a colt which no one had ridden before.

*Saying, "Go into the village opposite you, in which
as you enter you will find a colt tied, on which no
one yet has ever sat; untie it, and bring it here"*
(Luke 19:30).

*This is the statute of the law which the Lord has
commanded, saying, "Speak to the sons of Israel that
they bring you an unblemished red heifer in which is
no defect, and on which a yoke has never been placed"*
(Numbers 19:2).

At His death, Jesus was publicly declared King of Israel
just as He had been publicly announced at His birth by angels
and wise men.

To the Western mind the donkey is a lowly animal, but to the
Easterner, it is a noble animal. He rode in like a Prince, not as One
going out to war on a horse. By riding on a donkey He signified that
He was coming in peace. Although Jesus was not the political
conqueror that many Jews awaited, He was a Conqueror. He came
to conquer an enemy far greater than the Romans. The people greeted
Him as a Conqueror and sang:

Daniel's Prophecy

When Jesus rode into Jerusalem, it was the last day of Daniel's prophesied 69 weeks.

"Seventy weeks have been decreed for your people and your holy city, to finish the transgression, to make an end of sin, to make atonement for iniquity, to bring in everlasting righteousness, to seal up vision and prophecy, and to anoint the most holy place. So you are to know and discern that from the issuing of a decree to restore and rebuild Jerusalem until Messiah the Prince there will be seven weeks and sixty-two weeks; it will be built again, with plaza and moat, even in times of distress. Then after the sixty-two weeks the Messiah will be cut off and have nothing, and the people of the prince who is to come will destroy the city and the sanctuary..." (Daniel 9:24-26).

> *This is the day which the Lord has made; Let us*
> *rejoice and be glad in it. O Lord, do save, we beseech*
> *Thee; O Lord, we beseech Thee, do send prosperity!*
> (Psalm 118:24,25)

These verses were part of a collection of psalms known as the *Hallel*. The word *Hallel* means "Praise God." Every Jewish boy memorized them as part of his first memory assignment. These psalms were sung as great acts of praise and thanksgiving and used to welcome conquering heroes. As they shouted the words to Jesus, He knew He was the Conquering Hero, but not in the way they hoped.

What courage Jesus displayed! He knew the Jews were seeking to kill Him, yet he rode before them. It was as if He were extending one more invitation for them to come to Him for Living Water, the Bread of Life, and rest from their weariness.

Jesus was going to draw all men to Himself, but it would cost Him His life. After His crucifixion and resurrection He would put forth an invincible power to draw all those who were to be His elect. His Kingdom is scattered throughout the world, in every tribe and nation and in every age. A forceful example of this drawing power is seen in Judges 4:7:

> *And I will draw out to you Sisera, the commander of*
> *Jabin's army, with his chariots and his many troops*
> *to the river Kishon; and I will give him into your hand.*

In this case, God drew the enemy for defeat. In our case, He draws people to Himself to give them victory.

The Ultimate Gift

And Jesus answered them, saying, "The hour has come
for the Son of Man to be glorified. Truly, truly, I say to
you, unless a grain of wheat falls into the earth and
dies, it remains by itself alone; but if it dies, it bears
much fruit (John 12:23,24).

The full beauty of a seed is seen only after it is planted. Just so, we see the full beauty and love of Jesus when He gave His life—the glorious, triumphant Church, His Body, the result of that "planting."

As a result of His death we are able to overcome the world and cast out *its* ruler, Satan. There are four stages in the casting out of Satan in the Bible. First, he was cast out of heaven. Then he was cast out at the Cross (John 12:32). He will be cast into the bottomless pit and the final casting out is when he is cast into the lake of fire and brimstone:

> *And threw him into the abyss, and shut it and sealed it over him, so that he should not deceive the nations any longer, until the thousand years were complete; after these things he must be released for a short time* (Revelation 20:3).

> *And the devil who deceived them was thrown into the lake of fire and brimstone where the beast and the false prophet are also; and they will be tormented day and night forever and ever* (Revelation 20:10).

Yet, there *can be* another casting out of Satan and that is *whenever you use the Word* and **cast him out** of a situation in your own life. You can bind him; because his authority was utterly stripped from him at Calvary. You enforce victory over him when you use the Word, the name of Jesus, and submit yourself to God's power.

Preparations To Die

> *Now on the first day of Unleavened Bread the disciples came to Jesus, saying, "Where do You want us to prepare for You to eat the Passover?"* (Matthew 26:17).

Apparently, Jesus had already made arrangements with a certain man at a certain place in the city. He gave Peter and John specific instructions. They were to go into the city, meet a man carrying a pitcher of water, and follow him to the house where they were to prepare for the supper. (See Luke 22:8-13.)

Why such strange instructions? Why not give the address, or the name of the man? Judas had already schemed to betray Jesus. With these vague instructions, Judas would not be able to slip a message to the Jews telling them where Jesus was. He needed and desired that time with His disciples. Jesus worked precisely within the divine time frame. The disciples had no trouble following the directions. Carrying water was a woman's task. A man doing it would have been obvious.

In preparation for the feast, the disciples had to take the lamb to the Temple, make the offering at the altar, get the unleavened bread and grape juice, and any other supplies necessary for the meal.

When Jesus and the rest of the disciples arrived at the "large upper room" all was in readiness, and they sat down to celebrate the feast.

Teaching by Example

According to the Luke account, the disciples began to argue about who was to be the greatest among them:

> And there arose also a dispute among them as to which one of them was regarded to be greatest. And He said to them, "The kings of the Gentiles lord it over them; and those who have authority over them are called 'Benefactors.' But not so with you, but let him who is the greatest among you become as the youngest, and the leader as the servant. For who is greater, the one who reclines at the table, or the one who serves? Is it not the one who reclines at the table? But I am among you as the one who serves" (Luke 22:24-27).

Jesus dealt with the issue immediately. "You are not like the Gentiles who lord it over one another. No, in My kingdom the one who wants to be the greatest must be the one who serves."

That statement startled the disciples! They thought that special closeness to the Messiah meant special positions in the kingdom. Usually, the greater one *receives* service, but Jesus said, the greater one serves. They did not understand.

Imagine their amazement when Jesus demonstrated His teaching. They saw their Master Teacher rise, take a towel, wrap it around Himself, and wash their feet! They were awestruck! Jesus was doing the task of the most menial servant! When Jesus came to Peter, the disciple, he said, "Never shall you wash my feet!" It was an impetuous statement of false humility.

Jesus answered, "*...If I do not wash you, you have no part with Me*" (John 13:8). *"Lord,"* said Peter, *"Not my feet only, but also my hands and my head"* (John 13:9). Then Jesus washed the feet of the man who, within hours, would deny that he even knew his Master. Jesus said He would pray that Peter's faith would not fail. I believe as Jesus tenderly washed and dried those feet He was praying for the spiritual walk of the impetuous Peter. Notice that Jesus washed the feet of all—even of Judas, who raised up his heel against Him. *"Even my close friend, in whom I trusted, Who ate my bread, has lifted up his heel against me"* (Psalm 41:9).

There is a double washing for the believer. One washing is of your entire person and the other is for your feet alone. First Corinthians 6:10 lists the sins of the unrighteous man and then in I Corinthians 6:11 it says:

> *And such were some of you; but you were washed, but you were sanctified, but you were justified in the name of the Lord Jesus Christ, and in the Spirit of our God.*

Titus 3:5 also speaks of the washing of your entire being:

> *He saved us, not on the basis of deeds which we have done in righteousness, but according to His mercy, by the washing of regeneration and renewing by the Holy Spirit.*

That is the washing of the blood. Then there is the washing for

Marilyn Hickey Ministries

Marilyn was a public school teacher when she met Wallace Hickey. After their marriage, Wally was called to the ministry and Marilyn began teaching home Bible studies.

T he vision of Marilyn Hickey Ministries is to "cover the earth with the Word" (Isaiah 11:9). For more than 30 years, Marilyn Hickey has dedicated herself to an anointed, unique, and distinguished ministry of reaching out to people—from all walks of life—who are hungry for God's Word and all that He has for them. Millions have witnessed and acclaimed the positive, personal impact she brings through fresh revelation knowledge that God has given her through His Word.

Marilyn and Wally adopted their son Michael. Then through a fulfilled prophecy they had their daughter Sarah who, with her husband Reece Bowling, is now part of the ministry.

Marilyn has been the invited guest of government leaders and heads of state from many nations of the world. She is considered by many to be one of today's greatest ambassadors of God's Good News to this dark and hurting generation. The more Marilyn follows God's will for her life, the more God uses her to bring refreshing, renewal, and revival to the Body of Christ throughout the world. As His obedient servant, Marilyn desires to follow Him all the days of her life.

Marilyn founded her ministry "Life for Laymen" so that she could reach more people with her gift for practical Bible application.

Marilyn taught at Denver's "Happy Church"—now Orchard Road Christian Center (ORCC)—and hosted ministry conferences with husband Wally, pastor of ORCC.

At a retreat in 1976, Marilyn realized she was called to "cover the earth with the Word."

The ministry staff in the early days helped Marilyn answer the mail that came in response to her first 15-minute radio show.

Soon Marilyn realized she could reach more people through television. She and Wally hosted many well-known guests.

In Guatemala with former President Ephraim Rios-Mott

Marilyn has been the invited guest of government leaders and heads of state from many nations of the world.

In Egypt with Mrs. Anwar Sadat

In Venezuela with former first lady Mrs. Perez

Marilyn ministered to guerillas in Honduras and brought food and clothing to the wives and children who were encamped with their husbands.

The popular Bible-reading plan, *Time With Him,* began in 1978 and invited people to "read through the Bible with Marilyn." The monthly ministry magazine has since been renamed *Outpouring.* It now includes a calendar of ministry events, timely articles, and featured product offers.

Through Word to the World College (formerly Marilyn Hickey Bible College), Marilyn is helping to equip men and women to take the gospel around the world.

Sarah Bowling taught at Riverview Christian Academy for several years before her marriage, wrote correspondence courses for the Bible college...and has since joined the ministry full-time where she combines teaching at WWC with ministry trips and Crusades.

God opened doors for the supplying of Bibles to many foreign lands—China, Israel, Poland, Ethiopia, Russia, Romania, and the Ukraine, just to name a few.

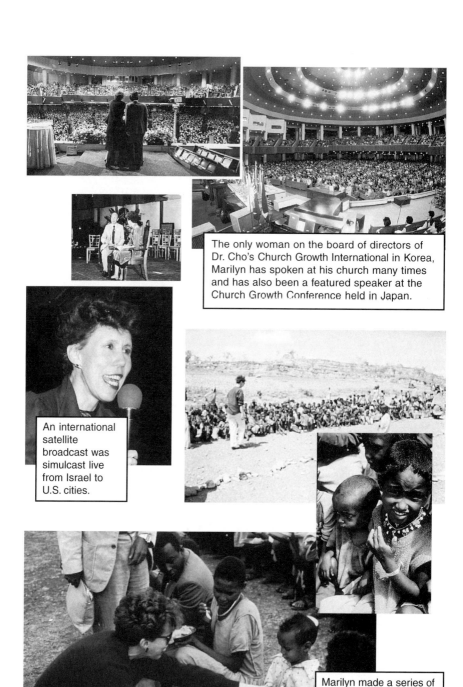

The only woman on the board of directors of Dr. Cho's Church Growth International in Korea, Marilyn has spoken at his church many times and has also been a featured speaker at the Church Growth Conference held in Japan.

An international satellite broadcast was simulcast live from Israel to U.S. cities.

Marilyn made a series of trips to African refugee camps, supplying food for feeding programs and Bibles for the famine- and war-stricken communities.

Sarah began traveling overseas with her parents at an early age and developed a heart for missions.

Both Marilyn and Sarah have a strong heart for China, and have distributed thousands of Bibles and tracts there and in Russia.

The ministry expanded from its beginnings in a cardboard box of files on a kitchen table, to its first International Ministry Center built in 1985, to its present headquarters located in Greenwood Village, Colorado.

FILL THE SHIP, a special project of the Marilyn Hickey Children's Fund, supplies food and Bibles to various Third World countries, such as Haiti, the Philippines, Ethiopia, Honduras, and El Salvador.

The prime time television special, "A Cry for Miracles," featured co-host Gavin MacLeod.

Marilyn has been a guest several times on the 700 Club with host Pat Robertson.

Marilyn ministered in underground churches in Romania before any of the European communist countries were officially open.

Marilyn Hickey's Prayer Center handles calls from all over the U.S.— ministering to those who need agreement in prayer.

More than 1,500 ministry products help people in all areas of their life.

Marilyn received her honorary doctorate from Oral Roberts University. She now serves as the chairman of the Board of Regents.

Sarah graduated from ORU, and later earned her master's degree in History.

Marilyn and her Faith Covenant Partners respond to countless needs across the world. . .the devastating earthquakes in Mexico City, Romanian orphans, leprosy victims in Africa, orphans in war-torn Rwanda, street children in Brazil. . . all are touched by God's power.

MHM supports Mission of Mercy in Calcutta, headed by Huldah Buntain. Marilyn has made several trips there.

Airlift Manila provided much-needed food, Bibles, and personal supplies to the Philippines; MHM also raised funds to aid in the digging of water wells for those without clean drinking water.

"Today With Marilyn," featuring Marilyn and Sarah teaching the Bible, is broadcast weekdays on TBN, BET, GEB, TLN, and several independent stations. The program is also seen overseas by millions through Christian Channel Europe, in Australia on Network 10, and in more than 80 other countries worldwide.

Marilyn ministers to and teaches thousands at Miracle Healing Crusades and meetings overseas, as well as in the U.S. Sarah has joined Marilyn in this endeavor, speaking in many churches throughout the U.S. and abroad.

Exciting ministry opportunities awaited Marilyn, Sarah, and their team of travelers in the Ukraine and Russia, as the doors opened for the Gospel.

Victim of the nuclear power plant disaster in Chernobyl

Marilyn has held Bible Encounters in Malaysia and Singapore. While traveling through Hong Kong she ministered to Vietnamese in a refugee camp.

National Women's Conferences and Pastors' Wives' Conventions were held across the U.S., exhorting women to "Change Their World!"

"Mastering Your Ministry: A Women's Mentoring Clinic" is Marilyn's new concept for providing in-depth teaching and personal ministry in an intimate setting.

The New York area Crusade hosted well-known national ministers and ministered to thousands at the Meadowlands Arena in New Jersey.

Ministry trips and cruises to places such as China, Indonesia, Russia, Greece, the Ukraine, Turkey, Africa, and Israel offer short-term missions' opportunities to travel to exotic places and minister with Marilyn and Sarah.

MHM now operates offices in several countries. Marilyn and Sarah also host yearly meetings, Crusades, and missions' projects in those countries.

Crowds of up to 200,000 attended the open-air Crusade in Bangalore, India.

In Islamabad, Pakistan, Marilyn held Ministry Training Schools. Total Crusade attendance was estimated at 70,000. Recent meetings in Karachi were estimated at 100,000!

Ministry Training Schools are held in many Third World countries, such as Sudan and Tanzania, and provide training and native language literature for local pastors and church leaders. Nightly Crusades are held to minister to the local populations.

your feet, your daily spiritual walk and is based on the blood
through the Word.

> *...Christ also loved the church and gave Himself up
> for her; that He might sanctify her, having cleansed
> her by the washing of water with the Word, that He
> might present to Himself the church in all her
> glory, having no spot or wrinkle or any such
> thing; but that she should be holy and blameless*
> (Ephesians 5:25-27).

This same distinction was held in the Old Testament. When
Aaron and his sons were consecrated, they were washed all over.

> *Then you shall bring Aaron and his sons to the
> doorway of the tent of meeting, and wash them with
> water* (Exodus 29:4).

> *Then Moses had Aaron and his sons come near, and
> washed them with water* (Leviticus 8:6).

> *And Aaron and his sons shall wash their hands and
> their feet from it;...So they shall wash their hands and
> their feet, that they may not die; and it shall be a perpetual
> statute for them, for Aaron and his descendants
> throughout their generations* (Exodus 30:19,21).

You need the daily cleansing of the Word! We are to wash
one another's feet. Which means, we are to humbly serve one
another. To wash someone's feet requires forgiving and forgetting
the past.

When Dying Isn't Death

Jesus warned Judas and extended His friendship, but Judas' heart
was not changed. Then Jesus said, *"...What you do, do quickly"*
(John 13:27). He warns them against misinterpreting His death:

When therefore he had gone out, Jesus said, "Now is the Son of Man glorified, and God is glorified in Him; if God is glorified in Him, God will also glorify Him in Himself, and will glorify Him immediately (John 13:31,32).

Jesus spoke of His death, not as martyrdom or disgrace. He spoke of His death as glorification! We may think it might have been more appropriate to speak of His baptism, or His transfiguration as glorifying, but Jesus considers His death as glorifying. The first Adam was *disobedient* unto death. The second Adam was *obedient* unto death. God was glorified when His Son laid down His life in submission to the Father. Christ's death caused the utter defeat of the enemy of God and man!

No one has taken it away from Me, but I lay it down on My own initiative. I have authority to lay it down, and I have authority to take it up again. This commandment I received from My Father (John 10:18).

He warned the disciples and Peter of His death.

Little children, I am with you a little while longer. You shall seek Me; and as I said to the Jews, I now say to you also, 'Where I am going, you cannot come' (John 13:33).

Jesus answered, "Will you lay down your life for Me? Truly, truly, I say to you, a cock shall not crow, until you deny Me three times" (John 13:38).

Peter was not a hypocrite, but he was over-confident. *Judas* pretended on the outside to be a disciple and *failed inwardly. Peter failed outwardly*, but on the inside was a disciple.

From the human point of view, Peter failed at his strongest point. He was a courageous person. He started to walk on the water.

He drew a sword in the garden. Yet he trembled in the presence of a sharp-tongued maiden. Without God, our strength is as weak as water. When we lay our weaknesses at Jesus' feet and receive His strength, we are made strong. We can learn to say:

> *Therefore I am well content with weaknesses, with insults, with distresses, with persecutions, with difficulties, for Christ's sake; for when I am weak, then I am strong* (II Corinthians 12:10).

Divine Directive

> *A new commandment I give to you, that you love one another, even as I have loved you, that you also love one another* (John 13:34).

The disciples of the Pharisees were known for their legalism. The disciples of John were known by their baptism. The disciples of Jesus are known by their love!

Giving extravagant worship and adoration to your Lord is a good thing! Do not worry about the opinions others have about your style of worship. Be concerned with the approval of your Master. Find as many ways as you can each day to pour out your love to the Lord!

Judas was a taker, not a giver. Jesus said, *"Give and it shall be given unto you."* Judas took and lost! He took the offering money and lost his position. He took the silver then threw it away. He took the sop, but not the friendship offered and finally, he took his life. He had not received eternal life and could not live with his guilt. Judas had many opportunities to receive Christ's love and become a giver, but refused! Look for opportunities to become an *abandoned* giver!

Jesus gave His life, the ultimate gift of love! He knew that the only way we could receive life was for Him to give His. He knew that a glorious Church could never bloom until He, the Seed, was planted in death. Jesus did not try an alternate route to kingship, He followed His Father's Word, timing, and plan. He died to give you life!

Personal Action Plan

1. What does John 12:26 mean to you? How are you serving the Lord today?

2. A *life principle* is "a guiding truth for an abundant life." Using this definition find as many life principles as you can in chapters 12 and 13.

3. Pray about how you can worship the Lord as the Kings of kings. (See John 12:13.)

4. What voice did Jesus hear coming from the heavens? What "voice" do you hear speaking to you about your personal ministry?

5. Meditate on what Jesus meant when He said, "You ought to wash one another's feet." See John 13:8,9. Write your thoughts down in a journal.

Chapter 8

THE
WAY
MAKER

The Way Maker

Jesus was about to suffer excruciating pain and humiliation on the Cross, yet He was concerned about the disciples. Jesus had said He would only be with them a little while longer and they already felt lonely. Then they received the shocking news that someone would betray their Master.

> When Jesus had said this, He became troubled in spirit, and testified, and said, "Truly, truly, I say to you, that one of you will betray Me" (John 13:21).

All of this caused a cloud of gloom to hang over Jesus' devoted group of disciples. It was into that depression that Jesus spoke comfort: "*Let not your heart be troubled; believe in God, believe also in Me*" (John 14:1). "Believe in God, believe also in Me." This could be translated: "You are depressed. Just believe in Us…trust Us. It is all part of the plan."

Promises, Promises

"*In My Father's house are many dwelling places…*" (John 14:2). The Father's house is where Jesus lives and His dwelling place is in heaven. Jesus is preparing a place for *us* in heaven. Looking at another aspect: where is the Father's dwelling place? Who is His temple? YOU are! You are the dwelling place of God! Jesus went to prepare a dwelling place in God for you and to prepare you to be God's dwelling place: " …*We will come to him, and make Our abode with him*" (John 14:23).

Jesus would return after His death and resurrection to receive the disciples into His Body (the Church) so that "*…where* [He]…[was], *there* [they] *may be also*" (John 14:3). There is the future promise of the Rapture and a glorious home in heaven.

So then you are no longer strangers and aliens, but
you are fellow citizens with the saints, and are of God's
household, having been built upon the foundation of
the apostles and prophets, Christ Jesus Himself being
the corner stone, in whom the whole building, being
fitted together is growing into a holy temple in the
Lord; in whom you also are being built together into a
dwelling of God in the Spirit (Ephesians 2:19-22).

The "Prepared" One(s)

How did Jesus prepare a place for us? What was involved in this preparation? Perhaps we will never fully understand the deep rift between God and sinful man. Sinners could never have been the temple of God—His dwelling place—without the sacrifice of Jesus.

Jesus offered His blood as an atonement for our sins (Hebrews 9:23-28). That made a way for us to have access to the Father: *"for through Him we both have our access in one Spirit to the Father"* (Ephesians 2:18). We have been reconciled to God; we are no longer enemies and aliens. Christ was the "prepared lamb" for sacrifice so that we could be made holy. (See Hebrews 10:5,13,14.)

As you therefore have received Christ Jesus the Lord,
so walk in Him. For in Him all the fullness of Deity
dwells in bodily form (Colossians 2:6,9).

God has chosen to live in us, by His Spirit, but we also look forward to living with Him where we will have total redemption of our body. One day, the last trumpet will sound, the dead in Christ will rise, and we will be "caught up" to meet him in the air. (See I Thessalonians 4:16,17) Heaven is a prepared place for a prepared people!

The Way, the Truth, the Life

"And if I go and prepare a place for you, I will come
again, and receive you to Myself; that where I am,

*there you may be also. And you know the way where
I am going." Thomas said to Him, "Lord, we do not
know where You are going, how do we know the way?"
Jesus said to him, "I am the way, and the truth, and
the life; no one comes to the Father, but through Me"*
(John 14:3-6).

The way to the Father is through the Son. First, Jesus brought
the Father to us. He came to do the works of the Father, speak the words
of the Father, and do the will of the Father. (See John 8:26-29.) Then, He
became the Way to *take us to the Father.*

He said to the disciples, "You know the way." But Thomas—
good, honest Thomas—who expressed his doubts to get God's view
on them, said, "But we don't know where You are going, so how can
we know the way?" Jesus answered:

*If you had known Me, you would have known My
Father also; from now on you know Him, and have
seen Him." Philip said to Him, "Lord, show us the
Father, and it is enough for us"* (John 14:7,8).

Jesus patiently explained, "If you know Me, you already
know the Father. I am in the Father and the Father is in Me. Know
Me...know My Father. Believe Me...believe My Father." Jesus was
telling them again, "I and the Father are One."

Man cannot manufacture a way to God, it *must be*
through Christ. Man finds ways that *seem* right to him, but
they all end up leading to death. (See Proverbs 14:12.) Satan
uses tricks and diversionary tactics to keep men from seeing
the true way—Jesus.

*"Teach me Thy way, O Lord; I will walk in Thy truth; unite
my heart to fear Thy name"* (Psalm 86:11). *"For Thy loving kindness
is before my eyes, and I have walked in Thy truth"* (Psalm 26:3).
Many men talk of truth, claim to show people the truth, preach
the truth, say they love the truth, but Jesus said, "I AM the Truth."

Jesus also said He is the Life. Proverbs speaks of the
"path of life."

For the commandment is a lamp, and the teaching is light; and reproofs for discipline are the way of life (Proverbs 6:23).

He is on the path of life who heeds instruction, But he who forsakes reproof goes astray (Proverbs 10:17).

Mankind is always seeking a better way of life and possessions that will make it worth living. But *real* life is not in "ways" and possessions...it is in a Person. *"I am the Life."* Jesus is your Life now and for eternity!

Works, Works, and Greater Works

Believe Me that I am in the Father, and the Father in Me; otherwise believe on account of the works themselves. Truly, truly, I say to you, he who believes in Me, the works that I do shall he do also; and greater works than these shall he do; because I go to the Father (John 14:11,12).

What Jesus did should be our example. He did the Father's work: to destroy the works of the devil. The Father now lives in us through the Holy Spirit and wants to do the same works Jesus did through us.

By this, love is perfected with us, that we may have confidence in the day of judgment; because as He is, so also are we in this world (I John 4:17).

The Father was doing His works through one Man, Jesus. Then Jesus died, rose again, sent the Holy Spirit to empower us, and now the Father is doing His works through millions of believers all over the world. God "sowed" one obedient Son, through whom He could speak His words and do His works, and "reaped" millions of obedient sons and daughters. That is why you can expect God to do miracles through you!

Jesus came to earth to bring the light of God to mankind. He became our Light. As we allow the Spirit to use us, God shines on everyone we meet. You are to be God's "light-holder," spreading light into every situation!

Jesus was leaving the earth, but what He began would go on and on, and become greater and greater. The disciples found that their ministry was like that of Jesus:

> *So then, when the Lord Jesus had spoken to them, He was received up into heaven, and sat down at the right hand of God. And they went out and preached everywhere, while the Lord worked with them, and confirmed the word by the signs that followed* (Mark 16:19,20).

The Power of "The Name"

And whatever you ask in My name, that will I do, that the Father may be glorified in the Son. If you ask Me anything in My name, I will do it (John 14:13, 14).

Soon Jesus would leave and His disciples were worried. He reassured them that distance would not be a problem. He would answer as if He were right there—and He was! They had heard Him speak to the Father repeatedly and make requests. They had seen the incredible results of this communication. Now Jesus said, "You will be able to talk to the Father like I do, in My name, and get the same results."

He had urged them to believe in Him as a Person sent from God, equal with God. Now He asked them to believe that praying *in His name* was the same as Christ Himself speaking to God. Jesus said, *"You may ask me for anything in My name, and I will do it"* (John 14:14 NIV).

The disciples would no longer be limited in their prayer life. Jesus said, "Ask anything...praying in my name." That means, Jesus is the name above every name. (See Ephesians 1:21.) He inherited that powerful name from his Father.

The Name of Jesus

Where two or three of us are gathered in His name, there He is in the midst. (See Matthew 18:20.) We are to do all things in that name:

And whatever you do in word or deed, do all in the name of the Lord Jesus, giving thanks through Him to God the Father (Colossians 3:17).

We are to give thanks always for "all things" in that name:

...Always giving thanks for all things in the name of our Lord Jesus Christ to God, even the Father (Ephesians 5:20).

We are washed, sanctified, and justified in that name:

And such were some of you; but you were washed, but you were sanctified, but you were justified in the name of the Lord Jesus Christ, and in the Spirit of our God (I Corinthians 6:11).

Taking the name of Jesus means you have the legal right to represent Him. You take His place in this world and act as His representative. You have been saved by the name of Jesus, and into that name you have been baptized:

But as many as received Him, to them He gave the right to become children of God, even to those who believe in His name (John 1:12).

That name was given to you at your new birth. Go ahead, use it to glorify the Father through the Son that your joy may be full!

...He sat down at the right hand of the Majesty on high; having become as much better than the angels, as He has inherited a more excellent name than they (Hebrews 1:3,4).

Jesus is the Heir of all things, and through Him, God made the worlds. God highly exalted Him and gave Him a name above every name:

Therefore, also God highly exalted Him, and bestowed on Him the name which is above every name, that at the name of Jesus EVERY KNEE SHOULD BOW, of those who are in heaven, and on earth, and under the earth (Philippians 2:9,10).

Jesus' name has authority in three worlds: heaven, earth, and hell. The name of Jesus, full of God's authority, was given *to you* to use. You have the right to use it in praise and worship, against your enemy, and when making requests to the Father! You have the name. It is *yours* to use. That name will never lose its power.

Never Alone

If you love Me, you will keep My commandments and I will ask the Father, and He will give you another Helper, that He may be with you forever; that is the Spirit of truth, whom the world cannot receive, because it does not behold Him or know Him, but you know Him because He abides with you, and will be in you (John 14:15-17).

"You mean I can ask anything I want and get it?" *Yes*, because if you love Him you want to obey Him and will ask for things in accordance with His will. You may say, "It is difficult to obey Him *all* the time."

Jesus knew our weaknesses. That is why He promised to send *another* Helper, or Counselor...One Who would be with us forever, the Spirit of Truth—the Holy Spirit.

"Helper" is the Greek word *parakletos*. Which means:

- one who gives witness in a court of law in someone's favor
- one who pleads the cause of someone charged with a serious crime
- one who is an expert that gives advice in a difficult situation
- one who encourages the troops!

The Holy Spirit brings *power* into our lives. He helps us to overcome our "inadequacies." Jesus was saying, "I am giving you a difficult assignment, but I am sending Someone Who will guide you and enable you to do it."

Jesus said, *"I will not leave you orphans...We will come and make Our abode with* [you]" (John 14:18,23). Jesus was going to die physically and leave them for a little while, but He *would* come back. He returned to them after the Resurrection; and He will come again in His glory at the Second-Coming!

What Do You Need?

But the Helper, the Holy Spirit, whom the Father will send in My name, He will teach you all things, and bring to your remembrance all that I said to you (John 14:26).

The Holy Spirit will bring the Word to your mind. All your decisions should be measured by what Jesus says—He is Truth and that truth applies to your everyday life. When you're worried and tired from trying to "keep it all together," the Word can put your thoughts into perspective. *"Let not your heart be troubled;...Come unto Me,...and I will give you rest"* (John 14:1; Matthew 11:28).

...That is the Spirit of truth, whom the world cannot receive, because it does not behold Him or know Him, but you know Him because He abides with you, and will be in you (John 14:17).

The Holy Spirit not only reminds you of the words of Jesus, but gives you the life of Jesus to live. You can live the truth because the Truth lives in you.

> *Peace I leave with you; My peace I give to you; not as the world gives, do I give to you. Let not your heart be troubled, nor let it be fearful* (John 14:27).

You have the peace of Christ if you will receive it. The world offers escape, avoidance, and denial, but Jesus offers peace and victory! No sorrow, situation, or danger, can take away Christ's peace—it operates within you, independent of circumstances.

You share in Jesus' victory over your enemy—the ruler of this world. Jesus said, *"The ruler of the world is coming, and he has nothing in Me"* (John 14:30). Jesus knew He would suffer, but He knew that the victory was His...and ours!

Twig, Vine, and Vineyard

"I am the true vine, and My Father is the vinedresser" (John 15:1). It is the vinedresser who plans the vineyard and plants each vine. He is the one who initiates the process that takes place in the vineyard:

> *Every branch in Me that does not bear fruit, He takes away; and every branch that bears fruit, He prunes it, that it may bear more fruit* (John 15:2).

It is the vinedresser's task to prune the plants. He takes out the branches that are dead, clips off unproductive twigs, redirects or removes growth that is going in the wrong direction. God has a special technique for each branch. Your fruit is unique and will serve many people, so God prepares each branch for its special purpose. (See Psalm 139:13-16.)

The Father has placed each of us exactly where He wants us in His garden. The branches do not tell the vinedresser where they would like to go. That job belongs to the One Who owns the vineyard.

*But God has placed the members each one of them, in
the body, just as He desired* (I Corinthians 12:18).

The Father Himself cares for the branches. He does not
allow anyone else to do it. He prunes or cleanses every branch
that bears fruit. *Cleansing* here means "washing off insects, moss,
or other parasites which would infect the plants." The water the
vinedresser uses is the water of the Word. The cleansing is not to
prepare us for heaven, but to make us more fruitful while we are
on earth.

A gardener gives the plants extra food when they need it and
makes sure they get all the sunshine and water needed for healthy
growth. God gives us His Word daily. We have the Bread of Life and
we can feast on His Word continually.

God does not always tell you the things you want to hear.
His Word always sounds sweet, but there are times when you
would rather hear something else! Fertilizer doesn't always smell
good. Yet you use it, because it is good for the plants. God, the
vinedresser, puts the Word deep into your spirit so that you will
be sure to hear it. When you obey His Word, growth takes place
in your life!

A good gardener protects plants from harmful diseases and
insects. God made provision for your protection, too. On the Cross,
Jesus stripped all power from Satan—who would try to destroy
you with disease and prevent your healthy growth. (See
Colossians 2:14,15.).

We live in a vineyard that has the most effective
pesticide and fungicide available. Pests cannot survive in a
Word-filled environment they *have to* leave; and although some
insecticides lose their potency over time, the Word of God never
loses its power!

*You are already clean because of the word which I
have spoken to you. Abide in Me, and I in you. As the
branch cannot bear fruit of itself, unless it abides in
the vine, so neither can you, unless you abide in Me*
(John 15:3,4).

Abundance Flows Through the Vine

Christ was made in *"the form of a servant"* (Philippians 2:7 KJV). God watched over Jesus as He matured—a tender plant and a root out of dry ground. Long before His birth, the Father prevented Joseph from putting away his wife Mary. Soon after His birth, God told Joseph to flee into Egypt. Herod would seek the young Child to destroy Him. These were absolute proofs of the Father's care for the Vine—Jesus. And the Father has the same loving care for the branches.

The seed must be planted, die, and be resurrected before there can be fruit. Fruit is mentioned eight times in these verses. Eight is the number of resurrection, of new beginnings, and of new creation. The kernel of wheat has to die before it sprouts, then there can be a resurrection of new life and a harvest of fruit. Jesus is your Resurrection and Life.

The Vine gives life to the branches, but what kind of life? The life that Jesus has was present at the creation. It is creative life.

> *...But if we walk in the light as He Himself is in the light,*
> *we have fellowship with one another, and the blood of*
> *Jesus His Son cleanses us from all sin* (I John 1:7).

Jesus is light. When we walk in the light with Him it is like walking in the presence of God's ability; nothing is dark and hopeless.

> *Truly, truly, I say to you, he who hears My word, and*
> *believes Him who sent Me, has eternal life, and does*
> *not come into judgment, but has passed out of death*
> *into life* (John 5:24).

Life in the Vine replaces death. Those who believe in Jesus pass from death to life.

> *The thief comes only to steal, and kill, and destroy; I*
> *came that they might have life, and might have it*
> *abundantly* (John 10:10).

Abundantly means lots and lots of life—more than you can use. You will never run out of ability, light, or anything else Jesus is, because He gives it abundantly—and keeps giving.

"Truly, truly, I say to you, he who believes has eternal life" (John 6:47). The life Christ gives never ends. Billions of years from now you will still have life—and it will be abundant and good.

> *Beloved, let us love one another, for love is from God;*
> *and everyone who loves is born of God and knows*
> *God. The one who does not love does not know God,*
> *for God is love* (I John 4:7,8)

Life in Jesus cannot be separated from love. Love permeates every other quality of the abundant life.

"He that is in you is greater than he that is in the world" (I John 4:4). In Christ, you are stronger than any force that can come against you—greater than Satan, greater than the law of sin and death, greater than your emotions, greater than any problem that could challenge you!

> *For by these He has granted to us His precious and*
> *magnificent promises, in order that by them you*
> *might become partakers of the divine nature, having*
> *escaped the corruption that is in the world by lust*
> (II Peter 1:4).

When we receive the life of Jesus Christ, the Vine, we receive divine life. We are made partakers of His divine nature. Think of it: we have *His* divine nature living in us.

God created this world so that everything produces after its kind. Vegetable life yields vegetables, birds bring forth birds, insects spawn insects. God created man after His image, so that divine life could flow through us. Human blood, untainted by sin, flowed in Jesus' veins and now divine life flows through us!

We Are the Branches

Bearing fruit is the result of abiding in the Vine. If you do not abide in the Vine, you cannot do anything worthwhile for God (John 15:5). The vinedresser's care is designed to produce fruit. You are the branches—your job is to abide in the Vine. *Your* life does not produce fruit, it is His life that is productive. His life is always successful—there is no failure in Jesus, no lack of power. We simply must *choose* to live in the Vine.

"*Abide in me.*" To be *in* Christ and to *abide* in Him are two different things: you have to be in Him before you can abide in Him, but to abide in God is to have continuous communion with Him (John 6:56). Using your faith is *abiding in Him*. Faith is the most necessary element of "abiding": without faith it is impossible to please Him. (See Hebrews 11:6.) Abiding involves obedience. (See John 15:10.) God wants us to believe Him, trust Him, and have utter faith in all that He is doing. As a result of faith, we will obey Him—because we trust Him and believe His way is always best.

Our relationship with Jesus differs from the picture of a vine and its branches because we have a choice to remain in the Vine or leave it. We can abide in the Vine and live, or go elsewhere and die! There is no other source of life. Jesus said, "I am the Way, the Truth and the *Life*."

Doin' What Comes Naturally

By this is My Father glorified, that you bear much fruit,
and so prove to be My disciples (John 15:8).

God calls His children "plants that flourish" and "trees that yield their fruit in their season." (See Psalms 1:3.)

Planted in the house of the Lord, they will flourish
in the courts of our God. They will still yield fruit in
old age; they shall be full of sap and very green
(Psalms 92:13,14).

Fruit is the natural result of living or abiding in the Vine. The

The Results of "Abiding" in Him

- **You can have an effective prayer life:**
  If you abide in Me, and My words abide in you, ask whatever you wish, and it shall be done for you (John 15:7).

- **The Father will be glorified:**
  By this is My Father glorified, that you bear much fruit, and so prove to be My disciples (John 15:8).

- **Your joy will be full:**
  These things I have spoken to you, that My joy may be in you, and that your joy may be made full (John 15:11).

- **You will keep His commandments and abide in His love:**
  If you keep My commandments, you will abide in My love; just as I have kept My Father's commandments, and abide in His love (John 15:10).

- **You will bear much fruit:**
  I am the vine, you are the branches; he who abides in Me, and I in him, he bears much fruit; for apart from Me you can do nothing (John 15:5).

branch doesn't work hard to have fruit. All the branch has to do is
be there. When we believe God, obey His Word, and love Him with
all our hearts, fruit will naturally result from our lives.

Fruit begins as a tiny, inconspicuous blossom, then the
fruit appears, and grows. It takes time. The vinedresser doesn't
look at the immature fruit, pluck it off and say, "That branch will
never make it." He waits for the fruit to mature. Your Father knows
you, your rate of development, and He has patience to wait for
mature fruit. He knows it will come if you abide in the Vine—that
Life does not fail to produce fruit.

The fruit the branch will produce is called the fruit of the
Spirit, which is found in Galatians 5:22 and 23: Love, joy, peace,
patience, kindness, goodness, faithfulness, gentleness, and self-
control. This fruit will affect everything else that you do. If they
rule, your life will be productive—you will be a soul-winner,
reproducing after your own kind!

The life of the Vine affects every area of your being. His life
flowing through you will affect the way you use your time. His
priorities will dictate what you do and when you do it. You will learn
to invest your time wisely.

His life flowing through you will affect the way you use your
body. You will want to use the members of your body to do what He
wants you to do. You will be His hands, feet, and lips—acting for
Him on this earth.

His life flowing through you will affect your emotions. His
life has joy, peace, and love. These three will affect every emotion
you have!

Your life will change. The more it changes to conform to the
Life flowing in you, the more productive you will be, bearing fruit—
thirty, sixty, and one-hundred fold!

He Is Your Friend

Jesus told His disciples that He was going to lay down His life for
the sheep. Then He told them that His life, that of the Vine, was
flowing through them, the branches. In John 15:13 He said that
they are to love each other just as He loves them—even to the

point of laying down their lives for one another. This can mean literally dying for a friend, but love often requires something equally difficult—consistently giving of yourself to meet the needs of others. Putting aside your desires and legitimate right to pleasure, in order that others may hear the Word and receive His joy—this kind of love will make an impact on others!

We know that Jesus is *our* Friend, but He calls us *His friends*. Why? Because we do what He commands. We obey, not as slaves, but as friends who know the purposes and plans of God. Jesus told us about them. He spared nothing. Abraham was called the friend of God because He shared His plans with Abraham. (See Genesis 18:17.)

We are children of Abraham—faith-filled believers whom God can call His "friends." We hear God's voice; we believe His word. Our faith pleases Him, and we are brought into holy, intimate communion with Him. Then—we can understand the "mysteries" of the kingdom.

> *And He was saying to them, "To you has been given the mystery of the kingdom of God; but those who are outside get everything in parables"...and He did not speak to them without a parable; but He was explaining everything privately to His own disciples* (Mark 4:11,34).

You, as God's friend, have a responsibility to obey Him. You have the privilege of constant fellowship with Him and of receiving revelation about His plans for the future. (See I Thessalonians 5:2-4.)

You are a beloved sheep in His pasture, a fruitful branch in His vineyard, but best of all you are His friend—and He chose you!

Personal Action Plan

1. What did Jesus mean when He said, *"...I go to prepare a place for you?"* (John 14:2). Tell a friend about this "place."

2. Why are you a friend of God? How does that make you feel? Write about it in your journal.

3. How did Jesus provide you a key to a powerful prayer life? How can you put that power into action today?

4. Meditate on John 14, verses 25-31. List the truths of these verses in your scripture notebook.

5. How will abiding in the Vine benefit you, your family, your work place, your church, and community?

Chapter 9

WHEN WORLD VIEWS COLLIDE

When World Views Collide

But these things I have spoken to you, that when their hour comes, you may remember that I told you of them. And these things I did not say to you at the beginning, because I was with you (John 16:4).

John wrote this letter during a time when the Church was already under heavy persecution—Christianity was illegal. If a person was a Christian, no matter how insignificant his crime, a magistrate could sentence him to death. Jesus had seen into the future and was warning and preparing His disciples about persecution. *"If the world hates you, you know that it has hated Me before it hated you"* (John 15:18).

Jesus looked beyond the present, and made every provision for you. He did not promise a trouble-free life; He did promise strength and wisdom in every situation. Jesus said He overcame the world. He lives in you. You walk as Jesus walked in this world! You are an overcomer. Jesus knew that persecution could tempt the disciples to make mistakes and fall away, so He carefully prepared them and warned them of things to come:

I have told you all these things so that you should not be offended—(taken unawares and falter, or be caused to stumble and fall away).[I told you to keep you from being scandalized and repelled] (John 16:1 TAB).

Jesus warned his disciples that they would stumble.

Then Jesus said to them, "You will all fall away because of Me this night, for it is written, 'I WILL STRIKE DOWN THE SHEPHERD, AND THE SHEEP OF THE FLOCK SHALL BE SCATTERED'" (Matthew 26:31).

Jesus told Peter to watch and pray when He knew Peter would deny Him three times. *"Keep watching and praying, that you may not come into temptation; the spirit is willing, but the flesh is weak"* (Mark 14:38).

He commanded the gospel to be preached to every creature when He knew that many would not listen. Jesus wanted to enforce their responsibility to His calling. We are responsible to obey Him, no matter what the world does, or how it reacts to us and the gospel. Jesus makes every provision for our victory, telling us of the pitfalls and dangers ahead of time.

Christ gradually unfolded to His disciples the negative reception they would get. He told them of persecution. (Also see Matthew 5:10,12.)

> *If the world hates you, you know that it has hated Me before it hated you. If you were of the world, the world would love its own; but because you are not of the world, but I chose you out of the world, therefore the world hates you. Remember the word that I said to you, "A slave is not greater than his master." If they persecuted Me, they will also persecute you; if they kept My word, they will keep yours also* (John 15:18-20).

The basic reason the world hated and persecuted the disciples was because it did not know the Father and therefore did not recognize Jesus as the Son. As a result, they would also hate those who went out in Jesus' name.

Trials, Troubles, and Tribulation

> *These things I have spoken to you, that in Me you may have peace. In the world you have tribulation, but take courage; I have overcome the world* (John 16:33).

All through the ages, godliness has met with hatred and

hostility. Cain, the first man to be born on this planet, opposed his godly brother and slew him. (See I John 3:12.) Since then, it has happened in every generation. *"An unjust man is abominable to the righteous, and he who is upright in the way is abominable to the wicked"* (Proverbs 29:27). *"They hate him who reproves in the gate, and they abhor him who speaks with integrity"* (Amos 5:10).

> *If you were of the world, the world would love its own; but because you are not of the world, but I chose you out of the world, therefore the world hates you* (John 15:19).

Persecution came to the early Christians because they put Christ first. He was and is the Lord of lords and the King of kings. For this, even now, persecution comes to Christians.

Hatred by the Romans was spontaneous when false rumors were spread concerning the Christians. They thought communion was cannibalism.

> *And when He had taken some bread and given thanks, He broke it, and gave it to them, saying, "This is My body which is given for you; do this in remembrance of Me." And in the same way He took the cup after they had eaten, saying, "This cup which is poured out for you is the new covenant in My blood"* (Luke 22:19,20).

Jesus' words at the celebration of the Last Supper were misunderstood. Stories were spread, and people believed the worst.

The Christians ate a weekly meal together and celebrated communion. It was called "Agape" or the "Love Feast." Christians also greeted each other with a kiss of peace. Rumors were spread that these feasts were really parties of sexual indulgence. The world twisted something beautiful and called it immoral!

Families were divided: if one member of a family was born again and the others refused, there was an inevitable division. This

Why the Romans Hated Christians

"The Romans distrusted and persecuted Christians because they were considered to be disloyal citizens. Rome did a lot for its subjects; it had brought peace and prosperity and a semblance of law and order. Their empire was vast and the people diverse, so they devised one unifying force—emperor worship. Caesar embodied all the Roman Empire had done for them. Though the practice was discouraged at first, the emperors saw how they could use this power to their advantage.

"So there came the day when once a year every inhabitant of the Empire had to burn his pinch of incense to the godhead of Caesar. By so doing, he showed that he was a loyal citizen of Rome. When he had done this, he received a certificate to say that he had done it.

"Here was the practice and the custom which made all men feel that they were part of Rome, and which guaranteed their loyalty to her. After he had burned his pinch of incense and said, "Caesar is Lord," a man could go away and worship any god he liked, so long as the worship did not affect public decency and public order. But that is precisely what the Christians would *not* do. They would call no man 'Lord' except Jesus Christ. They refused to conform, and therefore the Roman government regarded them as dangerous and disloyal."

From *The Gospel of John* by William Barclay

was never a goal of Christianity. Unity and restoration of families is always the goal. However, slanderous reports were circulated, with the help of unbelieving Jews, and those who felt threatened by the new church, and hatred was generated everywhere.

Synagogues threatened to cast out believers. Many Christians still worshiped in their synagogue. They believed in Judaism, and Christianity as its fulfillment. The disciples kept right on worshiping in the Temple. They had meetings in believers homes, but the Temple was still of great importance. To be cast out was a major consequence. It meant they would be cut off from former friendships and from the privileges of their own people.

In Judaism, there were many "zealots of the law" who thirsted for the blood of the Christians. Christianity was a great threat to their belief system.

Hatred from the world is still evident today. The world lives without God as its life Source. The world worships many gods; believers have but One—the true God. This creates a natural division. We are hated because we are different. Anyone who stands out from the crowd is noticed and often ridiculed. Another reason Christians are hated is that their lives bring conviction to the godless. It is uncomfortable to be made aware of sin, and striking back in anger temporarily relieves the pain of conviction.

World Overcomer

Yes, you are different. Your presence does convict because the Holy Spirit resides in you. The Holy Spirit convicts the world concerning sin, righteousness, and judgment. *"And He, when He comes, will convict the world concerning sin, and righteousness, and judgment"* (John 16:8).

The Holy Spirit also strengthens you—to stand against opposition. Pray for those who despitefully use you, intercede on their behalf.

You have authority in Jesus Christ to ask for favor in enemy territory to spread the gospel. Many times Paul had favor—with jailers, centurions, and the Roman government—which opened doors for the gospel. Even persecution was a means for getting the gospel to the most unlikely places. Paul was able to preach and teach for two years while held as a prisoner of Rome in his own rented house. He said:

> *Now I want you to know, brethren, that my circumstances have turned out for the greater progress of the gospel, so that my imprisonment in the cause of Christ has become well known throughout the whole praetorian guard and to everyone else, and that most of the brethren, trusting in the Lord because of my imprisonment, have far more courage to speak the word of God without fear* (Philippians 1:12-14).

No persecution or opposition can stop you and the Holy Spirit. Jesus said, "I have spoken these things to you so you won't stumble." Never allow opposition to keep you from doing what God told you to do when everything was going right!

Jesus has promised you wealth, victory, joy, peace, love—everything your heart, soul, and mind desires; but He has also warned you of battles, which are opportunities for success. Jesus said, *"...Take courage; I have overcome the world."* He lives within you. He is your life Source. You can be an overcomer!

The Convictor and Convincer

> *But I tell you the truth, it is to your advantage that I go away; for if I do not go away, the Helper shall not come to you; but if I go, I will send Him to you. And He, when He comes, will convict the world concerning sin, and righteousness, and judgment; concerning sin, because they do not believe in Me; and concerning righteousness, because I go to the Father, and you no longer behold Me; and concerning judgment, because the ruler of this world has been judged* (John 16:7-11).

When the Jews condemned Jesus to death and the Roman

soldiers nailed Him to the Cross, they did not believe they were doing anything wrong. However, a few weeks later, when Peter recounted the Crucifixion, he said they were *"...pierced to the heart"* (Acts 2:37). During that time, the Holy Spirit had done a work in their hearts! Why do men still, 2,000 years later, hear the story of Jesus and fall on their knees? It is the convicting work of the Holy Spirit!

The Holy Spirit convinces men of the righteousness of Jesus. Traveling on the road to Damascus to persecute Christians, Paul (thinking Jesus was an imposter) met Him face to face. Paul fell to the ground, and was, in one moment, convinced of Jesus' righteousness. Paul followed Jesus the rest of his life. Only the Holy Spirit could work such a change!

What causes men to know that there will one day be a judgment? The Holy Spirit convinces men that they will be responsible for their deeds at the end of their lives. They may not do anything about it, but most people know in their hearts they have a judgment day coming.

The Revealer of Truth

But when He, the Spirit of truth, comes, He will guide you into all the truth; for He will not speak on His own initiative, but whatever He hears, He will speak; and He will disclose to you what is to come (John 16:13).

The Holy Spirit shows us truths that only God can know, and often reveals them to us a little bit at a time. He teaches us the fundamentals first, and builds on them "precept upon precept." The Holy Spirit will teach you what you are able—and willing—to learn.

God reveals Himself in nature, through the prophets, through the Word, through Jesus Christ, and through His Holy Spirit— whatever He reveals is not just truth about Himself, but also about life and your part in it. He wishes to *continually* drop truth into your spirit about every situation.

Truth is not something men create or discover. It is a gift given by God Who reveals all truth! Truth is a continual revelation of Jesus Christ. Jesus said, "I am the Truth." His truth is inexhaustible. The Holy Spirit takes the words of Jesus and the concepts in the Word, and reveals them to us—concerning our lives, our beliefs, our society. Receiving revelation knowledge is really coming to know Jesus better and better.

> *These things I have spoken to you in figurative language; an hour is coming when I will speak no more to you in figurative language, but will tell you plainly of the Father. In that day you will ask in My name, and I do not say to you that I will request the Father on your behalf; for the Father Himself loves you, because you have loved Me, and have believed that I came forth from the Father.*
>
> *His disciples said, "Lo, now You are speaking plainly, and are not using a figure of speech. Now we know that You know all things, and have no need for anyone to question You; by this we believe that You came from God"* (John 16:25,27,29,30).

The "Spirit" of Christ

The Holy Spirit glorifies the character of Jesus. He is viewed in these verses as the *"Spirit of Christ."* Jesus had many things to tell the disciples, but they were not yet able to receive them without the Holy Spirit. *"I have many more things to say to you, but you cannot bear them now"* (John 16:12).

The disciples weren't ready for great revelations. They needed the inner working of the Holy Spirit to reveal His truth to them! (See John 16:13.) Jesus was merciful; He would not give them more than they could understand. On the other hand, had they been able to bear them, how much more would Jesus have shared with them? You *do* have the Holy Spirit, the Teacher within. Can the Father reveal many things to you? Are you able to "bear" them and receive them?

The Comforter will bring to remembrance things from the past.

> *But the Helper, the Holy Spirit, whom the Father*
> *will send in My name, He will teach you all things,*
> *and bring to your remembrance all that I said to*
> *you* (John 14:26).

He will bear witness in the "present" of Jesus (John 15:26), and He is also to reveal things of the future (John 16:13).

Christ is always the center of what the Holy Spirit says. The test of any religion, philosophy, or spirit is, "Does it magnify Christ?" Jesus reveals the Father, and the Holy Spirit unfolds to us the truths of Jesus Christ. By the Spirit, we understand the thoughts of God.

> *For to us God revealed them through the Spirit; for*
> *the Spirit searches all things, even the depths of God.*
> *For who among men knows the thoughts of a man*
> *except the spirit of the man, which is in him? Even*
> *so the thoughts of God no one knows except the Spirit*
> *of God. Now we have received, not the spirit of*
> *the world, but the Spirit who is from God, that*
> *we might know the things freely given to us by God*
> (I Corinthians 2:10-12).

As we learn to think God's thoughts and say God's words, we will overcome the world and do God's work!

A Seed of Sorrow for a Harvest of Joy

Christian joy can never be taken away but we can give it up. In the presence of Jesus your joy is enduring—it will last. The pain of trouble is soon forgotten, just as a woman forgets her labor pains when she first sees her baby. This joy can be ours now, in this life. Even now, it cannot be stolen from us. One day, in glory, our joy will be complete as we enjoy the wonders of heaven forever. In heaven there will be no more sorrow!

> *Truly, truly, I say to you, that you will weep and lament,*
> *but the world will rejoice; you will be sorrowful, but*

He Who Has an Ear

Seven times in the Book of Revelation the Holy Spirit gave John knowledge concerning Jesus Christ and the future:

1. *He who has an ear, let him hear what the Spirit says to the churches. To him who overcomes, I will grant to eat of the tree of life, which is in the Paradise of God* **(Revelation 2:7).**

2. *He who has an ear, let him hear what the Spirit says to the churches. He who overcomes shall not be hurt by the second death* **(Revelation 2:10,11).**

3. *He who has an ear, let him hear what the Spirit says to the churches. To him who overcomes, to him I will give some of the hidden manna, and I will give him a white stone, and a new name written on the stone which no one knows but he who receives it* **(Revelation 2:17).**

4. *And he who overcomes, and he who keeps My deeds until the end, to him I will give authority over the nations; and he shall rule them with a rod of iron, as the vessels of the potter are broken to pieces, as I also have* *received authority from My Father; and I will give him the morning star. He who has an ear, let him hear what the Spirit says to the churches* (Revelation 3:26-29).

5. *He who overcomes shall thus be clothed in white garments; and I will not erase his name from the book of life, and I will confess his name before My Father, and before His angels. He who has an ear, let him hear what the Spirit says to the churches* (Revelation 3:5,6).

6. *He who overcomes, I will make him a pillar in the temple of My God, and he will not go out from it anymore; and I will write upon him the name of My God, and the name of the city of My God, the new Jerusalem, which comes down out of heaven from My God, and My new name. He who has an ear, let him hear what the Spirit says to the churches* (Revelation 3:12,13).

7. *He who overcomes, I will grant to him to sit down with Me on My throne, as I also overcame and sat down with My Father on His throne. He who has an ear, let him hear what the Spirit says to the churches* (Revelation 3:21,22).

*your sorrow will be turned to joy. Whenever a woman
is in travail she has sorrow, because her hour has come;
but when she gives birth to the child, she remembers
the anguish no more, for joy that a child has been
born into the world. Therefore you too now have
sorrow; but I will see you again, and your heart will
rejoice, and no one takes your joy away from you* (John
16:20-22).

This was a sad time for the disciples, yet it turned to joy
when they heard the good news of Jesus' triumph over the grave.
*"And they departed quickly from the tomb with fear and great joy
and ran to report it to His disciples"* (Matthew 28:8).

*And when He had said this, He showed them both His
hands and His side. The disciples therefore rejoiced
when they saw the Lord* (John 20:20).

Later, when Jesus ascended on high, they worshiped Him
and returned to Jerusalem "with great joy."

In your life there will be times of sorrow. You might
even consider these to be times of failure. During these times
keep sowing the Word, both in your life and in the lives of
those around you. You may feel like you have been sowing in
tears, but God's promise is that you will reap with "joyful
shouting." (See Psalms 126:5,6.) Keep sowing the right seed
and you will reap a joyful harvest!

Prayer—Phoning the Father

Jesus had a habit of prayer. When being baptized, He was engaged
in prayer. (See Luke 3:21.) At the beginning of His public ministry,
Jesus prayed:

*"And in the early morning, while it was still dark, He
arose and went out and departed to a lonely place,
and was praying there"* (Mark 1:35).

On the eve of selecting the twelve apostles He prayed:

And it was at this time that He went off to the mountain to pray, and He spent the whole night in prayer to God. And when day came, He called His disciples to Him; and chose twelve of them, whom He also named as apostles (Luke 6:12,13).

Jesus was transfigured while He was praying:

And while He was praying, the appearance of His face became different, and His clothing became white and gleaming (Luke 9:29).

He prayed with His last breath:

And Jesus, crying out with a loud voice, said, "Father, INTO THY HANDS I COMMIT MY SPIRIT." And having said this, He breathed his last (Luke 23:46).

Jesus prayed as a priest and addressed God as "Father." In relation to the Father's whole family, Jesus is the first-born. (See Romans 8:29.)

For to which of the angels did He ever say, "THOU ART MY SON, TODAY I HAVE BEGOTTEN THEE"? And again, "I WILL BE A FATHER TO HIM, AND HE SHALL BE A SON TO ME"? And when He again brings the first-born into the world, He says, "AND LET ALL THE ANGELS OF GOD WORSHIP HIM" (Hebrews 1:5,6).

Jesus announced that His time had come. Seven times Jesus spoke of "His hour." And this was the last time. (See Chapter 1 of this book.)

These things Jesus spoke, and lifting up His eyes to heaven, He said, "Father, the hour has come, glorify Thy Son, that the Son may glorify Thee" (John 17:1).

Why did Jesus ask to be glorified? Because of His relationship with the Father. He asked to be glorified that He might glorify the Father. He also asked because the "appointed time" had arrived and He had been given authority over all mankind:

> ...*Even as Thou gavest Him authority over all mankind, that to all whom Thou hast given him, He may give eternal life* (John 17:2).

If Jesus was glorified, then eternal life could be given to the chosen and He could bring those who were His into knowledge of the Father. *"And this is eternal life, that they may know Thee, the only true God, and Jesus Christ whom Thou hast sent"* (John 17:3).

He had glorified the Father on earth and finished the work that was given to Him.

The Cross, a Conduit of Glory

The Cross was the completion of His work on earth. Christ came to earth to save sinners, and that plan included His sacrificial death. He went all the way—He finished His task. (See John 17:4,5.)

Obedience glorifies God. Children honor their parents by obeying them. Citizens honor their country when they obey the laws. A student honors his teacher when he follows his instructions. Jesus brought glory and honor to the Father by perfectly obeying the Father's plan.

> *And being found in appearance as a man, He humbled Himself by becoming obedient to the point of death, even death on a cross. Therefore also God highly exalted Him and bestowed on Him the name which is above every name* (Philippians 2:8,9).

The Cross was not the end; it was only the means to an end. Jesus was to die, but He would also rise from the dead. He was to succumb to death, but in that very act He would conquer death! He would pay for the sins of men, but He would also provide eternal life! Man and devil did their worst to Jesus Christ, but in the end, He conquered their efforts. *The glory of the Resurrection cancelled the shame of the Cross.*

Jesus gave up His glory when He came to earth. He limited Himself to a human body for thirty-three years. The time was approaching when He would be clothed with a resurrected body and return to the glory of His *true* home. He would again have the glory which was His before the world began!

The Prayer of Your Priest

Why did Jesus pray? *"...Those whom Thou hast given Me; for they are Thine"?* They belonged to Him, and He knew the Father would want to work on their behalf. They were His reward, part of His inheritance. *"Ask of Me, and I will surely give the nations as Thine inheritance, And the very ends of the earth as Thy possession"* (Psalms 2:8).

As High Priest, He appealed to His Father's love and personal interest in them:

> *I ask on their behalf; I do not ask on behalf of the world, but of those whom Thou hast given Me; for they are Thine; and all things that are Mine are Thine, and Thine are Mine; and I have been glorified in them* (John 17:9,10).

What belongs to the Father belongs to the Son—they are inseparable. Christ's disciples are the Father's children, the Son's Body, and the temple of the Holy Spirit.

> *And I am no more in the world; and yet they themselves are in the world, and come to Thee. Holy Father, keep them in Thy name, the name which Thou hast given Me, that they may be one, even as We are* (John 17:11).

Now that He was leaving them, they were even more vulnerable

When Jesus Prayed For the Disciples

- He prayed for their *preservation.* (See John 17:11.) Jesus did not pray for them to be taken out of the world, but that they would be victorious in the world. He wants us to be faithful in the battle, not abandon it.

- He prayed for their *joyfulness.* *"But now I come to Thee; and these things I speak in the world, that they may have My joy made full in themselves"* (John 17:13). Jesus does not just want your eternal joy in heaven. He requested that His joy be made full in you, in this world! His joy comes through fellowship with the Father.

- He prayed for their *protection* from evil. *"I do not ask Thee to take them out of the world, but to keep them from the evil one"* (John 17:15). With Christ praying for you, you are victorious. The evil one has no power over you. Christ defeated him, and He prayed that the Father would keep you from him!

- He prayed for their *sanctification*: *"Sanctify them in the truth; Thy word is truth"* (John 17:17). Jesus prayed that His disciples might be consecrated by the truth.

- He prayed for their *unification*: *"That they may all be one;..."* (John 17:21). Our relationship with the Father and the Son is based on love and obedience, and our relationship with one another is based on the same thing. The world will recognize our relationship to the Father by our love for one another.

- He prayed for their *association* with Him. Jesus wants His disciples to be close to Him. He longs to be reunited with us: *"Father, I desire that they also, whom Thou hast given Me, be with Me where I am, in order that they may behold My glory,..."* (John 17:24).

than before. Jesus committed their care into the Father's hands. *"I do not ask Thee to take them out of the world, but to keep them from the evil one"* (John 17:15). Jesus knew that the enemy would be working on His disciples. He prayed beforehand for their protection.

> I have given them Thy word; and the world has hated
> them, because they are not of the world, even as I am
> not of the world (John 17:14).

He set Himself apart to die. Jesus was giving His life as a sacrifice; He did not want that sacrifice to be in vain. *"And for their sakes I sanctify Myself, that they themselves also may be **sanctified** in truth"* (John 17:19).

The Greek word translated "consecrated" or "sanctified" is *hagiaze*. This word has two ideas in it: (1) It means "to set apart for a special task." Jeremiah was "set apart" from his mother's womb. (See Jeremiah 1:5.) (2) It means "to equip a man with the qualities of mind, heart, and character which are necessary for that task." God does not just choose you for a specific task: he also equips you with every quality you need to carry it out.

So Great a Love

Jesus loves you so much! He prayed for you long before you were born! As you study the requests he made for the disciples, you will notice how each prayer was designed to include **all** of Jesus' disciples down through the ages. Lest we have any doubts, Jesus plainly says, "I do not ask for these people alone, but for all who will believe in Me through their words." Jesus saw ahead and prayed for those who would have faith in Him! If you are His disciple, He prayed then and He prays now for you.

Jesus closed His prayer with a request that His love be in those that believe upon Him. Since He is Love and He dwells in you, you have His love and you love Him.

> ...And I have made Thy name known to them, and will
> make it known; that the love wherewith Thou didst love
> Me may be in them, and I in them (John 17:26).

> *...Jesus, knowing that His hour had come that He
> should depart out of this world to the Father, having
> loved His own who were in the world, He loved them
> to the end* (John 13:1).

Jesus interceded for you even before He went to the Cross. He had *you* in mind and *you* were on His heart when He went to the garden to pray and later when He gave His life. He prayed that *you* would be protected from the evil one, that *you* would be set apart and equipped for service by the truth. He prayed that you would become *one* with other believers as well as *one* with Him and the Father. Jesus prayed that *you* would, one day, be in heaven, where He is, to share His glory. He prayed that *you* would be filled with His joy. Jesus' prayers work—*you* have everything He asked for—receive it and live it!

Personal Action Plan

1. What promises of God can you claim, stand on, and put into action when you are persecuted? Encourage a fellow Christian with those promises.

2. Meditate on John 16:23-26. Write down specific things that the Holy Spirit reveals to you from these verses.

3. Do a brief study on joy answering questions such as: Where does it come from? How do I keep it? Why do I need it? What can rob me of joy?

4. Jesus interceded for you in His High Priestly prayer. How is He praying for you today?

5. Write out five phrases, in your scripture notebook, concerning your relationship to the world. Choose one relationship and find a scripture that tells how you can handle that relationship.

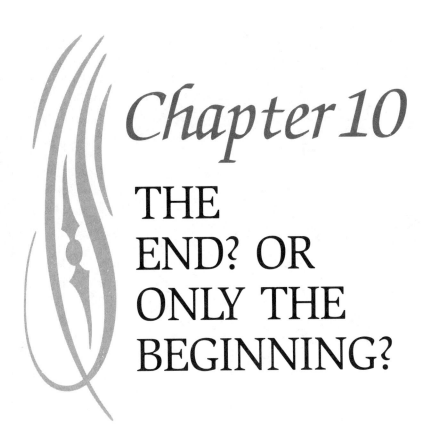

Chapter 10

THE
END? OR
ONLY THE
BEGINNING?

The End? Or Only the Beginning?

...He went forth with His disciples over the ravine of the Kidron, where there was a garden, into which He Himself entered, and His disciples (John 18:1).

Jesus crossed over the brook Kidron literally, but also symbolically. *Kidron* means "dark waters." He was crossing dark waters—this was to be one of the most difficult times of His life.

Jesus offered Himself for a sacrifice *outside* of Jerusalem. His sufferings began in the Garden of Gethsemane. He had to be betrayed outside the camp: in accordance with the teaching of the Day of Atonement, the sacrifice for the sin offering was made outside the camp.

> *Then he is to bring out the bull to a place outside the camp, and burn it as he burned the first bull; it is the sin offering for the assembly* (Leviticus 4:21).

> *Therefore Jesus also, that He might sanctify the people through His own blood, suffered outside the gate* (Hebrews 13:12).

By crossing the Kidron, an Old Testament type was fulfilled. David had crossed the same brook and wept when an intimate friend had betrayed him:

> *While all the country was weeping with a loud voice, all the people passed over. The king also passed over the brook Kidron, and all the people passed over toward the way of the wilderness* (II Samuel 15:23).

Jesus could have left His disciples in the upper room and

242

The Kidron Was Red With Blood

William Barclay describes the scene:

"When the last meal was finished and when Jesus' talk and prayer with his disciples were ended, he and his friends left the upper room. They were bound for the Garden of Gethsemane. They would leave by the gate, go down the steep valley and cross the channel of the brook Kidron. There a symbolic thing must have happened. All the Passover lambs were killed in the Temple, and the blood of the lambs was poured on the altar as an offering to God. The number of lambs slain for the Passover was immense.

"On one occasion, thirty years later than the time of Jesus, a census was taken and the number was 256,000. We may imagine what the Temple courts were like when the blood of all these lambs was dashed on to the altar. From the altar there was a channel down to the brook Kidron, and through that channel the blood of the Passover lambs drained away. When Jesus crossed the brook Kidron it would still be red with the blood of the lambs which had been sacrificed; and as he did so, the thought of his own sacrifice would surely be vivid in his mind."

From *The Gospel of John* by William Barclay

gone alone to pray, as He had done many times before. However, several prophecies had to be fulfilled in the garden that included the disciples. Also, the disciples were to be eyewitnesses that Jesus gave His life *willingly*. The soldiers did not have to force Jesus to go with them.

Jesus had foreseen that all His disciples would flee at His arrest, so He chose a place that would make it easy for them to escape. They were not to be arrested along with Him. Jesus loved His own to the end. (See John 13:1.)

In the garden He said, *"...If therefore you seek Me, let these go their way"* (John 18:8). Notice how easily He could have saved Himself. He spoke with authority, and commanded the soldiers to let the disciples go and they did. He could have commanded that they let Him go, too!

The Garden Of Grief

Jesus was about to do the work of High Priest—to make atonement for His people. He needed to be alone.

> *When he goes in to make atonement in the holy place, no one shall be in the tent of meeting until he comes out, that he may make atonement for himself and for his household and for all the assembly of Israel* (Leviticus 16:17).

In Matthew we are told how Jesus agonized alone in the garden (Matthew 26:36-45). This garden was a familiar place for Him. *Gethsemane* means "oil press." The press is where the oil was extracted from the olives which grew on the surrounding hills. Wealthy people had their gardens on this hill because of limited space within the city walls and because they were not allowed to use manure to fertilize the soil of the sacred city.

Some wealthy friend probably gave Jesus the key and the use of the garden when He was in Jerusalem. He went there often—Judas knew just where to find Him.

A False Arrest

Jesus therefore, knowing all the things that were coming upon Him, went forth, and said to them, "Whom do you seek?" They answered Him, "Jesus the Nazarene." He said to them, "I am He." And Judas also who was betraying Him, was standing with them. When therefore He said to them, "I am He," they drew back, and fell to the ground (John 18:4-6).

Jesus went to the garden knowing what would happen. He willingly offered Himself when He knew the hour had come. As soon as Jesus responded, *"I am He,"* the whole crowd fell backwards under the power of God. All it took for this group of strong men (including Judas) to fall down were two powerful words from Jesus: *"I am."* He had no weapons and used no force. He only spoke. The same power is in the Word for you to use!

So the Roman cohort and the commander, and the officers of the Jews, arrested Jesus and bound Him (John 18:12).

Judas had said, "Whoever I kiss, seize Him." (See Matthew 26:48.) His instructions implied that Jesus would need restraining. After all, Judas had seen Jesus work miracles. He knew they weren't arresting an ordinary man! They remembered what had happened on other occasions when arrest was attempted.

And they rose up and cast Him out of the city, and led Him to the brow of the hill on which their city had been built, in order to throw Him down the cliff. But passing through their midst, He went His way (Luke 4:29,30).

Everything that happened to Jesus fulfilled prophecy. Isaac was a type of Christ when sacrificed, and the first thing Abraham did to Isaac was bind him. (See Genesis 22:9.) It was also the first

Two Very Different Gardens

- In Eden, all was delightful—in Gethsemane, all was distasteful.
- In Eden, Adam and Eve conversed with Satan—in Gethsemane, Jesus, the second and last Adam, talked with God.
- In Eden, Adam sinned—in Gethsemane, Jesus suffered for sin.
- In Eden, Adam fell—in Gethsemane, Jesus conquered.
- In Eden, the conflict was by day—in Gethsemane it was by night.
- In Eden, Adam fell before Satan—in Gethsemane the soldiers fell before Jesus.
- In Eden, Adam took the fruit from Eve's hand—in Gethsemane Jesus took the cup from the Father's hand.
- In Eden, God sought Adam—in Gethsemane the soldiers hunted Jesus.
- Adam was driven from Eden—Christ was led from Gethsemane.
- In Eden, the sword was drawn—in Gethsemane the sword was returned to its sheath.

action in sacrificing animals. *"The Lord is God, and He has given us light; Bind the festival sacrifice with cords to the horns of the altar"* (Psalm 118:27). Ropes of some sort were used to bind our Lord when He was arrested. Before you came to know Jesus, you were bound by sin, iniquities, and all manner of evil. Jesus was bound that you might be set free!

A Pathetic Priesthood

And led Him to Annas first; for he was father-in-law of Caiaphas, who was high priest that year (John 18:13).

Jesus willingly submitted. They did not drag or carry Him. He was *led* to the high priest. Each animal that was sacrificed was also *led* first to the priest. (See Leviticus 11:5.)

The path that Jesus traveled from the garden to be questioned by the High Priest is significant. They passed through the "sheep gate" near the Temple. All sacrificial animals also passed through that gate—many of them coming from the meadows by the brook Kidron. The Lamb of God was to be sacrificed for the sins of the world: the Lamb would fulfill the type for every sacrifice man had made in accordance with God's Word. It was the last sacrifice God would accept from the Jews. The *perfect* sacrifice was about to take place!

Annas the old high priest was about 70 years of age. He was appointed in 6 A.D. and deposed in 15 A.D. However, he was always referred to as "high priest" for three reasons:

1. Though the Romans deposed high priests and appointed new ones, the Jews thought of it as an office for life.

2. The title "high priest" was given to members of a few priestly families from whom the high priests were drawn as well as those actually in office.

3. After being deposed Annas still had great influence on the office of high priest because all five of his sons succeeded him in office. The reigning high priest during Jesus' trial was his son-in-law, Caiaphas. Annas was the real, religious leader of the Jewish

nation, while his son-in-law was the professed leader.

Herod the Great had invited the family of Annas to come to Jerusalem from Alexandria, Egypt. They were Sadducees by religion— a cold, ambitious group, grasping for power and wealth.

Under the Roman governors the office of high priest became a matter for controversy and bribery. The position went to the highest bidder and the man most likely to cooperate with the Roman government. The family of Annas was immensely rich, and one by one members of his family bribed their way into office.

The way Annas made his money was despicable. In the court of the Gentiles were sellers of animals for sacrifice. The animals had to be without blemish. If a worshiper came with an animal not bought at the Temple, the "inspectors" would find a flaw. The worshiper would then be forced to buy a flawless animal from the sellers in the court. The catch was the price of the animals—the merchants charged many times the value of the animal. It was exploitation! (These were the sellers that Jesus drove out of the Temple.) The Jews themselves despised the family of Annas. It is now easy to understand the hatred Annas had for Jesus—he had been hurt in the pocketbook by Jesus, and he wanted revenge!

Trial by Mockers

Annas held the trial at night even though it was illegal. That way the multitude would not get involved in the proceedings. The purpose was to agree upon a sentence and get Jesus into the hands of the Romans.

Jesus would stand trial before both the Sanhedrin and the Roman governor, Pontius Pilate. There would also be a trial under Caiaphas since he was the recognized high priest. The Sanhedrin could judge and punish the guilty in regard to the Jewish law— except in the case of capital punishment.

Jewish law demanded at least two witnesses before a man could be condemned. The witnesses were to be interrogated—not the defendant. They could only present eyewitness evidence. According to Jewish law, a man could not receive the death penalty by his own confession, or even asked questions that would incriminate him.

When Annas interrogated Jesus about His teaching, our Lord boldly stated that He had done nothing in secret. For that answer Jesus received a blow to the face. Notice Jesus' reply: *"If I said something wrong...testify as to what is wrong, But if I spoke the truth, why did you strike me?"* (John 18:23 NIV).

Jesus, was reminding them of their laws. They had not properly charged Him, presented witnesses, or given opportunity for defense. Annas was frustrated, and sent Jesus, still bound, to Caiaphas.

In the trial under Caiaphas they tried to find witnesses who could condemn Jesus. Finally, two men came forward who reported that Jesus had declared, "I am able to destroy the temple of God and rebuild it in three days." (This was a perversion of what He *really* said.)

> *Jesus answered and said to them, "Destroy this temple, and in three days I will raise it up"* (John 2:19).

Caiaphas tore his clothes when he heard Jesus admit He was the Son of God and then say,

> *In the future you will see the Son of Man sitting on the right hand of the Mighty One and coming on the clouds of heaven,* (Matthew 26:64 NIV).

Peter—Hero or Heel?

> *Simon Peter therefore having a sword, drew it, and struck the high priest's slave, and cut off his right ear; and the slave's name was Malchus* (John 18:10).

In the garden, Peter acted in self-confident zeal of the flesh. He should have known that Jesus could have eluded the soldiers or called any number of angels to His defense. The truth had not yet reached Peter's spirit—Jesus was giving up His life.

> *But Jesus answered and said, "Stop! No more of this." And He touched his ear and healed him* (Luke 22:51).

Can you imagine the reaction of this huge group that came to arrest one man? How the miracle must have tugged at many of their hearts! They came with swords and clubs and when one of them was hurt, Jesus healed him! This was the last healing miracle Jesus performed. When Peter tried to be brave, his failure became an opportunity for a miracle.

Have you ever decided to do something for God—something really brave—and then blown it? How did you feel? If you allow Jesus to take control in those moments, He will take the botched-up situation and turn it into a miracle. Let Jesus have His way when you get into trouble!

Peter meant what he said; He *was* willing to die for Jesus. He loved Jesus that much. Peter fled the garden like the others, but stopped at a distance. There was another disciple with him who knew the high priest and could go right into the palace while Peter stayed outside the door. Jewish tradition states that the other disciple was John. Peter was, outside the place where they were going to press judgment on the Lord he loved.

> *And Simon Peter was following Jesus, and so was another disciple. Now that disciple was known to the high priest, and entered with Jesus into the court of the high priest, but Peter was standing at the door outside...* (John 18:15,16).

When Jesus heard the words, *"I will lay down my life for You,"* He knew Peter would allow fear to overcome Him. He said to Peter, *"...Truly, I say to you, a cock shall not crow, before you deny Me three times"* (John 13:38).

The *real* Peter gave his word of loyalty to Jesus, tried to protect Him, and followed Him. Jesus looked into the *failing* Peter and saw loyalty and love. Jesus loved Peter and forgave him. He loves you, too—even when you fail.

Each time Peter was asked if he was a disciple or had been with Jesus in the garden, he denied it. He really loved Jesus and longed to serve Him. Yet in this moment, surrounded by the enemy, he denied who he *really* was. *"The fear of man brings a*

The Cock's Crow

The cock here could have meant a literal rooster, but according to Jewish customs they were not allowed in the city, there might be another explanation.

The Roman military divided the night into four watches. After the third watch they changed guards. To mark its change there was a trumpet call at 3:00 A.M. The Greek word for "trumpet call" is *alektorophonia* which is the same word for *"cock crow."*

Jesus could have said, "Before the trumpet calls you will have denied me three times." Whether it was a rooster or a trumpet, Peter heard it loud and clear and remembered His Master's words. (See John 18:25-27.)

snare..." (Proverbs 29:25). Peter acted in fear and got caught in the snare of the enemy.

John does not complete the story of Peter's denial at this point, but Matthew closes his account with "...*immediately a rooster crowed. Then Peter remembered the word Jesus had spoken: 'Before the rooster crows you will disown me three times.' And he went outside and wept bitterly* (Matthew 26:74,75 NIV).

False Charges and Phony Proof

They led Jesus therefore from Caiaphas into the Praetorium, and it was early; and they themselves did not enter into the Praetorium in order that they might not be defiled, but might eat the Passover (John 18:28).

The Jews did not have the power to inflict the death penalty, therefore, they were forced to send Jesus to Pilate, the Roman governor for judgment. You will remember that they had attempted on various occasions to stone Jesus, but were unsuccessful. This time they sought to make His death sure...no slip-ups. They sent Jesus to the Romans— to His death.

The high priests condemned Jesus for blasphemy—and that offense carried the death penalty. *"Moreover, the one who blasphemes the name of the Lord shall surely be put to death;..."* (Leviticus 24:16).

How would they convince the Roman tribunal that He was worthy of death? "Blasphemy" would be a meaningless accusation to them. What could they accuse Him of that would stand up in a Roman court? They twisted the truth and said He claimed to be the King of the Jews. "We have no king but Caesar," they said. They knew that Jesus was no political threat to the Romans, however, He was definitely a threat to the Jewish religious establishment. It was convenient to charge Jesus with rebellion and political insurrection!

The Jews carried out capital punishment by stoning, but Jesus could not die that way. He had said, *"And I, if I be lifted up from the earth, will draw all men to Myself"* (John 12:32). He had to be crucified to fulfill prophecy and that was a Roman style of execution:

"That the word of Jesus might be fulfilled, which He spoke, signifying by what kind of death He was about to die" (John 18:32).

Pilate—The Cowardly Roman

In 4 B.C. Herod the Great died. He had been king of all Palestine and divided his kingdom among his three sons: Antipas became king of Galilee and Perea; Philip of the wild unpopulated areas of the northeast; and Archelaus of Idumea, Judea and Samaria. Pilate became the Roman agent over the entire area and ruled for nine years.

His rule was marked by several notorious incidents. In the situation concerning Jesus, Pilate knew the charges were false, and wanted nothing to do with them. *"...Take Him yourselves and judge Him according to your law..."* (John 18:31).

It was the custom to release a prisoner during the Passover. Pilate suggested releasing Jesus:

> But you have a custom, that I should release someone
> for you at the Passover; do you wish then that I release
> for you the King of the Jews? (John 18:39)

Then he tried to appease the Jewish leaders by scourging Jesus:

> Then Pilate therefore took Jesus, and scourged Him.
> And the soldiers wove a crown of thorns and put it on
> His head, and arrayed Him in a purple robe; and they
> began to come up to Him, and say, "Hail, King of the
> Jews !" and to give Him blows in the face. And Pilate
> came out again, and said to them, "Behold, I am
> bringing Him out to you, that you may know that I
> find no guilt in Him." Jesus therefore came out, wearing
> the crown of thorns and the purple robe. And Pilate
> said to them, "Behold, the Man!" (John 19:1-5).

Pilate could find no fault in Him and tried again to release

Him. Pilate thought that when the rulers saw the bleeding, beaten Jesus they would have compassion and not ask for the death penalty. He did not have the courage to make the right decision himself.

Pilate was curious about Jesus. He wanted to know more about Him—not because he wanted to believe, but because he was superstitious. What if there was something to the claims this Man made? What if a god did have something to do with this Man? Pilate was caught between two fears: fear of the Jews, and the superstitious fear that Jesus was linked to a higher power.

> *Pilate therefore said to Him, "So You are a king?" Jesus answered, "You say correctly that I am a king. For this I have been born, and for this I have come into the world, to bear witness to the truth. Everyone who is of the truth hears My voice." Pilate said to Him, "What is truth?" And when he had said this, he went out again to the Jews, and said to them, "I find no guilt in Him"* (John 18:37-38).

This question, "what is truth" may have puzzled Pilate for years, and he stood before Truth Himself. What an opportunity! He asked a most important question but turned to go without waiting for an answer.

How many times have people—or have you—asked a question of God concerning the truth but not waited for an answer? Pilate's eternal destiny could have been changed at that moment had he waited to receive Jesus' answer.

Jesus was not caught in a web of circumstances over which He had no control. Pilate thought he had authority and that he had the power to release Jesus or order Him crucified. Jesus said, "No, you have no authority over Me unless it had been given you from above." (See John 19:11.)

The soldiers amused themselves with cruel games. "He said He was a king? Let's treat Him like one!" They put a crown of thorns on His head, clothed Him in purple, and began to mock Him: "Hail O king of the Jews!" In their jest they called Him "King" but they

The Death by Crucifixion

"There was no more terrible death than death by crucifixion. Even the Romans themselves regarded it with a shudder of horror. Cicero declared that is was 'the most cruel and horrifying death.' Tacitus said that it was a 'despicable death.' It was originally a Persian method of execution. It may have been used because, to the Persians, the earth was sacred, and they wished to avoid defiling it with the body of an evildoer. So they nailed him to the cross and left him to die there, looking to the vultures and the carrion crows to complete the work. The Carthaginians took over crucifixion from the Persians; and the Romans learned it from the Carthaginians.

"Crucifixion was never used as a method of execution in the homeland, but only in the provinces, and there only in the case of slaves. It was unthinkable that a Roman citizen should die such a death."

From *The Gospel of John* by William Barclay

had no revelation of the truth of that statement!

As soon as a man was condemned, they gave him to four soldiers. They always scourged him first, then put his cross on his back and made him carry it through the streets. An officer walked before him carrying a placard, which stated his crime. This was done for two reasons: to put fear of committing a crime in those watching and also to give anyone an opportunity to plead his innocence if they had more evidence. In that case, they would halt the procession and retry the case. Pilate wrote the "crime" of Jesus in three languages: Jesus was KING.

Last Words

...He said to His mother, "Woman, behold, your son!"
Then He said to the disciple, "Behold, your mother!"
And from that hour the disciple took her into his own
household (John 19:26,27).

Mary, His mother was there, and Jesus committed her to John because His brothers did not yet believe on Him. Jesus was the eldest son; therefore she was His responsibility.

He said, *"I am thirsty"* (John 19:28). Jesus said this to fulfill Scripture (Psalms 69:21). Those close by used hyssop to give Jesus a drink of *vinegar.* When John says they used hyssop, he is pointing back to the first Passover. Jesus was the Passover Lamb.

He declared, *"It is finished!"* (John 19:30).The other three Gospels say He died with a great shout. Jesus died with a shout of triumph! *"And Jesus cried out again with a loud voice, and yielded up His spirit"* (Matthew 27:50).

To Kill a God

But one of the soldiers pierced His side with a spear,
and immediately there came out blood and water
(John 19:34).

The Death of Jesus

1. **God's view—it was a conciliation:**
   Whom God displayed publicly as a propitiation in His blood through faith. This was to demonstrate His righteousness, because in the forbearance of God He passed over the sins previously committed: for the demonstration, I say, of His righteousness at the present time, that He might be just and the justifier of the one who has faith in Jesus (Romans 3:25,26).

2. **Jesus' view—it was a sacrifice, an offering, an act of obedience:**
   And being found in appearance as a man, He humbled Himself by becoming obedient to the point of death, even death on a cross (Philippians 2:8).

3. **The believers' view—it was a substitution:**

For Christ also died for sins once for all, the just for the unjust, in order that He might bring us to God, having been put to death in the flesh, but made alive in the spirit (I Peter 3:18).

4. Satan's view—it was a triumph and defeat, a bruised heel, the power of death destroyed:
   Since then the children share in flesh and blood, He Himself likewise also partook of the same, that through death He might render powerless him who had the power of death, that is, the devil (Hebrews 2:14).

5. The world's view—it was a brutal murder:
   But put to death the Prince of life, the one whom God raised from the dead, a fact to which we are witnesses (Acts 3:15).

The Jews were not to leave a dead body on the cross overnight. (See Deuteronomy 21:22,23.)

If the criminal was still alive on the cross, the execution was completed by beating him with mallets. They did not break a bone of Jesus—He was the Passover Lamb.

> *They shall leave none of it until morning, nor break a bone of it; according to all the statute of the Passover they shall observe it* (Numbers 9:12).

When they came to Him, they saw that He was already dead. Then one of the soldiers thrust a spear in His side, and another scripture was fulfilled.

> *And I will pour out on the house of David and on the inhabitants of Jerusalem, the Spirit of grace and of supplication, so that they will look on Me whom they have pierced; and they will mourn for Him, as one mourns for an only son, and they will weep bitterly over Him, like the bitter weeping over a first-born* (Zechariah 12:10).

Beginning or End?

When Jesus crossed the Kidron He made the final decision to give His life as a sacrifice for mankind. He pleaded with the Father, but submitted to the Father's will. Jesus took each step toward His goal, making sure every detail of prophecy was fulfilled along the way. He took care of His disciples, commanding the soldiers to let them go; then He submitted to the soldiers' authority, knowing He had the power to kill them with a word. How great was the love of our Savior—He willingly gave Himself!

Can you imagine the irony of Jesus—the Holy Son of God, the believers' High Priest forever—being condemned by a high priest whose motivation was greed and lust for power? Jesus stood in front of the man who had made His Father's house a den of thieves and listened to *his* condemnation. Annas pronounced the death penalty after he learned that Jesus claimed to be the Son of God. His soul and conscience were seared. Annas, along with the rest of the Sanhedrin, were too blind to recognize the Messiah, the Son of Jehovah—the God they pretended to worship!

Pilate, although he had power and authority, did not use his power to release Jesus when he judged Him innocent. He delivered the King of kings to be crucified like a common criminal! Pilate's soldiers blindly called Jesus "King" and nailed Him to the Cross!

Jesus' death looked unjust. He was falsely condemned. There was no concern for the law or even justice when the chief priests condemned Jesus, or when Pilate turned Him over to the crucifixion squad. However, God was in control, and justice for all mankind was being served. God's wrath for all of mankind's sin was answered by Jesus' death. Man had violated God's laws and God's judgment was satisfied by the death of His own Son!

Personal Action Plan

1. Meditate on why Jesus went to the Cross for you. Share your answers with a friend.

2. Read the verses that examine Peter's behavior immediately before Jesus' arrest. Have you ever done something "foolish"?

3. Pray and meditate on what Jesus meant concerning the kingdom in John 18:36. Write your thoughts in your scripture notebook or journal.

4. What was Jesus' specific promise to Peter? What is His specific promise to *you* in times of failure or distress?

5. How does the death of Jesus bring you triumph? Find a verse in the Bible that supports your answer.

Chapter 11

FATAL VICTORY

Fatal Victory

Now in the place where He was crucified there was a garden; and in the garden a new tomb, in which no one had yet been laid (John 19:41).

Jesus was buried in a garden. It is interesting that in the Garden of Eden, Adam sowed the seed of sin that reaped death for mankind. In another garden, Jesus, the second Adam, *the* Seed, was sown to reap eternal life for all who believe.

They laid Jesus in a new, clean tomb where no one had yet been laid. (See John 19:41.) The ashes of a sacrificial heifer were also to be laid in a "clean place." (See Numbers 19:9.) The sacrifices of the Old Testament predicted the death and burial of Jesus.

The Resurrection—No Surprise

Noah, surviving the flood waters of judgment, is a foreshadowing of the Resurrection:

> *Who once were disobedient, when the patience of God kept waiting in the days of Noah, during the construction of the ark, in which a few, that is, eight persons, were brought safely through the water. And corresponding to that, baptism now saves you—not the removal of dirt from the flesh, but an appeal to God for a good conscience—through the resurrection of Jesus Christ* (I Peter 3:20,21).

The deliverance of Isaac from the sacrificial altar after he had been committed to death three days earlier is a type of the Resurrection.

> *On the third day Abraham raised his eyes and saw
> the place from a distance* (Genesis 22:4).

Jonah was in the fish's belly three days and three nights, and then delivered—a sign of the Resurrection on the third day!

> *For just as Jonah was three days and three nights in
> the belly of the sea monster, so shall the Son of Man
> be three days and three nights in the heart of the earth*
> (Matthew 12:40).

Triumph Over the Tomb

The Resurrection was brought about by the joint action of all three Persons of the Trinity, as were Jesus' incarnation and baptism.

• **The Father**

> *Therefore we have been buried with Him through
> baptism into death, in order that as Christ was raised
> from the dead through the glory of the Father, so we
> too might walk In newness of life* (Romans 6:4).

• **The Son**

> *For this reason the Father loves Me, because I lay down
> My life that I may take it again. No one has taken it
> away from Me, but I lay it down on My own
> initiative. I have authority to lay it down, and I
> have authority to take it up again. This
> commandment I received from My Father*
> (John 10:17,18).

• **The Spirit**

> *But if the Spirit of Him who raised Jesus from the
> dead dwells in you, He who raised Christ Jesus from*

*the dead will also give life to your mortal bodies
through His Spirit who indwells you* (Romans 8:11).

The Bible records numerous eyewitness accounts of Jesus
reappearing after His resurrection:

*Now on the first day of the week Mary Magdalene
came early to the tomb, while it was still dark, and
saw the stone already taken away from the tomb.
"...they have taken away my Lord, and I do not know
where they have laid Him." When she had said this,
she turned around, and beheld Jesus standing there,
and did not know that it was Jesus* (John 20:1,13,14).

He appeared to the women returning from the grave. (See
Matthew 28:9,10.) Disciples going to Emmaus recognized Him and
others testified that Simon Peter saw Him:

*And He went in to stay with them. And it came
about that when He had reclined at the table with
them, He took the bread and blessed it, and breaking
it, He began giving it to them. And their eyes were
opened and they recognized Him; and He vanished
from their sight....[And they said], "The Lord has
really risen, and has appeared to Simon" And they
began to relate their experiences on the road and
how He was recognized by them in the breaking of
the bread. (Luke 24:29,30,31,34,35).*

He appeared to the ten disciples in the Upper Room. (See
John 20:19-24.) Later, He appeared to all eleven disciples, including
Thomas, in the Upper Room:

*And after eight days again His disciples were inside,
and Thomas with them. Jesus came, the doors having
been shut, and stood in their midst, and said, "Peace
be with you." Thomas answered and said to Him, "My*

Lord and my God!" Jesus said to him, "Because you have seen Me, have you believed? Blessed are they who did not see, and yet believed" (John 20:26,28,29).

Jesus showed Himself to the seven disciples fishing at the Tiberias sea (see John 21:1) and again in Galilee: *"But the eleven disciples proceeded to Galilee, to the mountain, which Jesus had designated"* (Matthew 28:16). First Corinthians 15:6 says that He showed Himself to about 500 brethren at once and then to James and all the apostles:

After that He appeared to more than five hundred brethren at one time, most of whom remain until now, but some have fallen asleep; then He appeared to James, then to all the apostles.

The disciples on the Mount of Olives saw Him at His Ascension:

And after He had said these things, He was lifted up while they were looking on, and a cloud received Him out of their sight (Acts 1:9).

He appeared to Stephen:

But being full of the Holy Spirit, he gazed intently into heaven and saw the glory of God, and Jesus standing at the right hand of God; and he said, "Behold, I see the heavens opened up and the Son of Man standing at the right hand of God" (Acts 7:55,56).

The resurrected Jesus appeared to Saul on the way to Damascus. (See Acts 9:3-6.) He appeared to John on the Isle of Patmos:

And when I saw Him, I fell at His feet as a dead man. And He laid His right hand upon me, saying, "Do not be afraid; I am the first and the last" (Revelation 1:17).

Angelic Announcement

In John's account, angels are seen sitting at either end of the sepulchre. Arthur W. Pink comments:

"This is the only place in Scripture where we see angels sitting. The fact that they were sitting in the place where 'the body of Jesus had lain' was God's witness unto the rest which was secured by and proceeds from the finished work of the Lord Jesus. It is in striking accord with the character of this fourth Gospel that it was reserved for John to mention this beautiful incident.

"Who can doubt that the Holy Spirit would have us link up this verse with Exodus 25:17-19, *'And thou shalt make a mercy seat of pure gold...and thou shalt make two cherubims of gold, of beaten work shalt thou make them, in the two ends of the mercy seat.'* More remarkable still is the final work which Jehovah spake unto Moses concerning the mercy-seat: *'And there I will meet with thee, and I will commune with thee from above the mercy seat from between the two cherubims'* (Exodus 25:22). Here, then, in John's Gospel, do we learn once more that Christ is the true Meeting Place between God and man!"

From *The Exposition of the Gospel of John* by Arthur W. Pink

No more personal appearances are recorded after that, but Jesus has appeared to many of His disciples since that day. You may not have seen Jesus with your physical eyes, but you have seen Him through spiritual eyes. One day, you will see Him when He raptures His church.

> *For the Lord Himself will descend from heaven with a shout, with the voice of the archangel, and with the trumpet of God; and the dead in Christ shall rise first. Then we who are alive and remain shall be caught up together with them in the clouds to meet the Lord in the air, and thus we shall always be with the Lord* (I Thessalonians 4:16,17).

God cared enough to send angels to bring comfort to Mary Magdalene. *"For He will give His angels charge concerning you, to guard you in all your ways"* (Psalm 91:11). Angels announced the resurrection of Jesus:

> *And it happened that while they were perplexed about this, behold, two men suddenly stood near them in dazzling apparel; and as the women were terrified and bowed their faces to the ground, the men said to them, "Why do you seek the living One among the dead? (Luke 24:4-5)*

Forever Changed

Tradition says that Mary Magdalene was a prostitute. The Bible adds that she had seven demons cast out of her.

> *And also some women who had been healed of evil spirits and sicknesses: Mary who was called Magdalene, from whom seven demons had gone out* (Luke 8:2).

Mary Magdalene had been delivered from her old life—she was a new creature in Christ. Jesus had forgiven her sins and cast the demons out of her life. She was free—free to live a new lifestyle, and free to follow a new Master. She loved Jesus because of all that she had been through.

> *For this reason I say to you, her sins, which are many, have been forgiven, for she loved much; but he who is forgiven little, loves little* (Luke 7:47).

Mary Magdalene came to the tomb very early. (See John 20:1.) The Greek word for early is *proli* which means "between 3 and 6 a.m."

It was the custom to visit the tomb of a loved one after three days. They believed that for three days the spirit of the person hovered around the tomb; then the spirit departed because the body was decaying. Jesus' friends couldn't come on the Sabbath...that would have violated the Law. So on the first day of the week, they came and Mary Magdalene was the first to arrive.

When she arrived, she was surprised to see the stone at the entrance to the tomb rolled away. Originally, the tomb had been sealed by the authorities and the stone's removal was illegal. (See Matthew 27:66.) She might have thought two things: first, that the Jews had taken His body to hide it, wanting to further humiliate Him; or, that grave robbers had stolen Him. Either thought was horrible.

She returned to the city to tell Peter and John and then returned to the tomb with them:

> *Peter therefore went forth, and the other disciple, and they were going to the tomb. And the two were running together; and the other disciple ran ahead faster than Peter, and came to the tomb first; and stooping and looking in, he saw the linen wrappings lying there, but he did not go in. Simon Peter therefore also came, following him, and entered the tomb; and he beheld the linen wrappings lying there, and the face-cloth, which had been on His head, not lying with the linen wrappings, but rolled up in a place by itself* (John 20:3-7).

Then John went in. He saw and he believed.

> *So the other disciple who had first come to the tomb*
> *entered then also, and he saw and believed. For as yet*
> *they did not understand the Scripture, that He must*
> *rise again from the dead* (John 20:8,9).

John didn't understand yet, but he believed. Many times you have to believe by faith, before you really understand what is going on. Love gave him believing eyes and a heart that received truth. Later that same day, Jesus opened the Scriptures to the disciples so that they might also understand with their minds. *"Then He opened their minds to understand the Scriptures"* (Luke 24:45).

Weeper to Worshiper

Peter and John, jubilant with new truth, went away to their own homes. Meanwhile, Mary Magdalene, probably left behind by the runners, arrived at the tomb a second time.

> *But Mary was standing outside the tomb weeping; and*
> *so, as she wept, she stooped and looked into the tomb;*
> *and she beheld two angels in white sitting, one at the*
> *head, and one at the feet, where the body of Jesus had*
> *been lying* (John 20:11,12).

Mary looked into the tomb and wept. She was weeping so hard that at first she did not see the two angels sitting there. They asked her why she was weeping. She answered, *"Because they have taken away my Lord, and I do not know where they have laid Him."* Then something must have caused her to turn. As she did, she saw Jesus standing there. But she did not recognize Him! She was too busy crying. How many times have we been so preoccupied with our sorrow and pain that we didn't know Jesus was standing beside us?

Her sorrow was for Someone within arm's reach. Mary wanted to know where Jesus had been taken, but He was standing in front of her. Sometimes, as believers, we can be so distraught over the absence of a blessing and weep for it with such intensity that we are blind to it when it comes. Expect and believe that God is sending good things your way.

> *Jesus said to her, "Woman, why are you weeping? Whom are you seeking?" Supposing Him to be the gardener, she said to Him, "Sir, if you have carried Him away, tell me where you have laid Him, and I will take Him away"* (John 20:15).

Mary heard the words, but did not recognize the voice. She was totally absorbed with her personal sorrow. She supposed everyone would know for Whom she was looking. *"Jesus said to her, 'Mary!' She turned and said to Him in Hebrew, 'Rabboni' (which means, Teacher)"* (John 20:16).

The first time He spoke, Jesus called her *"woman."* He was God and she was one of His creations. He was exalted high above every human relationship. But the second time He spoke, He called her *"Mary."* He was identifying Himself as her friend, her Savior, her Good Shepherd, the one Who calls His sheep by name.

> *To him the doorkeeper opens, and the sheep hear his voice, and he calls his own sheep by name, and leads them out* (John 10:3).

By calling her name, Jesus transformed her from a weeper to a worshiper. After His first words, she turned away from Him, and looked back toward the tomb. But when He called her by name, she turned her back on the tomb and fell at His feet.

The Invisible Man

> *"...Stop clinging to Me, for I have not yet ascended to the Father; but go to My brethren and say to them, 'I ascend to My Father and your Father and My God and your God'"* (John 20:17).

"Stop Clinging to Me"

There is another possible explanation for this command from our Lord. Gordon Lindsay says, "There is some mystery in these words, yet the meaning seems not too difficult. Later we are told that the other women saw Jesus and 'held him by the feet, and worshipped him' (Matthew 28:9). It would appear, therefore, that Jesus spoke to Mary as the High Priest fulfilling the day of atonement (Leviticus 16). After leaving Mary, He presents the sacred blood in heaven, then returns for the meeting of Matthew 28:9. Mary knew Christ only after the flesh, and having found Him alive again wanted to hold on to Him in the old relationship.

"'And He died for all, that they who live should no longer live for themselves, but for Him who died and rose again on their behalf. Therefore from now on we recognize

no man according to the flesh; even though we have known Christ according to the flesh, yet now we know Him thus no longer. Therefore if any man is in Christ, he is a new creature; the old things passed away; behold, new things have come'
(II Corinthians 5:15-17).

"After His resurrection Jesus was about to assume a new relation and He would show Mary that she must not attempt to hold Him on earth, but to carry the message of the resurrection to others at once."
(See John 20:17.)

From *The Life and Teachings of Christ* by Gordon Lindsay

Mary wanted to hold on to Jesus and resume their relationship. He would be the Master and she would follow Him and minister to His needs. Jesus was saying, "No, do not cling to me. Know Me in the Spirit now. You will still be My follower, but you will be obeying the Spirit—not following a visible Man."

Mary was the first witness of Christ's resurrection. A woman had been the first to anoint Jesus for burial (see John 12) and a woman was the first to whom Christ revealed Himself. Now He told her to go and tell the others. "*...Go to My brethren...*" (John 20:17).

Mary went and told the disciples that she had seen the Lord. Mary not only told them Jesus was *risen*, but also that He was *returning to the Father*. Through a woman who anointed Jesus came the *first* message of His death. Now, Jesus chose a woman to spread the *first* message of **resurrection life!**

Sown in Weakness, Raised in Power

*When therefore it was evening, on that day, the first day of the week, and when the doors were shut where the disciples were, for fear of the Jews, **Jesus came and stood in their midst**, and said to them, "Peace be with you." And when He had said this, He showed them both His hands and His side. The disciples therefore rejoiced when they saw the Lord. Jesus therefore said to them again, "Peace be with you; as the Father has sent Me, I also send you." And when He had said this, He breathed on them, and said to them, "Receive the Holy Spirit. If you forgive the sins of any, their sins have been forgiven them; if you retain the sins of any, they have been retained"* (John 20:19-23).

When Jesus suddenly appeared in that room with the disciples, He had no words of reproach for them although most of them had scattered, leaving Him alone with the soldiers, and one had even denied Him three times. They were hiding like defeated men—afraid of the Jews. Yet Jesus' first words were, *"Peace be with you."* He wanted to dispel fear of His sudden appearance. He wanted to remind them of the last words He said before He left: *"These things have I spoken to you that you might have peace…"* (John 16:33).

John called this group *"apostles,"* not *"disciples."* Apostle is "one who is sent forth." There and then they were still with Christ; they had not yet been commissioned. *"The doors were shut where the disciples were."* The word *shut* signifies "barred" in the Greek. They were huddling in fear. They had heard Christ was alive, yet they sat frightened behind locked doors. Locked doors meant nothing to the risen Lord. His body, though sown in weakness, had been raised in power. It no longer had physical limitations.

Jesus wanted His disciples to be sure that He was in fact their Lord—*not* a ghost. In Luke 24:39, He said,

> *See My hands and My feet, that it is I Myself; touch Me and see, for a spirit does not have flesh and bones as you see that I have.*

The disciples rejoiced when they saw the Lord. They had been frightened, sad, and angry at the Jews, emotions had overcome them. In fact, they hadn't all believed that Jesus was alive. Then Jesus came! A look at Him, a Word from His mouth, and they were filled with joy, delight, exultation, and ecstasy. Jesus had fulfilled His promise—their sorrow had turned to joy.

> *Therefore you too now have sorrow; but I will see you again, and your heart will rejoice, and no one takes your joy away from you* (John 16:22).

Notice that Jesus did not change their circumstances—they were still hiding behind closed doors. However, He changed *them.* That's what happens when Jesus is allowed to take preeminence over a gloomy, sad, or frightening situation.

Jesus said a second time, *"Peace be with you."* The first time it was *positional* peace: Jesus' death had bought them peace with God.

> *Therefore having been justified by faith, we have peace*

with God through our Lord Jesus Christ (Romans 5:1).

The second time He said, "peace," He was speaking peace to the situation they were in—the peace of God.

> *And the peace of God, which surpasses all comprehension, shall guard your hearts and your minds in Christ Jesus* (Philippians 4:7).

They would be going out into a hostile world—one that would try to steal their peace. They would need a reliable and inexhaustible source of peace—Jesus Himself!

Primed With Power and Purpose

• Prayerfully

Jesus had prayed about this moment in His High Priestly prayer. He knew that the world would hear the gospel because of His disciples. *"As Thou didst send Me into the world, I also have sent them into the world"* (John 17:18).

> *I do not ask in behalf of these alone, but for those also who believe in Me through their word* (John 17:20).

• Powerfully

Jesus was sent by the Father with a message of love and grace for a sinful world—so are you. Power backed up Jesus' message—and yours too. When you have the message of Jesus—His words, His life, and His command to go—you go forth in power!

• Confidently

Jesus showed His relationship to the Church. The Church is *"...His body, the fullness of Him who fills all in all"* (Ephesians 1:23).

For even as the body is one and yet has many members,
and all the members of the body, though they are many,
are one body, so also is Christ (I Corinthians 12:12).

Jesus had such confidence in His Church that He said, *"I send you,"* and expected the job to be done! That is the way it gets done today—through His Body!

The Breath of God

Jesus gave them the Holy Spirit. (See John 20:22.) Jesus entered the ministry anointed by the Holy Spirit—so would His disciples.

In Genesis 2:7 God breathed into Adam the breath of life. Now Jesus was breathing into His disciples the breath of *new* life. This was the beginning of a new creation. The first Adam received the breath of life from God. The second Adam [Jesus] was **giving** life from God:

So also it is written, "The first MAN, Adam, BECAME
A LIVING SOUL." The last Adam became a life-giving
spirit (I Corinthians 15:45).

We have the authority to declare the forgiveness of sins to all who repent, and also the solemn responsibility to warn that there is no forgiveness outside of repenting and receiving Jesus Christ as Lord. The power of forgiving sins belongs to God:

I, even I, am the one who wipes out your transgressions
for My own sake; and I will not remember your sins
(Isaiah 43:25).

Paul forgave others in the person of Christ.

But whom you forgive anything, I forgive also; for
indeed what I have forgiven, if I have forgiven
anything, I did it for your sakes in the presence of
Christ (II Corinthians 2:10).

A Day of New Beginnings

• Christ is known in a new way, no longer *"after the flesh,"* but in the Spirit (John 20:17).

• Believers were given a new title: *"brethren"* (John 20:17).

• Believers have a new position with God as Father. *"I ascend to My Father and your Father"* (John 20:17).

• Believers have a new blessing—peace (John 20:19,20).

• Believers were given a new privilege—having Jesus in their midst anywhere and anytime (Matthew 28:20).

• Believers receive a new commission. As the Son was sent by the Father, they are sent by the Son (John 20:21).

• Believers received new life when Jesus breathed on them (John 20:22).

• Believers became the temple in which the Holy Spirit would dwell (John 20:22). This all happened on the first day of the week—the time of new beginnings!

From a Pessimist to True Believer

When Jesus went to Jerusalem after they tried to kill Him, all Thomas could think of was death—not only the death of Jesus but of all of them. He was a natural pessimist. In John 14:5 Thomas said, *"Lord, we don't know where you are going and we don't know the way."* Jesus had just promised that He would be back and He had just said that they did know where He was going or the way there. Thomas chose to ignore the promises and stay with the gloomy mood of uncertainty.

"But Thomas, one of the twelve, called Didymus, was not with them when Jesus came" (John 20:24). John believed in the Resurrection, but many of the others were skeptical. They gathered together in mutual fellowship and support. However, Thomas was not with them. He withdrew from fellowship and missed the first appearance of Jesus to His disciples. Do not be like Thomas and shut yourself off when you are depressed! Seek fellowship!

The disciples had a tender attitude toward their brother, Thomas, who had "missed it." They did not say with an air of superiority, "He should have been here. Let's not share the news. He chose to be away; it's his fault!" No, they told him the wonderful news, *"The other disciples therefore were saying to him, 'We have seen the Lord!'"* (John 20:25).

We have to be prepared for people who will not receive our message. Some feel that the gospel is just too good to be true, even though they have seen many miracles.

> Mary Magdalene came, announcing to the disciples, "I have seen the Lord," and that He had said these things to her....The other disciples therefore were saying to [Thomas], "We have seen the Lord!" But he said to them, "Unless I shall see in His hands the imprint of the nails, and put my finger into the place of the nails, and put my hand into His side, I will not believe" (John 20:18,25).

Thomas had seen the lame walk, the blind see, the dumb

talk. He even witnessed the resurrection of Lazarus who had been dead for four days. He heard Jesus' promise to rise from the dead on the third day, yet Thomas persisted in doubt and unbelief and explained the precise conditions for him to believe. This is the only place in the New Testament where the nails that pierced Jesus' hands and feet are mentioned. It not only shows that prophecy was literally fulfilled; it proves that Jesus was nailed to the Cross and not bound as was sometimes the case.

> *For dogs have surrounded me; a band of evildoers has encompassed me; they pierced my hands and my feet* (Psalm 22:16).

The next Sunday, the disciples were once again assembled and this time Thomas was with them. The doors were locked and once more Jesus suddenly appeared in their midst with the greeting *"Peace be with you!"* It was exactly as the first time—all for the benefit of Thomas!

Jesus loved Thomas, and knew his basic nature was to be pessimistic. He knew how hard it was for Thomas to commit himself totally until he was sure. Jesus also knew that Thomas had great courage and that once he was convinced he would become a loyal and powerful believer. Jesus patiently "replayed" the whole scene just for one doubting Thomas.

Then He said to Thomas,

> *Reach here your finger and see My hands; and reach here your hand, and put it into My side; and be not unbelieving, but believing* (John 20:27).

Jesus knew the very words that Thomas had used to express his doubts. In one moment the doubter became a worshiper. He saw Jesus and exclaimed, *"My Lord and my God!"* Thomas had a revelation that Jesus was really God. This is the only time in the Gospels that someone actually called Jesus *"God."* Yet Thomas did not just call Jesus *Lord and God* He said, *"**MY** Lord and **MY** God."*

The Victory of Death

In the Old Testament there are many references to the death of Christ, and to His resurrection. God planned all along that His Son would die, and that He would rise again to receive a name above every name and give resurrection life to all who believed on His name.

When Jesus arose from the dead He did not keep it a secret. He appeared to His disciples that same day. Then, for the next forty days, He appeared to believers. Once, five hundred people saw Him. Jesus wanted His disciples to know that He was truly alive. Christ's resurrection day began a new era for believers. They were now new creatures, born again, raised to a new life with Christ.

Mary Magdalene was also transformed by the words of the risen Lord. She wept at his death, and was devastated to discover that His body was gone! Her tears caused her vision to be impaired— she did not recognize that she was talking to angels; she even thought Jesus was a gardener. Her attention was absorbed with her sorrow and loss, but when she heard her Shepherd call her name, she knew His voice. She responded and fell to her knees, and the weeper become a worshiper.

Jesus came to comfort the frightened disciples when they were behind locked doors! He came with peace—showing His scars, the price He paid for that peace. It was a peace *with* God—there were now no barriers between man and his Creator. It was also the peace *of* God—peace that could face frightening and difficult circumstances in the world. Seeing Jesus and hearing His words brought delight to the disciples. He had loved them to the end, then returned to change their sorrow into joy—just as He had promised. Jesus breathed new life into them. They received the Holy Spirit and were *born again.* They too, had risen to life with Christ!

Personal Action Plan

1. Find three key words in John 20 and write a paragraph about each in your scripture notebook.

2. Pray about how Jesus speaks to you when you are suffering grief or sorrow. Is there someone to share this with this week?

3. Describe the peace God gives you. Where in your life do you need peace?

4. Why should we be believers and not doubters? Find several Bible verses that discuss this issue.

5. Meditate on the chief purpose of this Gospel. (See John 20:31.) What actions does God want you to take?

Chapter 12

LORD OF THE SECOND CHANCE

Lord of the Second Chance

After these things Jesus manifested Himself again to the disciples at the Sea of Tiberias, and He manifested Himself in this way (John 21:1).

It was at the waterfront that several disciples first made the life-changing decision to follow Jesus, instead of pursuing their fishing trade. (See Luke 5:1-11.) Things had not turned out as they planned. Jesus was alive, but they were not sure of the next step. Peter, a man of action, decided to go fishing—back to the life he knew.

But the eleven disciples proceeded to Galilee, to the mountain which Jesus had designated (Matthew 28:16).

The disciples went to the Sea of Galilee (the Sea of Tiberias, is its Latin name.) They chose that location because Jesus had given the women at the tomb a message for the disciples: *"Go and take word to My brethren to leave for Galilee, and they shall see Me"* (Matthew 28:10). The disciples had gone there in response to Christ's command.

They were to go to Galilee, but *not* fishing. They left that occupation to follow Jesus. Notice all the disciples were there, including Peter, who denied Him, and Thomas, who doubted Him. Both were completely forgiven. The Holy Spirit made sure they were mentioned first—to emphasize the grace and forgiveness of God.

Jesus told them He would make them "fishers of men"—not fishermen. They spent the whole night working, fruitlessly getting nowhere but hungry *"...and that night they caught nothing."* The disciples learned, by firsthand experience, the truth of John 15:5, *"Without Me, you can do nothing."*

When Peter decided to go fishing, the others agreed to go
with him. (See John 21:3.) They had not stopped to ask whether
they *should* go, they were merely following the crowd. Always be
sure that you ask *God* for directions. Then you will be following the
Spirit and not acting in the strength of your own flesh.

From Empty Nets to Full

When Jesus stood on the shore, the disciples did not recognize
Him. Their spiritual faculties were not as sharp as they could
have been. They were obviously not expecting Him. The disciples
were so involved with the "calling" of their former life that they
did not recognize the Lord. After the Resurrection, Jesus was only
visible when He desired to be. The disciples saw Jesus when He
appeared to them. Jesus was beginning to teach His disciples to
believe in His presence whether they saw Him or not—to recognize
Him by the Spirit—and not by the flesh. They were to "walk by
faith, not by sight."

> *Jesus therefore said to them, "Children, you do not
> have any fish, do you?" And they answered Him, "No"*
> (John 21:5).

In saying *children,* Jesus used a distant term for the disciples.
In John 13:33, He spoke to them as children in training: *"Little
children, I am with you a little while longer..."* (John 13:33).

Jesus knew the answer before He asked the question, but the
disciples needed to admit their weakness before they could receive
His strength. It's still that way. Jesus comes to you when you are
struggling. Sometimes you feel desperately alone, as the disciples
did that night. At times you don't recognize Him because you are so
deeply involved in your problems. But He *does* come—or rather He
is always there. He does speak and always has a solution.

> *And He said to them, "Cast the net on the right-hand
> side of the boat, and you will find a catch." They cast
> therefore, and then they were not able to haul it in*

because of the great number of fish (John 21:6).

Jesus told them to cast the net on the right-hand side of the boat to find a catch. They obeyed and had a net full of fish. Christ's power drew the fish into the net. They had toiled uselessly all night, yet when Jesus directed their energies, they had a full catch. So it is with us. We cannot be fishers of men in our own energy, but we can "catch" every person the Father draws into our net.

The Big Fisherman

The multitude of fish demonstrated the power of the Word. (See John 21:6.) The fishermen had worked all night using their expertise, but nothing happened. Then came the Word. Their obedience to the Word caused an abundant harvest of fish. How true Psalm 19:11 is: *"In keeping of them* [His commandments] *there is great reward."* Expect results when you obey the Word.

> *That disciple therefore whom Jesus loved said to Peter,*
> *"It is the Lord." And so when Simon Peter heard that*
> *it was the Lord, he put his outer garment on (for he*
> *was stripped for work), and threw himself into the sea*
> (John 21:7).

John was one of the first who believed in the Resurrection after he saw the grave clothes in the empty tomb. The great catch of fish caused John to recognize the hand of the Lord. John seemed to be the most devoted and to possess the most spiritual discernment. He was the one who leaned on his Master's breast; he was the one who was given charge of the Lord's mother. A heart that truly loves his Lord will be sensitive to recognize His hand in any situation.

> *There was reclining on Jesus' breast one of His disciples,*
> *whom Jesus loved. Simon Peter therefore gestured to*
> *him, and said to him, "Tell us who it is of whom He is*
> *speaking." He, leaning back thus on Jesus' breast, said*
> *to Him, "Lord, who is it?" Jesus therefore answered,*

"That is the one for whom I shall dip the morsel and give it to him. So when He had dipped the morsel, He took and gave it to Judas, the son of Simon Iscariot (John 13:23-26).

So the other disciple who had first come to the tomb entered then also, and he saw and believed (John 20:8).

John's response to the full net was "It is the Lord!" He gave the glory to the right source. (See John 21:7.) Instead of talking about their great success, he turned to the Giver of success. That should always be your attitude when you experience a measure of triumph because of the Word—turn your attention to the Lord—give Him the praise!

John may have been first to *recognize* Jesus, but Peter was the first to *act*. He jumped into the sea (though he stopped long enough to put on his outer garment). Peter also loved Jesus, and he put his love into action. It was Peter who stepped out of the boat and walked on the water toward Jesus in Matthew 14:28. He couldn't wait for Jesus to get to him. Now he left the boat again—this time, swimming to reach Jesus. The abundant catch of fish was nothing compared to being with Jesus.

But the other disciples came in the little boat, for they were not far from the land, but about one hundred yards away, dragging the net full of fish (John 21:8).

People respond differently to Jesus. John recognized the Word in action; Peter responded with a move towards Jesus; others respond by using the gifts that Jesus has given them. All responded differently to Jesus; all were blessed, and the fish were brought safely to shore. When souls are saved, we should recognize the Holy Spirit as the source of the drawing power and move toward Jesus in a special declaration of love and praise. New converts also need to be carefully taken nearer to Jesus.

The fish were caught close to shore. This was an unlikely place for such a large catch of fish. Souls, too, can be won in the strangest places. Follow Jesus' Word, His leading, and you will soon produce a harvest.

> *Simon Peter went up, and drew the net to land, full of large fish, a hundred and fifty-three; and although there were so many, the net was not torn* (John 21:11).

It is interesting that the net was very heavy, too heavy for the disciples to haul ashore. They had to drag it. (See John 21:8.) What six men had trouble doing, one man, Peter, did by himself. He drew the net to land! Peter was at that moment in a place of strength, at the feet of Jesus. Spend time in the presence of Jesus and you will find *your* strength greatly increasing.

> *He gives strength to the weary, and to him who lacks might He increases power. Though youths grow weary and tired, and vigorous young men stumble badly, yet those who wait for the Lord will gain new strength; they will mount up with wings like eagles, they will run and not get tired, they will walk and not become weary* (Isaiah 40:29-31).

> *Wait for the Lord; be strong, and let your heart take courage; yes, wait for the Lord* (Psalms 27:14).

The fish that were brought to Jesus were counted and accounted for—there were 153. This is important. These fish are symbolic of people brought into the kingdom of God. They are rejoiced over, each is counted and considered precious.

The Lord Your Provider

> *And so when they got out upon the land, they saw a charcoal fire already laid, and fish placed on it, and bread* (John 21:9).

Jesus knew they had toiled all night. He loved them, and

love always serves. When the men came ashore, Jesus was cooking fish—He even had bread for them. How thoughtful and compassionate; He knows we have human needs: *"For He Himself knows our frame; He is mindful that we are but dust"* (Psalms 103:14).

Where did Jesus get the fish and bread? I believe it was a miracle. For Jesus it would have been easy to create food for His hungry disciples. By feeding them, He also reminded them of the miracle of feeding the five thousand and Jesus' teaching, *"I am the bread of life."* It was a practical demonstration that Jesus would meet their needs—even the physical ones.

As our example, Jesus willingly served and met the needs of others. It is important for us to serve each other and help to meet the needs of those around us. Even a cup of water given in Jesus' name will receive a reward. He shows us that those who *labor* also need warming and feeding from the Bread of Life!

Jesus can meet your needs supernaturally. He already had the fish and bread prepared before the disciples arrived. He was not dependent upon a human source! Generally, God uses people, His body, to meet the needs of others. However, He is not restricted to working through us. Jesus does miracles, and uses His ministering angels to meet our needs. God has unlimited ways to provide for you. Depend on Him!

Jesus wants the laborers to have fellowship and to enjoy the fruit of their labor. *"Jesus said to them, 'Bring some of the fish which you have now caught'"* (John 21:10).

> *Already he who reaps is receiving wages, and is gathering fruit for life eternal; that he who sows and he who reaps may rejoice together* (John 4:36).

The Lord desires to share the joy of the salvation of sinners with His servants.

> *And when he comes home, he calls together his friends and his neighbors, saying to them, "Rejoice with me, for I have found my sheep which was lost!"* (Luke 15:6).

7 Marks of a Good Pastor

• Personal knowledge: no stranger to God or gospel experiences (John 10:5; II Corinthians 5:17; Galatians 5:16-26; I Corinthians 12)
• Divine call: not based on avarice, personal ambition, respect, honor, self-interest, or love of ease (John 10:2; Acts 13:3; I Corinthians 12:28; Ephesians 4:11; Romans 11:29)
• Consecrated motives: God's will and glory, salvation of lost souls, and the best interests of the Church and all men (John 10:9-13; Luke 19:10; Acts 20:28; II Corinthians 5:4-21; Ephesians 4:12)
• Divine anointing: not only human education, wisdom, polish, and effort, but also divine leading and help (Luke 11:13; Luke 24:49; John 7:37-39; John 14:12-17, 26; John 15:26; Acts 1:4-8; I Corinthians 2:1-10; 12:1-11; II Corinthians 3)
• Personal interest: acquaintance with his flock, private and public instruction, and helpfulness in all problems (John 10:3,9; Acts 20:26-35; Ephesians 1:15-19; 3:13-21; I Thessalonians 2:4-13; II Timothy 4:1-5; Hebrews 13:7,17)
• Good example: lead, not drive; feed, not destroy; and live what is preached (John 10:3,4; I Corinthians 4:9-13; II Corinthians 4:8-18; 6:1-10; I Timothy 3:1-13; 4:11-16, II Timothy 2; Titus 1).
• Divine success: be zealous and fearless to protect, heal, preserve, increase, sacrifice, and visit the flock (John 10:9-18; Mark 16:17,18; James 5:14-16; Luke 19:10; Jeremiah 23:1-8; Ezekiel 13:1-9,34).

From *Dake's Annotated Reference Bible*

To those who overcome He will give to eat of the Tree of Life and the hidden manna.

> *He who has an ear, let him hear what the Spirit says to the churches. To him who overcomes, I will grant to eat of the tree of life, which is in the Paradise of God. He who has an ear, let him hear what the Spirit says to the churches. To him who overcomes, to him I will give some of the hidden manna, and I will give him a white stone, and a new name written on the stone which no one knows but he who receives it* (Revelation 2:7,17).

Restored by the Lord

You will recall, it was by another fire that Peter denied his Lord:

> *Now the slaves and the officers were standing there, having made a charcoal fire, for it was cold and they were warming themselves; and Peter also was with them, standing and warming himself* (John 18:18).

Imagine Peter's conscience as he sat beside the Lord's fire. Jesus did not say a word about the denial—He let Peter judge himself. Fire then, as now, spoke of judgment. Peter had repented; now he needed full restoration of fellowship.

> *So when they had finished breakfast, Jesus said to Simon Peter, "Simon, son of John, do you love Me more than these?" He said to Him, "Yes, Lord; You know that I love You." He said to him, "Tend My lambs"* (John 21:15).

"*Simon, son of John.*" Jesus used Peter's original name, not the new one He had given him. (See John 1:42.) He was reminding Peter that he had acted out of his natural man—his old self.

At one point, Peter had said, "*Though all be offended, yet will I not."* He had declared that he would remain faithful even if the others did not. Now Jesus asked, *Do you love Me more than these?—* that is,...more than these disciples love Me?" Peter had an opportunity to retract his former boast. (See John 21:15.) He did so, saying, *"Yes, Lord; you know that I love you."* He rested on the Lord's knowledge of his love. He was saying, "You know I love you in spite of my awful failure."

Jesus restored Peter by giving him the only true motive for service—love. He accepted Peter's declaration of love, then gave him an assignment: *"Feed My Lambs."* The picture was changed from fishing for men to caring for sheep. Those who are saved need feeding and shepherding. Peter was exhorted to feed lambs—small, weak sheep that need the most attention. Whose lambs are they? Jesus called them, *"My lambs."* They belong to Him. He appoints under-shepherds to feed His flock.

> *Jesus said to Peter a second time, "Simon, son of John, do you love Me?" He said to Him, "Yes, Lord; You know that I love You." He said to him, "Shepherd My sheep"* (John 21:16).

Jesus asked Peter a second time, "Do you love Me?" This was strong, agape love. "Do you love Me with an unconditional love?" But Peter answered with a lesser kind of love. The Greek text uses two different kinds of love here. Peter said, "You know I have affection for you." He was no longer boasting of a superior love. He was stating affection only.

Jesus knew Peter's heart, and gave him the command, *"Feed My sheep."* This word for *feed* means to "rule and discipline." Again, Jesus calls them *His* sheep. Peter was not to have his own flock; he was to rule and discipline the flock of the Chief Shepherd.

> *He said to him the third time, "Simon, son of John, do you love Me?..." And he said to Him, "Lord, You know all things; You know that I love You." Jesus said to him, "Tend My sheep"* (John 21:17).

This time Jesus Himself used the weaker term in speaking to Peter, "Do you have affection for Me?" Peter was grieved that the Lord asked him the third time. *Grieved* here does not mean that he was offended, but that he was "deeply sorrowful." Perhaps he was remembering his three-fold denial and was deeply moved.

In his first question the Lord challenged the superiority of Peter's love. In the second question the Lord challenged whether Peter had any love at all. Here, in His third question, the Lord now challenges even his affection, and it had the desired effect.

"Lord, You know all things, you know I love You" (John 21:17). Peter rests his case with the Lord Who knows all things. There is no boast. Peter is humbled before Him and casts himself upon His mercy.

Jesus showed Peter that he was fully restored to apostleship. He said, *"Feed My sheep."* This word *feed* is the same one used in John 21:15, meaning "to minister spiritual nourishment to the people of God." Peter and others are entrusted with Jesus' own sheep to do what is necessary to rule and discipline them—perhaps force feed them sometimes, but to spiritually nourish them. Peter must have felt completely forgiven, accepted, and even trusted!

Not Ashamed of the Gospel

> *Truly, truly, I say to you, when you were younger, you used to gird yourself, and walk wherever you wished; but when you grow old, you will stretch out your hands, and someone else will gird you, and bring you where you do not wish to go* (John 21:18).

Jesus told Peter that in the future he would again be faced with a choice of denying Him or holding fast to his confession; and this time Peter would be true until death. Even a martyr's cross would not cause Peter to deny His Lord again!

> *Now this He said, signifying by what kind of death he would glorify God. And when He had spoken this, He said to him, "Follow Me!"* (John 21:19).

This kind of suffering glorifies God—when threats or physical torment cannot change a believer's confession. Jesus said to Ananias about Paul, *"For I will show him how much he must suffer for My name's sake"* (Acts 9:16).

The author of Hebrews said:

> *But remember the former days, when, after being enlightened, you endured a great conflict of sufferings, partly, by being made a public spectacle through reproaches and tribulations, and partly by becoming sharers with those who were so treated* (Hebrews 10:32,33).

Peter's love for the Lord brought him a task, *"Feed My sheep."* It also brought him a cross. History says that Peter died for his Lord. When he went to the cross, Peter asked to be nailed upside down because he didn't feel worthy to die as his Lord had died. Peter loved his Lord until the end.

Jesus made a statement about Peter's future faithfulness, and Peter lived up to it. In His Word, God makes many good faith statements about His children. He knows you can live victoriously all the days of your life, no matter what comes your way!

"And when He had spoken this, He said to him, 'Follow Me!'" (John 21:19). Peter had judged himself, discovered his own weakness, and been fully restored. He had received a commission, and now he received a final command, *"Follow Me!"*

When Peter knew what it would take to follow Jesus, he turned and looked at John to compare his ministry with John's and said, "Lord, what about this man?" Jesus cautioned him not to look around.

Jesus answered, *"If I want him to remain until I come, what is that to you? You follow Me!"* Peter needed to take care of the ministry given to him, not wonder about another's, comparing either difficulty or glory. Your task is to run the race that is set before *you*, not the one set before someone else. Instead of comparing your ministry with someone else's, keep your eyes on your Lord, follow Him, get direction from Him, and your work will glorify Him. Paul said to

A True Minister

TRUE MINISTERS MUST BE:

• United to the vine—John 15:6
Chosen of God to do the work—
John 15:15

• Ordained of God for the work
Laborers to bring forth fruit, not
idlers—John 6:27; 15:16

• Goers to the work, not waiters for the
work—Matthew 28:19-20; Mark 4:35-38;
16:15-20; Acts 1:4-8

• Preservers of their fruit, not
destroyers of it—John 15:16; 6:27

• Pray-ers who get results—John 15:16

• Lovers of all men—John 15:12-17;
I John 3:4-18; I Corinthians 13

From *Dake's Annotated Reference Bible*

Timothy, *"Pay close attention to yourself...."* (I Timothy 4:16).

It is interesting that John does not record the Ascension of Jesus. The last picture we have is Jesus with His disciples—a true picture. Jesus is still here on earth with us through the Holy Spirit. He is still ministering the joy of life, the Bread of life, the water of life, and the Word of life. He is teaching us all things by the Holy Spirit. He is still asking, "Do you really love Me?" He is even now declaring to each of us, *"Follow Me!"* Can you say, "Yes, Lord, I love You. Yes, I will follow You to the end. You are my love, my light, and my life."

Power Living

The disciples went fishing, going back to a former way of life. They went in the energy of the flesh without direction from the Lord, and the result was—no fish. *"Without Me you can do nothing,"* Jesus said. They were so busy they did not even recognize Jesus when He came to them in the morning. Be sure to get instructions from the Lord, and not embark on ventures that are purely of the flesh. They will not be successful and will keep you from recognizing Jesus in life's situations.

Things changed when Jesus came on the scene and His Words were obeyed. Immediately, they had success and immediately John recognized the Lord's hand in it. Jesus had them admit their failure (they caught no fish), and then He told them where to cast the net. Jesus' power drew many fish into the net. He also wants to draw many "fish" into your soul-winning net. Obey His instructions, and you will be a soul-winner.

Jesus served His disciples breakfast. It was a reminder that He loved them and wanted to take care of them. It was also reminiscent of His feeding the five thousand with bread and fish. This time the bread and fish had come from nowhere. Jesus was demonstrating one final time that He was their Source. He was their Bread of Life. God is not limited to human ways to meet your needs. He can do anything. Trust Him.

By one fire Peter denied Jesus three times, and by another fire declared his love for Jesus three times. Jesus gave Peter the true motive for serving Him—love. It was out of love for his Lord that Peter was to take care of Jesus' lambs and sheep. Jesus also revealed to Peter that he would be faithful—that he would even die for Jesus. His love for his Savior would be true to the end!

Personal Action Plan

1. Meditate on John 21:12,13. Does this passage remind you of other similar events in this book?

2. Pray about the different kinds of love mentioned in this chapter. How do they apply to you today?

3. Have you ever felt as Peter did— grieved that you didn't do something the Lord asked of you? What is the Lord saying to you about your failure?

4. Review the book of John briefly. What were Christ's seven "I am" statements? Write them in your scripture notebook.

5. State very briefly the most important truth you have learned from the book of John. Write it in your journal and share it with someone you know.

Chapter 13

LIFE-
CHANGING
REVELATION
UNIQUE
TO JOHN

Life-Changing Revelation Unique to John

Parables Found Only in John

Jesus was a great storyteller—I think He loved to tell parables. Over the course of His ministry, Jesus taught kingdom principles in many different ways—by example, by preaching, even by demonstration—yet, the writers of the Gospels record 70 parables. Parables (stories with spiritual meanings) were surely Jesus' favorite way to teach. I strongly suggest that you study and meditate on every parable. You will discover yourself and a life-changing nugget of truth in each and every one.

In John's Gospel, we discover two parables that can't be found anywhere else in the Bible—and for a very good reason. John presents the most powerful case in all of Scripture for the deity of Jesus—the incarnate Son of God. To make the point, John recounts the seven times that Jesus said, "I am." You'll recall that God revealed Himself to Moses as, "I AM." The two *new* parables in John, on which I want to teach, are used to richly explain two of Jesus' "I am" statements. (You can find more information about the "I am" statements of Christ later in this chapter.)

• The Good Shepherd

> ***I am the good shepherd***; *the good shepherd lays down His life for the sheep. He who is a hireling, and not a shepherd, who is not the owner of the sheep, beholds the wolf coming, and leaves the sheep, and flees, and the wolf snatches them, and scatters them. He flees because he is a hireling, and is not concerned about the sheep. I am the good shepherd; and I know My —*

John—The Author

And going on a little farther, He saw James the son of Zebedee, and John his brother, who were also in the boat mending the nets. And immediately He called them; and they left their father Zebedee in the boat with the hired servants, and went away to follow Him (Mark 1:19,20).

John's mother was Salome, probably a sister of Mary, mother of Jesus. *"Among whom was Mary Magdalene, along with Mary, the mother of James and Joseph, and the mother of the sons of Zebedee"* (Matthew 27:56).

And there were also some women looking on from a distance, among whom were Mary Magdalene, and Mary the mother of James the Less and Joses, and Salome (Mark 15:40).

John was a partner in a fishing business with his brother James and with Peter and Andrew. He quit to follow Jesus: *"And going on from there He saw two other brothers, James the son of Zebedee, and John his brother, in the boat with Zebedee their father, mending their nets; and He called them. And they immediately left the boat and their father, and followed Him"* (Matthew 4:21,22).

John was one of the first disciples of John the Baptist and probably the companion of Andrew mentioned in John 1:40. He was with Jesus on His first tour in Galilee. Jesus called John and his brother James the "sons of thunder,"a name they earned.

And James, the son of Zebedee, and John the brother of James (to them He gave the name Boanerges, which means, "Sons of Thunder") (Mark 3:17).

And John answered and said, "Master, we saw someone casting out demons in Your name; and we tried to hinder him because he does not follow along with us"....And He sent messengers on ahead of Him. And they went, and entered a village of the Samaritans, to make arrangements for Him. And they did not receive Him, because He was journeying with His face toward Jerusalem. And when His disciples James and John saw this, they said, "Lord, do You want us to command fire to come down from heaven and consume them?" (Luke 9:49,52-54).

John leaned on Jesus at the last supper: *"There was reclining on Jesus' breast one of His disciples, whom Jesus loved"* (John 13:23). John witnessed the trial and death of Jesus and took care of Jesus' mother Mary after His death (John 19:26,27). John was also one of the first to come to the empty tomb: *"So the other disciple who had first come to the tomb entered then also, and he saw and believed"* (John 20:8).

Though John began full of fire and as a "son of thunder," he became an apostle of love. John was the only apostle who was not martyred and was the author of the book of Revelation. He probably lived until the end of the first century.

own, and My own know Me, even as the Father knows Me and I know the Father; and I lay down My life for the sheep. And I have other sheep, which are not of this fold; I must bring them also, and they shall hear My voice; and they shall become one flock with one shepherd (John 10:11-16).

In this parable Jesus said, "I am the Good Shepherd"—not someone *hired* to take care of sheep, but the *owner* of the flock. In many countries the shepherd is not the owner, but a hireling who takes turns watching the flock. A shepherd who owned his flock usually did not own much land or have an expensive home; his wealth was in his flock. In Latin, the word for money is related to the word for sheep, because to the early Romans, as with many ancient people, wool was wealth and their fortune *was* the flock.

For Jesus, the Good Shepherd, we are His wealth. If you asked Him about His riches, Jesus would tell you of *"...the riches of the glory of His inheritance in the saints..."* (Ephesians 1:18). In Malachi 3:17 (KJV), God calls us His "jewels." In Deuteronomy 32:9, when portioning out wealth and lands to mankind, he declares *"...the Lord's portion is His people...."* In the Old Testament, God gave land and even countries to His people, but in the New Testament, Jesus so loved His flock—the Church—that He gave His life for it.

As our Shepherd, Jesus is our Caretaker. His relationship with the Church didn't begin and end on the Cross. He is a full-time Shepherd, always on duty—never sleeping or slumbering—because somewhere there is always a lamb sick, hurting, or with a problem. We need all kinds of things and He is the Provider of them all.

A shepherd is the sheep's leader and sometimes He makes us "lie down in green pastures." That's a hard thing for sheep because we want to run around. Nevertheless, we can trust in His abundant care; He never makes us lie down in dry spots, but in lush green pastures. We can count on Him to lead and guide us safely through every circumstance of life.

Jesus is our Defender. There are always wolves sneaking around to attack the sheep but our Defender *"...will neither slumber nor sleep"* (Psalms 121:4). We can put fears for our present situations and future problems confidently into His hands because He is *the* Good Shepherd. There are no other *good* shepherds; Jesus is the only one. Like anyone proud of their work, Jesus repeats again and again in this parable that He is the "Good Shepherd."

Jesus declares that He "knows" His sheep. He knows their number and intimately understands each individual of His flock— the number of hairs on each of their heads, their thoughts, their trials, and their sins. He didn't buy His sheep in the dark; He knew what He was getting when He acquired you and me. He didn't purchase us at a discount or find us in the bargain sheep pen. Jesus paid the full, complete price for each of us—there was nothing left owed and nothing left to pay. He gave everything He had to get YOU and me.

John tells us that Jesus is the "Good Shepherd," but in Hebrews 13, He is called the "*Great* Shepherd." As the Good Shepherd, He died for the sheep, but He arose from death as the "*Great Shepherd*" Who guides us in our new covenant with God purchased by His blood. In I Peter 2:25, Jesus is pictured as the Overseer or Over-shepherd of His flock (the Church).

Three times in John's Gospel, Jesus calls Himself the "Good Shepherd," and twice He speaks about laying down His life for the sheep. In the original Greek text, this expression has two meanings: first, it means paying a pledge or paying a price; second, it means to lay aside His life like a garment. Remember, Jesus *gave* His life, no one took it from Him. He could have called 12 legions of angels to His defense. Yet, gladly, Jesus gave His life so that we could have life eternal. Sheep—listen to His voice! Follow your Shepherd! Only when you *follow* Him will you have a full and complete life.

• **The True Vine**

> *I am the true vine, and My Father is the vinedresser.*
> *Every branch in Me that does not bear fruit, He takes*
> *away; and every branch that bears fruit, He prunes*
> *it, that it may bear more fruit. You are already clean*
> *because of the word which I have spoken to you.*

Abide in Me, and I in you. As the branch cannot bear fruit of itself, unless it abides in the vine, so neither can you, unless you abide in Me. I am the vine, you are the branches; he who abides in Me, and I in him, he bears much fruit; for apart from Me you can do nothing. If anyone does not abide in Me, he is thrown away as a branch, and dries up; and they gather them, and cast them into the fire, and they are burned.

If you abide in Me, and My words abide in you, ask whatever you wish, and it shall be done for you. By this is My Father glorified, that you bear much fruit, and so prove to be My disciples. Just as the Father has loved Me, I have also loved you; abide in My love. If you keep My commandments, you will abide in My love; just as I have kept My Father's commandments, and abide in His love. These things I have spoken to you, that My joy may be in you, and that your joy may be made full.

This is My commandment, that you love one another, just as I have loved you. Greater love has no one than this, that one lay down his life for his friends. You are My friends, if you do what I command you. No longer do I call you slaves, for the slave does not know what his master is doing; but I have called you friends, for all things that I have heard from My Father I have made known to you. You did not choose Me, but I chose you, and appointed you, that you should go and bear fruit, and that your fruit should remain, that whatever you ask of the Father in My name, He may give to you (John 15:1-16).

This parable contains some of the last words spoken by Jesus to His disciples before the Crucifixion. In His final hours of earthly life, Jesus shared one of His most important truths—"I am the vine."

The disciples had watched in amazement as Jesus turned

water into wine—His first miracle—and now He revealed that the source of the wine is the vineyard and that He is the *true* vine. The vine was a symbol for the divinely chosen nation, Israel. (See Hosea 10:1; Matthew 21:33; Luke 13:6.) Israel had become an *empty* vine and Jesus had come as the *true* vine.

Jesus wasn't saying that He was separate from the vine of Israel. A vine has both unity and diversity—roots, stems, branches, leaves, tendrils, and grapes are all unique aspects of the vine but all of them are *of the vine.* As twigs or branches, we must be di-vine-ly connected to Him to fulfill the function for which we were created— to bear fruit. Severed from Him, we are useless.

Throughout the vine's branches and roots flows sap. The sap connects each part to the other and brings life and nutrients that empower the branches to bear fruit. The sap that flows in Jesus' vine is the "zoe" life Jesus referred to in John 10:10, *"...I came that they may have* [zoe] *life, and might have it abundantly."* Remember, we do not produce fruit—we bear it. It is the Holy Spirit operating in and through our lives (like the sap in a vine) Who produces the fruit! Our job is to cooperate with Him.

• **Four conditions to fruitfulness:**

1. Fruit will lead to holiness: *"But now having been set free from sin, and having become slaves of God, you have your fruit to holiness, and the end, everlasting life"* (Romans 6:22 NKJ).

2. You need God's pruning to become even more fruitful. There are three kinds of fruit spoken of in the Bible, each is better than the preceeding—"more fruit," "better fruit," and "remaining" fruit." As the Keeper of the vineyard, God is always working with you to help you to improve your performance as a Christian.

3. Fruitfulness is only possible when we learn to "abide." Abiding in Jesus is remaining in union with Him, the vine, and constantly receiving a flow of sap or "zoe" life. Abiding is resting, obeying, and living in unbroken fellowship with God.

4. Those who bear fruit must "ask" things of the Father. There is no conflict between the more passive "abiding" and the more active "asking." A branch that abides in the vine is always asking for more sap. As we abide in Him, we listen to Him, then ask for things that are in harmony with His will.

Please note: fruit-bearing branches are not perfect. God, unlike a natural gardener, does not use a knife or pruning shears on us, He uses His Word:

> *For the word of God is living, and active, and sharper than any two-edged sword, and piercing even to the dividing of soul and spirit, of both joints and marrow, and quick to discern the thoughts and intents of the heart* (Hebrews 4:12 ASV).

In this parable, Jesus told His disciples, *"You are already clean* [pruned] **because of the word** *which I have spoken to you* (John 15:3). That is why I can't say often enough, "Read, read, read the Word." Do you want to have a ministry? Read the Word! Want a bigger, better ministry? Read the Word! Are there things in your life that you want to get rid of? Read God's Word!

Although you may not enjoy the pruning process, you will enjoy its results. Growing in place of those things God prunes (traits that have held you back and kept you from being all that you can be in Christ), will be the fruit of the Spirit: *"...love, joy, peace, patience, kindness, goodness, faithfulness, gentleness, self-control; against such things there is no law"* (Galatians 5:22,23).

The Seven "I Ams" of Jesus Found in John

1. I am the Bread of Life.
Sign: feeding of the five thousand

> *Jesus said to them, "I am the bread of life; he who comes to Me shall not hunger, and he who believes in Me shall never thirst"* (John 6:35,36).

2. I am the Light of the world.
Sign: restoring the blind man's sight

> *Then spake Jesus again unto them, saying, I am the light of the world: he that followeth me shall not walk in darkness, but shall have the light of life* (John 8:12).

3. I am the door.
Sign: making the sick man well

> *I am the door: by me if any man enter in, he shall be saved, and shall go in and out, and find pasture* (John 10:9).

4. I am the Good Shepherd.
Sign: catch of fishes after the Resurrection

> *I am the good shepherd; and I know My own, and My own know Me* (John 10:14).

5. I am the resurrection and the life.
Sign: raising Lazarus from the dead

> *Jesus said to her, "I am the resurrection and the life; he who believes in Me shall live even if he dies,"* (John 11:25).

6. I am the way, the truth, and the life.
Sign: healing the official's son

> *Jesus said to him, "I am the way, and the truth, and the life; no one comes to the Father, but through Me"*
> (John 14:6).

7. I am the true vine.
Sign: changing water into wine

> *I am the true vine, and My Father is the vinedresser*
> (John 15:1).

Light Vs. Darkness—A Theme of John

A major theme throughout the Gospel of John is the battle between darkness and light. Jesus was Life, and therefore the Light of men, *"...the true Light that gives light to every man..."*
(John 1:9 NIV).

John recognized that the greatest kind of life is eternal life. Nevertheless, he recognized that all men possess some kind of life. They possess reason and conscience, enough to leave them with no excuse if they ignore the Divine Light that is Jesus. You can almost feel the frustration John felt, that drove him to write this Gospel. Even though Jesus had brought light to a dark world, some still loved the darkness. *"This is the verdict: Light has come into the world, but men loved darkness instead of light because their deeds were evil"* (John 3:19 NIV).

If you are a burglar, which houses do you choose to rob? The darkest ones, of course. Evil men love the dark, because it hides their sin. It is painful to have the light of day shone upon your wrongdoing, so many will avoid the light of God's Word out of fear and out of guilt. *"Everyone who does evil hates the light, and will not come into the light for fear that his deeds will be exposed"* (John 3:20 NIV). It is sad that these folks do not realize that the very light that exposes their sin also washes it away! *"But whoever lives by the truth comes into the light, so that it may be seen plainly that what he has done has been done through God"* (John 3:21 NIV).

Darkness is the realm of spiritual evil, the state of the world under Satan's command. Darkness does not understand its opposite, light. Man, in his sinful state, cannot understand the enormous love that Jesus has for mankind. Jesus' gift of Himself as the sacrifice that paid for all of our sins is simply beyond his comprehension. Evil does not understand the Light, Satan cannot overcome it. Praise God, the Light is the everlasting winner in the battle of light versus darkness. *"The light shines in the darkness, but the darkness has not understood it"* (John 1:5 NIV). Through one unbelievable act of selflessness, Jesus, the Light, defeated the darkness on our behalf.

John stressed that the Light is meant for *every* person. Jewish scholars taught that a Messiah would come to redeem Israel. It was a great surprise to those who received Jesus that His gift of salvation was for the Gentiles as well as the Jews. John illustrates this in the story of the Samaritan woman at the well. The disciples were amazed when Jesus conversed with her, for Jews traditionally despised and would not even speak to a Samaritan. Imagine their astonishment when Jesus stayed for two days with these people (John 4:4-42). The Light of life is a treasure meant for every person on earth. We have only to open our eyes, ears, and hearts to Him!

It is strange how hard the Jews of that time worked to keep from seeing the light!

> When Jesus spoke again to the people, he said, "I am the light of world. Whoever follows me will never walk in darkness, but will have the light of life" (John 8:12 NIV).

Jesus was referring to the prophetic writings of Isaiah:

> The people walking in darkness have seen a great light; on those living in the land of the shadow of death, a light has dawned (Isaiah 9:2 NIV).

What a beautiful revelation of all that had been promised in the Old Testament, yet many continued to walk in the darkness. Jesus' message to non-Jews was also revealed by the prophet Isaiah,

> *...I will also make you a light for the Gentiles, that*
> *you may bring my salvation to the ends of the earth*
> (Isaiah 49:6 NIV).

There was nothing confusing about Jesus' message to Jews and Gentiles alike: in Him is light, life, and salvation. That message is the same for you and me, and for every person in this world.

Once we have received the Light that conquers the darkness of the world, it is our responsibility to spread that Light to others. Share the Light of Jesus—today!

Personal Action Plan

1. After studying the parable of the Good Shepherd tell how we should respond to Him.

2. Meditate on how Jesus is your Defender and wants you to rest in Him.

3. If Jesus is the vine, then what are you? Write your answers in your journal or scripture notebook.

4. Pray about how to apply the concept of Jesus as the "I AM..." to difficult circumstances. How does this meet your need?

5. Light has defeated darkness for all mankind. Who could you share this truth with this week? How can this truth change the way you pray for your unsaved loved ones?

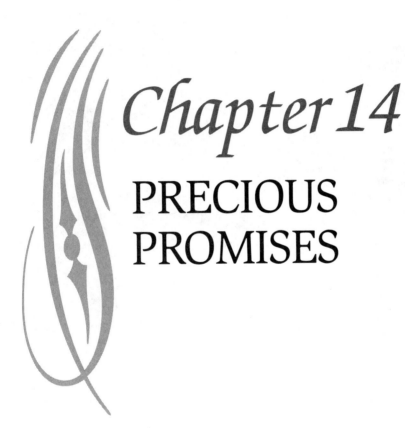

Chapter 14

PRECIOUS PROMISES

Precious Promises

What the Gospel of John Has To Say About...
Eternal Life

"And this is the witness of John, when the Jews sent to him priests and Levites from Jerusalem to ask him, 'Who are you?' And he confessed, and did not deny, and he confessed, 'I am not the Christ.' And they asked him, 'What then? Are you Elijah?' And he said, 'I am not.' 'Are you the Prophet?' And he answered, 'No.' They said then to him, 'Who are you, so that we may give an answer to those who sent us? What do you say about yourself?'" (John 1:19-22).

"And as Moses lifted up the serpent in the wilderness, even so must the Son of Man be lifted up; that whoever believes may in Him have eternal life" (John 3:14,15).

"The Father loves the Son, and has given all things into His hand. He who believes in the Son has eternal life; but he who does not obey the Son shall not see life, but the wrath of God abides on him" (John 3:35,36).

"Jesus answered and said to her, 'Everyone who drinks of this water shall thirst again; but whoever drinks of the water that I shall give him shall never thirst; but the water that I shall give him shall become in him a well of water springing up to eternal life'" (John 4:13,14).

"Truly, truly, I say to you, he who hears My word, and believes Him who sent Me, has eternal life, and does not come into *judgment, but has passed out of death into life"* (John 5:24).

"Not that any man has seen the Father, except the One who is from God; He has seen the Father. Truly, truly, I say to you, he who believes has eternal life" (John 6:46,47).

"I am the living bread that came down out of heaven; if anyone eats of this bread, he shall live forever; and the bread also which I shall give for the life of the world is My flesh" (John 6:51).

"Truly, truly, I say to you, if anyone keeps My word he shall never see death" (John 8:51).

"Jesus said to her, 'I am the resurrection and the life; he who believes in Me shall live even if he dies, and everyone who lives and believes in Me shall never die. Do you believe this?'" (John 11:25,26).

What the Gospel of John Has To Say About...
God's Love for You

"For God so loved the world, that He gave His only begotten Son, that whoever believes in Him should not perish, but have eternal life" (John 3:16).

"He who has My commandments and keeps them, he it is who loves Me; and he who loves Me shall be loved by My Father, and I will love him, and will disclose Myself to him" (John 14:21).

"Jesus answered and said to him, 'If anyone loves Me, he will keep My word; and My Father will love him, and We will come to him, and make Our abode with him'" (John 14:23).

"Just as the Father has loved Me, I have also loved you; abide

in My love. If you keep My commandments, you will abide in My love; just as I have kept My Father's commandments, and abide in His love" (John 15:9,10).

"If the world hates you, you know that it has hated Me before it hated you. If you were of the world, the world would love its own; but because you are not of the world, but I chose you out of the world, therefore the world hates you" (John 15:18,19).

"I in them, and Thou in Me, that they may be perfected in unity, that the world may know that Thou didst send Me, and didst love them, even as Thou didst love Me" (John 17:23).

"A new commandment I give to you, that you love one another, even as I have loved you, that you also love one another" (John 13:34).

What the Gospel of John Has To Say About...
Growing Spiritually

"But he who practices the truth comes to the light, that his deeds may be manifested as having been wrought in God" (John 3:21).

"Jesus therefore was saying to those Jews who had believed Him, 'If you abide in My word, then you are truly disciples of Mine; and you shall know the truth, and the truth shall make you free'" (John 8:31,32).

"Jesus said to him, 'I am the way, and the truth, and the life; no one comes to the Father, but through Me'" (John 14:6).

"Sanctify them in the truth; Thy word is truth" (John 17:17).

"Pilate therefore said to Him, 'So You are a king?' Jesus answered, 'You say correctly that I am a king. For this I have been born, and for this I have come into the world, to bear witness to the truth. Everyone who is of the truth hears My voice'" (John 18:37).

What To Do When...
You Need Assurance of Salvation

"The next day he saw Jesus coming to him, and said, 'Behold, the Lamb of God who takes away the sin of the world!'" (John 1:29).

"For God did not send the Son into the world to judge the world, but that the world should be saved through Him" (John 3:17).

"Truly, truly, I say to you, he who hears My word, and believes Him who sent Me, has eternal life, and does not come into judgment, but has passed out of death into life" (John 5:24).

"And if anyone hears My sayings, and does not keep them, I do not judge him; for I did not come to judge the world, but to save the world" (John 12:47).

What To Do When...
You Need Comfort

"Let not your heart be troubled; believe in God, believe also in Me" (John 14:1).

"And I will ask the Father, and He will give you another Helper, that He may be with you forever;" (John 14:16).

"I will not leave you as orphans; I will come to you" (John 14:18).

What To Do When...
You Feel Condemned

"...We are Abraham's offspring, and have never yet been enslaved to anyone; how is it that You say, 'You shall become free'? Jesus answered them, 'Truly, truly, I say to you, everyone who commits sin is the slave of sin. And the slave does not remain in the house forever; the son does remain forever. If therefore the Son shall make you free, you shall be free indeed'" (John 8:33-36).

What To Do When...
You Need Joy

"Come, see a man who told me all the things that I have done; this is not the Christ, is it?" (John 4:29).

"These things I have spoken to you, that My joy may be in you, and that your joy may be made full" (John 15:11).

"Truly, truly, I say to you, that you will weep and lament, but the world will rejoice; you will be sorrowful, but your sorrow will be turned to joy" (John 16:20).

"Until now you have asked for nothing in My name; ask, and you will receive, that your joy may be made full" (John 16:24).

"But now I come to Thee; and these things I speak in the world, that they may have My joy made full in themselves" (John 17:13).

What To Do When...
You Need Security

"...What is this that He says, 'A little while'? We do not know what He is talking about. Jesus knew that they wished to question Him, and He said to them, 'Are you deliberating together about this, that I said,...'" (John 16:18,19).

"And I am no more in the world; and yet they themselves are in the world, and I come to Thee. Holy Father, keep them in Thy name, the name which Thou hast given Me, that they may be one, even as We are" (John 17:11).

"I do not ask Thee to take them out of the world, but to keep them from the evil one." (John 17:15).

Truth From the Gospel of John About...
Forgiveness

"And the scribes and the Pharisees brought a woman caught in adultery, and having set her in the midst, they said to Him, 'Teacher, this woman has been caught in adultery, in the very act. Now in the Law Moses commanded us to stone such women; what then do You say?'"

"And they were saying this, testing Him, in order that they might have grounds for accusing Him. But Jesus stooped down, and with His finger wrote on the ground. But when they persisted in asking Him, He straightened up, and said to them, 'He who is without sin among you, let him be the first to throw a stone at her.' And again He stooped down, and wrote on the ground."

"And when they heard it, they began to go out one by one,

beginning with the older ones, and He was left alone, and the woman, where she was, in the midst. And straightening up, Jesus said to her, 'Woman, where are they? Did no one condemn you?' And she said, 'No one, Lord.' And Jesus said, 'Neither do I condemn you; go your way. From now on sin no more'" (John 8:3-11).

Truth From the Gospel of John About...
The Gifts of the Spirit

"...I have beheld the Spirit descending as a dove out of heaven, and He remained upon Him. And I did not recognize Him, but He who sent me to baptize in water said to me, 'He upon whom you see the Spirit descending and remaining upon Him, this is the one who baptizes in the Holy Spirit'" (John 1:32,33).

"Jesus answered, 'Truly, truly, I say to you, unless one is born of water and the Spirit, he cannot enter into the kingdom of God. That which is born of the flesh is flesh, and that which is born of the Spirit is spirit'" (John 3:5,6).

"For He whom God has sent speaks the words of God; for He gives the Spirit without measure" (John 3:34).

"God is spirit, and those who worship Him must worship in spirit and truth" (John 4:24).

"It is the Spirit who gives life; the flesh profits nothing; the words that I have spoken to you are spirit and are life" (John 6:63).

"He who believes in Me, as the Scripture said, 'From his innermost being shall flow rivers of living water.' But this He spoke of the Spirit, whom those who believed in Him were to

receive; for the Spirit was not yet given, because Jesus was not yet glorified" (John 7:38,39).

"And I will ask the Father, and He will give you another Helper, that He may be with you forever; that is the Spirit of truth, whom the world cannot receive, because it does not behold Him or know Him, but you know Him because He abides with you, and will be in you" (John 14:16,17).

"But the Helper, the Holy Spirit, whom the Father will send in My name, He will teach you all things, and bring to your remembrance all that I said to you" (John 14:26).

"When the Helper comes, whom I will send to you from the Father, that is the Spirit of truth, who proceeds from the Father, He will bear witness of Me" (John 15:26).

"But when He, the Spirit of truth, comes, He will guide you into all the truth; for He will not speak on His own initiative, but whatever He hears, He will speak; and He will disclose to you what is to come. He shall glorify Me; for He shall take of Mine, and shall disclose it to you. All things that the Father has are Mine; therefore I said, that He takes of Mine, and will disclose it to you" (John 16:13-15).

"And when He had said this, He breathed on them, and said to them, 'Receive the Holy Spirit'" (John 20:22).

Jesus Is Your...
Abundant Life

"...I am the bread of life; he who comes to Me shall not hunger, and he who believes in Me shall never thirst. But I said to you, that you have seen Me, and yet do not believe" (John 6:35,36).

"All that the Father gives Me shall come to Me, and the one who comes to Me I will certainly not cast out" (John 6:37).

"...If any man is thirsty, let him come to Me and drink. He who believes in Me, as the Scripture said, 'From his innermost being shall flow rivers of living water'" (John 7:37,38).

"The thief comes only to steal, and kill, and destroy; I came that they might have life, and might have it abundantly" (John 10:10).

Jesus Is Your...
Light in Times of Darkness

"In Him was life, and the life was the light of men. And the light shines in the darkness, and the darkness did not comprehend it" (John 1:4,5).

"There was the true light which, coming into the world, enlightens every man" (John 1:9).

"And this is the judgment, that the light is come into the world, and men loved the darkness rather than the light; for their deeds were evil. For everyone who does evil hates the light, and does not come to the light, lest his deeds should be exposed. But he who practices the truth comes to the light, that his deeds may be manifested as having been wrought in God" (John 3:19-21).

"Again therefore Jesus spoke to them, saying, 'I am the light of the world; he who follows Me shall not walk in the darkness, but shall have the light of life'" (John 8:12).

"Jesus therefore said to them, 'For a little while longer the light is among you. Walk while you have the light, that darkness may not overtake you; he who walks in the darkness does not know where he goes. While you have the light, believe in the light, in order that you may become sons of light.' These things Jesus spoke, and He departed and hid Himself from them" (John 12:35,36).

"I have come as light into the world, that everyone who believes in Me may not remain in darkness" (John 12:46).

Jesus Is Your...
Peace in Troubled Times

"I will not leave you as orphans; I will come to you" (John 14:18).

"Peace I leave with you; My peace I give to you; not as the world gives, do I give to you. Let not your heart be troubled, nor let it be fearful" (John 14:27).

"These things I have spoken to you, that in Me you may have peace. In the world you have tribulation, but take courage; I have overcome the world" (John 16:33).

Personal Action Plan

1. What promises of eternal life can you freely share with an unsaved loved one?

2. How does the truth about forgiveness affect your relationship with God?

3. Do a word study on light in your scripture notebook. What have you learned about Jesus as the Light?

4. What new commandment did Jesus give His disciples? Share it with a friend today.

5. What should you do when the devil tries to condemn you?

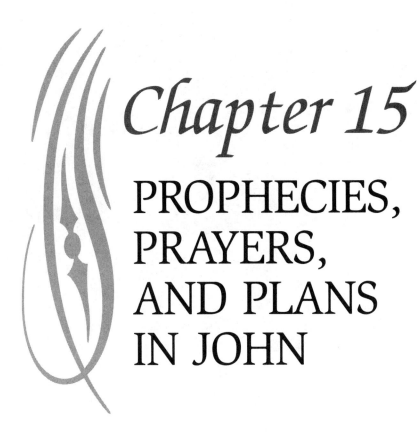

Chapter 15

PROPHECIES, PRAYERS, AND PLANS IN JOHN

Prophecies

OLD TESTAMENT PROPHECIES FULFILLED IN JOHN

John the Baptist

Prophecy:

> *A voice is calling, "Clear the way for the LORD in the wilderness; make smooth in the desert a highway for our God"* (Isaiah 40:3).

Fulfillment:

> *...I am a voice of one crying in the wilderness, "Make straight the way of the Lord," as Isaiah the prophet said* (John 1:23).

Zeal for the Temple

Prophecy:

> *For zeal for Thy house has consumed me, and the reproaches of those who reproach Thee have fallen on me* (Psalm 69:9).

Fulfillment:

> *And the Passover of the Jews was at hand, and Jesus went up to Jerusalem. And He found in the temple those who were selling oxen and sheep and doves, and the moneychangers seated. And He made a scourge of cords, and drove them all out of the temple, with the sheep and the oxen; and He poured out the coins of the moneychangers, and overturned their tables; and to those who were selling the doves He said, "Take*

these things away; stop making My Father's house a house of merchandise." His disciples remembered that it was written, "Zeal for Thy house will consume me"(John 2:13-17).

Bread of Heaven

Prophecy:

> *When the layer of dew evaporated, behold, on the surface of the wilderness there was a fine flake-like thing, fine as the frost on the ground* (Exodus 16:14).

> *Thou didst provide bread from heaven for them for their hunger, Thou didst bring forth water from a rock for them for their thirst, and Thou didst tell them to enter in order to possess the land which Thou didst swear to give them* (Nehemiah 9:15).

> *And He rained down manna upon them to eat, and gave them food from heaven. Man did eat the bread of angels; He sent them food in abundance* (Psalm 78:24,25).

Fulfillment:

> *Our fathers ate the manna in the wilderness; as it is written, "He gave them bread out of heaven to eat."Jesus therefore said to them, "Truly, truly, I say to you, it is not Moses who has given you the bread out of heaven, but it is My Father who gives you the true bread out of heaven. For the bread of God is that which comes down out of heaven, and gives life to the world"* (John 6:31-33).

Taught of the Lord

Prophecy:

> *And all your sons will be taught of the LORD; and the well-being of your sons will be great* (Isaiah 54:13).

Fulfillment:

> *No one can come to Me, unless the Father who sent*
> *Me draws him; and I will raise him up on the last day.*
> *It is written in the prophets, "And they shall all be*
> *taught of God." Everyone who has heard and learned*
> *from the Father, comes to Me. Not that any man has*
> *seen the Father, except the One who is from God; He*
> *has seen the Father* (John 6:44-46).

Son of God

Prophecy:

> *...You are gods, and all of you are sons of the Most*
> *High* (Psalm 82:6).

Fulfillment:

> *...Has it not been written in your Law, "I said, you are*
> *gods?" If he called them gods, to whom the word of*
> *God came (and the Scripture cannot be broken), do*
> *you say of Him, whom the Father sanctified and sent*
> *into the world, "You are blaspheming," because I said,*
> *"I am the Son of God?" If I do not do the works of My*
> *Father, do not believe Me;* (John 10:33-37).

King on a Donkey

Prophecy:

> *Rejoice greatly, O daughter of Zion! Shout in triumph,*
> *O daughter of Jerusalem! Behold, your king is coming*
> *to you; He is just and endowed with salvation, humble,*
> *and mounted on a donkey, even on a colt, the foal of*
> *a donkey* (Zechariah 9:9).

Fulfillment:

> *And Jesus, finding a young donkey, sat on it; as it is*
> *written, "Fear not, daughter of Zion; behold, your King*
> *is coming, seated on a donkey's colt"* (John 12:14,15).

Blind Eyes and Deaf Ears

Prophecy:

> *Who has believed our message? And to whom has the arm of the LORD been revealed?* (Isaiah 53:1).

> *Render the hearts of this people insensitive, their ears dull, and their eyes dim, lest they see with their eyes, hear with their ears, understand with their hearts, and return and be healed* (Isaiah 6:10).

Fulfillment:

> *But though He had performed so many signs before them, yet they were not believing in Him; that the word of Isaiah the prophet might be fulfilled, which he spoke, "Lord, who has believed our report? And to whom has the arm of the Lord been revealed?" For this cause they could not believe, for Isaiah said again, "He has blinded their eyes, and He hardened their heart; lest they see with their eyes, and perceive with their heart, and be converted, and I heal them." These things Isaiah said, because he saw His glory, and he spoke of Him* (John 12:37-41).

Eat and Betray

Prophecy:

> *Even my close friend, in whom I trusted, who ate my bread, has lifted up his heel against me* (Psalm 41:9).

Fulfillment:

> *I do not speak of all of you. I know the ones I have chosen; but it is that the Scripture may be fulfilled, "He who eats My bread has lifted up his heel against Me"* (John 13:18).

Gamble for His Garments

Prophecy:

> *They divide my garments among them, and for my clothing they cast lots* (Psalms 22:18).

Fulfillment:

> *The soldiers therefore, when they had crucified Jesus, took His outer garments and made four parts, a part to every soldier and also the tunic; now the tunic was seamless, woven in one piece. They said therefore to one another, "Let us not tear it, but cast lots for it, to decide whose it shall be"; that the Scripture might be fulfilled, "They divided My outer garments among them, and for My clothing they cast lots"* (John 19:23,24).

Pierced—Not Broken

Prophecy:

> *It is to be eaten in a single house; you are not to bring forth any of the flesh outside of the house, nor are you to break any bone of it* (Exodus 12:46).

> *They shall leave none of it until morning, nor break a bone of it; according to all the statute of the Passover they shall observe it* (Numbers 9:12).

> *He keeps all his bones; not one of them is broken* (Psalm 34:20).

> *And I will pour out on the house of David and on the inhabitants of Jerusalem, the Spirit of grace and of supplication, so that they will look on Me whom they have pierced; and they will mourn for Him, as one mourns for an only son, and they will weep bitterly over Him, like the bitter weeping over a first-born* (Zechariah 12:10).

Fulfillment:

> *...But coming to Jesus, when they saw that He was already dead, they did not break His legs; but one of the soldiers pierced His side with a spear, and immediately there came out blood and water. And he who has seen has borne witness, and his witness is true; and he knows that he is telling the truth, so that you also may believe. For these things came to pass, that the Scripture might be fulfilled, "Not a bone of Him shall be broken." And again another Scripture says, "They shall look on Him whom they pierced"* (John 19:33-37).

NEW TESTAMENT PROPHECIES IN JOHN

Transfiguration

Prophecy:

> *And He said to him, "Truly, truly, I say to you, you shall see the heavens opened, and the angels of God ascending and descending on the Son of Man"* (John 1:51).

Fulfillment :

> *And He was transfigured before them; and His face shone like the sun, and His garments became as white as light....While he was still speaking, behold, a bright cloud overshadowed them; and behold, a voice out of the cloud, saying, "This is My beloved Son, with whom I am well-pleased;..."* (Matthew 17:2,5).

Crucifixion

Prophecy:

> *But a certain one of them, Caiaphas, who was high priest that year, said to them, "You know nothing at all, nor do you take into account that it is expedient for you that one man should die for the people, and*

that the whole nation should not perish." Now this he did not say on his own initiative; but being high priest that year, he prophesied that Jesus was going to die for the nation, and not for the nation only, but that He might also gather together into one the children of God who are scattered abroad. So from that day on they planned together to kill Him (John 11:49-53).

Fulfillment:

...Christ also died for sins once for all, the just for the unjust, in order that He might bring us to God, having been put to death in the flesh, but made alive in the spirit... (I Peter 3:18).

Resurrection

Prophecy:

You heard that I said to you, "I go away, and I will come to you." If you loved Me, you would have rejoiced, because I go to the Father; for the Father is greater than I. And now I have told you before it comes to pass, that when it comes to pass, you may believe. I will not speak much more with you, for the ruler of the world is coming, and he has nothing in Me; but that the world may know that I love the Father, and as the Father gave Me commandment, even so I do. Arise, let us go from here (John 14:28-31).

...What is this thing He is telling us, "A little while, and you will not behold Me; and again a little while, and you will see Me"; and, "because I go to the Father"? And so they were saying, "What is this that He says,...? We do not know what He is talking about." Jesus knew that they wished to question Him, and He said to them, "Are you deliberating together about this,...? Truly, truly, I say to you, that you will weep and lament, but the world will rejoice; you will be sorrowful, but your sorrow will be turned to joy. Whenever a woman is in

travail she has sorrow, because her hour has come; but when she gives birth to the child, she remembers the anguish no more, for joy that a child has been born into the world. Therefore you too now have sorrow; but I will see you again, and your heart will rejoice, and no one takes your joy away from you" (John 16:16-22).

Fulfillment:

Jesus answered and said to them, "Destroy this temple, and in three days I will raise it up." The Jews therefore said, "It took forty-six years to build this temple, and will You raise it up in three days?" But He was speaking of the temple of His body. When therefore He was raised from the dead, His disciples remembered that He said this; and they believed the Scripture, and the word which Jesus had spoken (John 2:19-22).

Judas' Betrayal

Prophecy:

Jesus answered them, "Did I Myself not choose you, the twelve, and yet one of you is a devil?" Now He meant Judas the son of Simon Iscariot, for he, one of the twelve, was going to betray Him" (John 6:70-71).

When Jesus had said this, He became troubled in spirit, and testified, and said, "Truly, truly, I say to you, that one of you will betray Me." The disciples began looking at one another, at a loss to know of which one He was speaking. There was reclining on Jesus' breast one of His disciples, whom Jesus loved. Simon Peter therefore gestured to him, and said to him, "Tell us who it is of whom He is speaking." He, leaning back thus on Jesus' breast, said to Him, "Lord, who is it?" Jesus therefore answered, "That is the one for whom I shall dip the morsel and give it to him." So when He had dipped the morsel, He took and gave it to Judas, the son of

Simon Iscariot. And after the morsel, Satan then entered into him. Jesus therefore said to him, "What you do, do quickly" (John 13:21-27).

Fulfillment:

Then when Judas, who had betrayed Him, saw that He had been condemned, he felt remorse and returned the thirty pieces of silver to the chief priests and elders, saying, "I have sinned by betraying innocent blood" (Matthew 27:3,4).

Peter's Denial

Prophecy:

Jesus answered, "Will you lay down your life for Me? Truly, truly, I say to you, a cock shall not crow, until you deny Me three times" (John 13:38).

Fulfillment:

Then he began to curse and swear, "I do not know the man!" And immediately a cock crowed. And Peter remembered the word which Jesus had said, "Before a cock crows, you will deny Me three times." And he went out and wept bitterly (Matthew 26:74,75).

Persecution of Christians

Prophecy:

These things I have spoken to you, that you may be kept from stumbling. They will make you outcasts from the synagogue, but an hour is coming for everyone who kills you to think that he is offering service to God. And these things they will do, because they have not known the Father, or Me. But these things I have spoken to you, that when their hour comes, you may remember that I told you of them. And these things I did not say to you at the beginning, because I was with you (John 16:1-4).

Fulfillment:

>...*And on that day a great persecution arose against the church in Jerusalem; and they were all scattered throughout the regions of Judea and Samaria,...* (Acts 8:1).

Peter's Execution

Prophecy:

>*Truly, truly, I say to you, when you were younger, you used to gird yourself, and walk wherever you wished; but when you grow old, you will stretch out your hands, and someone else will gird you, and bring you where you do not wish to go* (John 21:18).

Fulfillment:

>The early church fathers recorded and documented the well-known fact of Peter's martyrdom.

Prayers

One of the most famous and heart-touching prayers in the Bible is found in the Gospel of John, Chapter 17. Jesus and His disciples had just finished the Passover dinner, and Jesus knew He would soon be arrested and crucified.

This prayer is actually three prayers in one. The first prayer is Jesus' prayer for Himself. The second is a prayer for those closest to Him, His disciples. The third is a prayer for the church—for all believers.

Jesus Prays for Himself

Father, the hour has come; glorify Thy Son, that the Son may glorify Thee, even as Thou gavest Him authority over all mankind, that to all whom Thou hast given Him, He may give eternal life. And this is eternal life, that they may know Thee, the only true God, and Jesus Christ whom Thou hast sent. I glorified Thee on the earth, having accomplished the work which Thou hast given Me to do. And now, glorify Thou Me together with Thyself, Father, with the glory which I had with Thee before the world was (John 17:1-5).

Is it surprising that the Son of God prayed first for Himself? Even Jesus needed prayer! Often, we are so busy praying for others that we forget to pray for ourselves. Try Jesus' method: pray for yourself first!

In this prayer, Jesus dedicates everything He has done to the glory of God. When you pray, dedicate yourself and your actions to the glory of God. Ask God to forgive and forget the things you have done that were not in His will. Then seek His guidance in all you do, so that your life, too, can be for His glory.

Jesus prays for His disciples:

> *I manifested Thy name to the men whom Thou gavest*
> *Me out of the world; Thine they were, and Thou gavest*
> *them to Me, and they have kept Thy word. Now they*
> *have come to know that everything Thou hast given*
> *Me is from Thee; for the words which Thou gavest Me*
> *I have given to them; and they received them, and*
> *truly understood that I came forth from Thee, and they*
> *believed that Thou didst send Me. I ask on their behalf;*
> *I do not ask on behalf of the world, but of those whom*
> *Thou hast given Me; for they are Thine; and all things*
> *that are Mine are Thine, and Thine are Mine; and I*
> *have been glorified in them.*
>
>   *And I am no more in the world; and yet they*
> *themselves are in the world, and I come to Thee. Holy*
> *Father, keep them in Thy name, the name which Thou*
> *hast given Me, that they may be one, even as We are.*
> *While I was with them, I was keeping them in Thy*
> *name which Thou hast given Me; and I guarded them,*
> *and not one of them perished but the son of perdition,*
> *that the Scripture might be fulfilled. But now I come*
> *to Thee; and these things I speak in the world, that*
> *they may have My joy made full in themselves. I have*
> *given them Thy word; and the world has hated them,*
> *because they are not of the world, even as I am not of*
> *the world. I do not ask Thee to take them out of the*
> *world, but to keep them from the evil one. They are*
> *not of the world, even as I am not of the world.*
> *Sanctify them in the truth; Thy word is truth. As*
> *Thou didst send Me into the world, I also have sent*
> *them into the world. And for their sakes I sanctify*
> *Myself, that they themselves also may be sanctified*
> *in truth* (John 17:6-19).

In the second prayer, Jesus asked God's protection for those

He loved. He knew that His disciples would face fear, confusion, and persecution in the days and years ahead. He asked God to protect them from the world, from the evil one. What is the power that will protect them?

It is hard not to be fearful when we know that our loved ones are making their way in a dangerous world. Follow Jesus' example, and pray for their safety and sanctity. When you pray for your family and friends, ask for protection in the name of Jesus, His name is more powerful than the world, more powerful than Satan.

Jesus Prays for All Believers

I do not ask in behalf of these alone, but for those also who believe in Me through their word; that they may all be one; even as Thou, Father, art in Me, and I in Thee, that they also may be in Us; that the world may believe that Thou didst send Me. And the glory which Thou hast given Me I have given to them; that they may be one, just as We are one; I in them, and Thou in Me, that they may be perfected in unity, that the world may know that Thou didst send Me, and didst love them, even as Thou didst love Me.

Father, I desire that they also, whom Thou hast given Me, be with Me where I am, in order that they may behold My glory, which Thou hast given Me; for Thou didst love Me before the foundation of the world. O righteous Father, although the world has not known Thee, yet I have known Thee; and these have known that Thou didst send Me; and I have made Thy name known to them, and will make it known; that the love wherewith Thou didst love Me may be in them, and I in them (John 17:20-26).

Finally, Jesus prayed for all who hear His Word and believe in Him. He prayed that they would be witnesses to the world, so the world will believe that Jesus was sent from God.

Your prayers should include the entire church, throughout the world. Ask for God's blessings on those who have heard and believed, and pray that their witnessing will bring more and more people into the glory of God. Jesus' reason for this prayer is so lovely! He simply wants everyone, everywhere, to share in God's salvation and love. Perhaps the best insight into Jesus' prayers is that they were always answered. Look at John 12:27-29:

> *Now My soul has become troubled; and what shall I say, "Father, save Me from this hour"? But for this purpose I came to this hour. Father, glorify Thy name. There came therefore a voice out of heaven: "I have both glorified it, and will glorify it again." The multitude therefore, who stood by and heard it, were saying that it had thundered; others were saying, "An angel has spoken to Him."*

You may not hear a thundering voice, but know that if you pray in Jesus' name, your prayers are always heard, and always answered.

Plans

The Plan of Salvation in John

The book of John is sometimes called the evangelist's net. Why is it that brand-new Christians are almost always told to read the book of John first? What is it about this Gospel that speaks to those who are searching for spiritual truth? Should you be using John in your own discipleship?

Unlike the other three Gospels, John is not a chronological story of the life of Jesus. It is the only Gospel without a genealogy of Jesus. It speaks much less of the kingdom of God, but concentrates on rebirth, and on the gift of eternal life lived in fellowship with God. That life, John tells us, begins now, not after death. It is a permanent and immediate gift.

Much of the emphasis of this life-changing Gospel is on the choice that all of us must make: the choice between good and evil, between light and darkness, between eternal life and ruin. We all make this choice every day, every minute. The Gospel of John hammers home the message that making the right choice brings with it the most glorious gifts!

How does this Gospel speak so deeply to our hearts? John uses simple language and lots of imagery. His Gospel is not an intellectual analysis of the life of Jesus, but the story of personal commitment. Just look at the glorious opening words:

In the beginning was the Word, and the Word was with God, and the Word was God. He was in the beginning with God (John: 1,2).

Immediately John tells us that this Gospel is the story of the Son of God. This Gospel will contain the words of Jesus, but far more importantly, Jesus IS the Word. Jesus IS God.

The Gospel of John continues on with proof of Jesus' diety. The events recorded in this Gospel are topical. There are nine stories of how God as Life meets the needs of nine different kinds of people. Each of us can find ourselves in at least one of these stories. Are you the woman at the well? Are you the new believer, Nicodemus? Maybe you are the official with the sick son or the crippled man who waited by the crowded pool for a miracle. When you are witnessing, this Gospel truly has something for everyone.

Perhaps most memorable of all is the story of Thomas, whose doubts plague all new believers. Touching the nail holes in Jesus' hands, Thomas cries, "My Lord and my God!" and Jesus says:

> *Because you have seen me you have believed. Blessed*
> *are those who have not seen and yet have believed"*
> (John 20:29 NIV).

This Gospel calls out to those who would choose light over darkness. John himself tells us that this is why he wrote this book:

> *But these are written you may believe that Jesus is the*
> *Christ, the Son of God, and that by believing you may*
> *have life in his name* (John 20:31 NIV).

I pray that you will reach out to the lost ones around you, as John reached out to all of us in this precious Gospel.

There is a very simple, Scriptural approach to these life-changing decisions, and I want to share it with you.

A Plan for Leading a Person to Christ

1. Open a Bible to Romans 10. Have the candidate read verses 9 and 10 aloud. Explain to the candidate that because these scriptures say that "confession is made unto salvation," you are going to lead him in a short prayer. Ask the candidate to repeat after you as you pray.

2. Allow the Holy Spirit to guide your prayer so that the candidate will be sure to: acknowledge that he is a sinner (repentance); ask the Father to cleanse him, by the blood of Jesus, from every sin he has committed from the day he was born to this very moment; invite Jesus to come into his heart and be Master and Lord of his life; thank God for saving his soul.

3. Ask the candidate to read Romans 10:13 aloud. Now, ask him to read it again, but this time have him substitute his own name for "whosoever" in this verse. The candidate will realize that he has fulfilled the simple requirements of verse 13 and that he is saved according to God's Word—*whether or not he feels any differently!* You may warmly affirm this momentous decision and welcome your new brother or sister to the Body of Christ.

Bibliography

Barclay, William. *The Gospel of John Volume 1*. Revised ed. Philadelphia: The Westminister Press, 1975.

Hunt, Gladys. *John: Eyewitness*. Wheaton, IL.: Harold Shaw Publishers, 1971.

Kent, Homer A. Jr. *Light in the Darkness, Studies in the Gospel of John*. Grand Rapids: Baker Book House, 1974.

Lindsay, Gordan. *The Life and Teachings of Christ, Volume 3*. Dallas: Christ for the Nations, 1978.

Metzgar, Bruce and Michael Coogan eds. *The Oxford Companion to the Bible*. Oxford University Press, 1993.

Pink, Arthur W. *Exposition of the Gospel of John.*. Grand Rapids: Zondervan Publishing House, 1975.

Walvoord, John and Roy Zuck. *The Bible Knowledge Commentary*. Victor Books, 1986.

Prayer Request(s)

Let us join our faith with yours for your prayer needs. Fill out the coupon below and send to Marilyn Hickey Ministries, P.O. Box 17340, Denver, CO 80217.

Prayer Request(s) _____

_____

_____

_____

_____

_____

Signed _____ Date_____

Name _____

Address _____

City _____ State/Province _____

Zip/Postal Code _____ Country _____

Phone (H) (   )_____

Give us your email address, so we can send you periodic updates. Email Address _____

If you want prayer immediately, call our Prayer Center, TOLL-FREE (U.S. only) at 1-877-661-1249, anytime.

Receive Jesus Christ as Lord and Savior of Your Life.

The Bible says, *"That if thou shalt confess with thy mouth the Lord Jesus, and shalt believe in thine heart that God raised him from the dead, thou shalt be saved. For with the heart man believeth unto righteousness; and with the mouth confession is made unto salvation"* (Romans 10:9,10).

To receive Jesus Christ as Lord and Savior of your life, sincerely pray this prayer from your heart:

Dear Jesus,

I believe that You died for me and that You rose again on the third day. I confess to You that I am a sinner and that I need Your love and forgiveness. Come into my life, forgive my sins, and give me eternal life. I confess You now as my Lord. Thank You for my salvation!

Signed _____ Date _____

Please print.

Mr. & Mrs.
Mr.
Miss
Name Mrs. _____

Address _____

City _____ State/Province _____

Zip/Postal Code _____ Country _____

Phone (H) ( ) _____

Give us your email address, so we can send you periodic updates. Email Address _____

Write or call... We will send you information to help you with your new life in Christ: Marilyn Hickey Ministries • P.O. Box 17340 • Denver, CO 80217 •
For prayer call: TOLL-FREE (U.S. only) at 1-877-661-1249, anytime. For product orders call
TOLL-FREE (U.S. only) at 1-888-637-4545.
On the worldwide web at **www.mhmin.org**

BOOKS BY MARILYN HICKEY

A Cry for Miracles $7.95
Acts of the Holy Spirit $7.95
Angels All Around $7.95
Armageddon $4.95
Ask Marilyn $9.95
Be Healed $9.95
Bible Encounter Classic Edition $24.95
Break the Generation Curse $7.95
Break the Generation Curse–Part 2 .... $9.95
Building Blocks for Better Families $4.95
Daily Devotional $7.95
Dear Marilyn $7.95
Devils, Demons, and Deliverance $9.95
Freedom From Bondages $7.95
Gift-Wrapped Fruit $2.95
God's Covenant for Your Family $7.95
God's Rx for a Hurting Heart $4.95
How to Be a Mature Christian $7.95
Know Your Ministry $4.95
Maximize Your Day . . . God's Way $7.95
Miracle Signs and Wonders $24.95
Names of God (The) $7.95
Nehemiah—Rebuilding the Broken Places in Your Life $7.95
No. 1 Key to Success—Meditation (The) $4.95
Psalm 119 Classic Library Edition $24.95
Psalms Classic Library Edition $24.95
Proverbs Classic Library Edition $24.95
Release the Power of the Blood Covenant $4.95
Satan-Proof Your Home $7.95
Signs in the Heavens $7.95
What Every Person Wants to Know About Prayer $4.95
When Only a Miracle Will Do $4.95
You Can Bounce Back From Your Setback $19.95
Your Miracle Source $4.95
Your Total Health Handbook—Body • Soul • Spirit $9.95

Word to the World College

Explore your options and increase your knowledge of the Word at this unique college of higher learning for men and women of faith. Word to the World College offers **on-campus and correspondence courses** that give you the opportunity to learn from Marilyn Hickey and other great Bible scholars. WWC can help prepare you to be an effective minister of the gospel. Classes are open to both full- and part-time students.

For more information, complete the coupon below and send it to:

Word to the World College
P.O. Box 17340 • Denver, CO 80217
1-303-770-0400 • www.mhmin.org
Call now for a FREE information packet.
TOLL-FREE (U.S. only) at 1-888-637-4545
or email wwcinfo@mhmin.org

Mr. & Mrs.   Please print.
Mr.
Miss
Name Mrs. _____

Address _____

City _____

State/Province _____

Zip/Postal Code _____

Country _____

Phone (H) (   ) _____

(W) (   ) _____

Give us your email address, so we can send you periodic updates. Email Address _____

For Your Information
Free Monthly Magazine

❏ Please send me your free monthly magazine, OUTPOURING (including daily devotionals, timely articles, and ministry updates)!

Tapes and Books

❏ Please send me your latest product catalog.

Mr. & Mrs.   Please print.
Mr.
Miss
Name Mrs. _____

Address _____

City _____ State/Province _____

Zip/Postal Code _____

Country _____

Phone (H) (   ) _____

Give us your email address, so we can send you periodic updates. Email Address _____

Mail to:
Marilyn Hickey Ministries
P.O. Box 17340
Denver, CO   80217
1-303-770-0400
www.mhmin.org

Visit

Marilyn
Hickey Ministries'

Website

www.mhmin.org